MW01291895

Damn, I Shot My Horse

Damn, I Shot My Horse

Damn, I Shot My Horse

By

Fred Hauptmann

Damn, I Shot My Horse

Published 2016 by Fred Hauptmann
Copyright © 2015 by Fred Hauptmann

ISBN 978-1-329-90559-7   9000

Damn, I Shot My Horse
Fred Hauptmann –Fourth Edition
Author's e-mail: fredruns@outlook.com

·

Book design by Fred Hauptmann
Cover artwork and back photography by Fred Hauptmann

Printed at Lulu Enterprises, Inc.
www.lulu.com

Manufactured in the United States of America
10 9 8 7 6 5 4 3 2 1

Fred Hauptmann

To my wife Marsha

Without you,
this never would have been completed

Damn, I Shot My Horse

The stories in this book took place between 1959 and 1973.

I have changed the names of certain characters in these stories except those of my immediate family. I didn't change the names of my horse Pinto and my five dogs either (because they won't give a damn), Thanks to my wife's encouragement I managed to complete this. Also, a big thank you to the other people who helped me with their support and kind words.

It was supposed to be a small twenty-page compilation, viewed only by my immediate family. So much for self-control.

Damn, I Shot My Horse

Table of Contents

Damn, I Shot My Horse

THE EARLY YEARS

The year was 1959 and I was eleven years old. My world was full of wonder and excitement. Every day after school on my way home the route took me past a pasture full of horses of all descriptions. Stopping and watching them I would dream of being a cowboy on the range, roping and riding the days away. In 1959, what wondrous dreams these were.

One day I watched a hugely overweight man make his way from the house towards the barn. He saw me and shouted in my direction, asking if I could give him a hand catching one of the horses. Running over to him I dropped my book bag by a corner post and replied "Yes!" The horse was easy to catch.

"If you want to brush him down and ride him for an hour I'll give you a dollar." He was short of breath just uttering this sentence.

"I don't know anything about riding horses, but if you show me, I will", I replied excitedly. His instructions were friendly and he helped me get started. I would have done it for nothing.

The man explained, "My wife usually does this, but she's not feeling well. If you want to come back tomorrow, you can do it again with a different horse."

All my dreams were being fulfilled by one lucky turn of events. Being an hour late I ran home to share the news with my family but no one was there. Doing my homework when they arrived, the news of a possible job fell on deaf ears. No questions about where I had been or no explanations about where they had gone. Very typical, a family of few words and even less concern.

My new "Boss" was a horse trader. Every month he would drive his truck to Los Angeles and buy eight horses at auction bringing them back to Sacramento to sell. Every day I would stop after school and ride one or two horses. On weekends I would spend all day riding as many as possible. When a buyer would come my job was to demonstrate a particular animal. As a horse gets older a sunken spot would appear above the eyes, he taught me how to use a syringe and fill the void with air that would last several days.

On one of his trips, a horse had fallen down in the truck. All the way back to Sacramento he had been stepped and crapped on by the other horses. What a mess. We washed and doctored him but we couldn't do a thing about all the hide and hair missing. Nothing serious was wrong but he sure limped. The next day, two of the sweetest ladies came by looking for a horse with a quiet disposition. The beaten up animal was tied to a hitching post in preparation for his doctoring that morning. The ladies expressed some concern about his well-being.

"That is a very valuable horse." My boss assured them. "He was a Hollywood horse of some renown. They used him in an episode of Rawhide to leap over a cliff. The hair will grow back and he'll be as good as new. The studio was so impressed with him they decided he deserved retirement. They made me promise to find the kindest people possible for him." He continued on in this vein while I stood by stroking the poor animals neck.

The ladies were cooing and clucking like two hens. Nothing could stop them now from purchasing this bedraggled beast. He mentioned some outrageous sum, but they were not to be dissuaded. He promised immediate delivery as a bonus. With smiles all around, even I was inclined to believe this long litany of B.S. Thus it started, all winter. Every horse had a story, mostly untrue.

Summer was coming quickly, another month and school would be out. My grades were good. My parents did little to influence my life. My father was well on his way to becoming a full time alcoholic. There was never any physical abuse, mostly he left me alone but his words would cut so deep and painful. My two sisters, both older than myself seemed to get along well with him. My mother, a very stoic person was slowly losing her enjoyment of life. Maybe sensing some dark clouds on the horizon.

As a family we had immigrated from Germany to Canada when I was five years old. Both my parents lost a large amount of their family during World War II. From there we moved to West Sacramento when I was ten years of age. My father was a mason, mostly in stone but he could work with brick and block as well. He was a skilled craftsman and rarely lacked for employment. My mother would work in local factories as an assembly line worker to fill her days.

One fine spring Saturday as I was throwing a saddle on my first horse, a stranger and my boss walked over, the stranger introducing himself as Joe. He needed several horses and would like to try them out. Making his selection on the first horse he invited me to join him on a ride. A little gruff, he seemed to be all that a real cowboy should be. Straw cowboy hat, boots with spurs, a strong craggy face with an unfiltered cigarette in the corner of his mouth, sitting his horse like he was born there; I had stumbled onto my hero.

We rode side by side, not saying much. He took out his pack

of Lucky Strike cigarettes, putting one in his mouth he looked across at me and asked if I wanted one. Both my parents smoked and I would on occasion steal one and smoke it where no one could see me. I was no stranger to them so I gladly took one, thanking him. He acted neither surprised nor concerned.

Riding back to the stables Joe asked what my plans were for the summer. I answered, "Don't have any. Probably ride horses as long as I'm needed."

"If you want I'll give you a job. It's on a big cattle ranch north of town. The pay's sixty bucks a month, room and board. The work's hard and you won't have any days off." I knew Joe's offer was sincere.

There was no need to think about it, I could hardly contain my excitement.

"I'll come over to your house and talk to your folks, get their okay when we get done here." Joe stated.

I told him where we lived, but said he didn't need to, since I doubted anyone cared. "I do," he said. So we left it at that.

That evening introductions were made between my parents and Joe. My mother excused herself shortly after. The plans for me hadn't been discussed yet, but they had already consumed several shots of whiskey. They persuaded me to have a cigarette and shot of whiskey with them. I obliged but not gladly. I stole away at the first chance. They were to become good drinking friends. I'm not sure if my summer plans ever came up, somehow my future didn't look as bright as it had earlier that day.

Four weeks later school ended. Joe came and picked me up as promised. Everyone was gone that morning so without fanfare I threw my meager belongings in the back of his pickup and we drove to the ranch.

A small bunkhouse would be my home for the next three months. There was a tiny kitchen, a bathroom, and a cot to sleep on. Small but adequate.

The ranch itself was sixteen hundred acres of irrigated pasture and dry fields for wintering the cattle. There were four hundred head to take care of and move on a rotation schedule. The work was hard as promised and the days were long. Many times I would go out alone at midnight or later if irrigation water needed to be changed. It was much easier to use a horse to get around the wet pastures. Plus, I felt like I had some protection from the things that lurked in the dark, just waiting to pounce on my back while I was bent over a ditch at three o-clock in the morning. Miles from the safety of your bunkhouse, all alone on a fog shrouded lane, surrounded by large overhanging trees you just knew that the wooly-buggers were waiting to pounce and eviscerate you. It never happened, but many nights were spent riding with my head turned backwards.

Joe was a true horse and cattleman. A bachelor, short but very wiry and strong, he was as lively at the end of a long day as the beginning of it. We got on very well. Most days we worked together, at nights we worked alone as needed. He would tell me what time to get up and where the water needed to be changed. I had my own alarm clock so he left me alone to get things done. I was dependable, it was very important to me.

Most days were just as I hoped they would be. The majority of the time was spent on horseback, riding side by side down tree covered lanes, smoking cigarettes. Checking and moving the cattle, he never tired of explaining things to me.

On occasion he would invite me over to his much larger house. We would smoke and drink a shot or two of whiskey, sometimes not saying much at all. We didn't have a need to I guess. Such a fine way for a young man to grow up, I thought, often devoid of TV or even a phone. I celebrated my twelfth birthday in just such a manner. Joe didn't know and I'm not sure it would have mattered. Turning twelve didn't seem like such a milestone anyway. On occasion I would get lonely, wishing there were other kids around.

My father came to the ranch several times that summer. It was to drink with Joe, and drink they did. When I knew he was there, I would become scarce. In the rare event that I crossed paths with my father that summer, we were friendly but cordial. He had no need to be demonstrative and mine was becoming less so. Joe and I never discussed my family life. He must have thought it was none of his business or he just didn't care. I was never reprimanded by Joe about my work and there were the rare words of praise. All things considered I thought of myself as well off.

Back to school that fall. Seventh grade, and all the kids were talking about Frankie Avalon, Elvis Presley and other singers whom I had never heard about, shows on the television I had never seen. Though the summer was spent on a horse, wearing Levis and cowboy boots, at school, slacks and a white shirt were my everyday clothes. I liked dressing neatly and giving a well-groomed appearance. Some other kids would make fun of me but for the most part I was left alone or accepted. This may have stemmed from my first four years of school being under the yardsticks of Catholic nuns. My one and only act of defiance ever to take place in these younger years happened in the classrooms under the tutelage of these battle-hardened and children hating nuns. Quite often the knuckles of one hand would receive a fast painful rap from the yard stick of some sexually frustrated, penguin-attired woman. One moment in particular was brief and decisive. With a smacking sound that reverberated off the walls, the instrument landed. "Damn that hurts!" It was out before I could even begin to stop it. With audible gasps, and horrified looks my classmates waited for Satan to come and burn me with his pitchfork.

He didn't. My tormenter, her eyes squinted, and lips compressed into a thin line, stared at me. Slowly, through clenched teeth she uttered, "Put out the other hand." Squirming so bad from fright, it's a wonder my back wasn't thrown out. I tried in vain to say the Rosary to myself, but there was no room in my brain for anything but fear. She slowly raised the wooden stick that served no other purpose than to instill a brain numbing fear. It did. I tried to close my eyes but couldn't. She stared in rapture at it, as if it alone could end all the misery in the world. So swiftly it descended and hit that the sound was gone before the pain came. And come it did. Unsuccessfully, I tried to shake the misery away. I couldn't and didn't cry. This must have sated some vengeance for her barren, wasted life. It sure as hell cured me of ever testing her or any others again.

I enjoyed the seventh grade. School came pretty easy for me, especially if a small effort was made in some of the harder courses. Track was my sport of choice. Sprints were a good fit, coming mostly first or second. There was one boy my own age. He was a Russian immigrant and would beat me at times when my training wasn't done regularly. I thought smoking might be hindering my running efforts, but it fit too well with my cowboy lifestyle and the addiction had taken root.

Most of my hours after school and track practice were spent at the horse trader's, riding and training. Getting them ready to show for potential buyers. Don, the horse trader, was glad to have me whenever possible and paid me weekly. It was a good arrangement and made me feel important.

The weekends at times were spent out at Gibson Ranch working for Joe. He hired another person to help with feeding and other chores. Mostly we would ride horses, checking, doctoring and moving the cattle as needed. It was such a good, fulfilling life for someone twelve years of age, well on my way to becoming an adult. School caused me no problems, I had more employment than I could handle and money in my pockets. My parents felt no need to intervene in my life. Cigarettes and whiskey were always at hand.

Joe and I were spending the day riding. "Do you want your own horse and saddle?" The question was unexpected.

"Yes." I responded without hesitation, followed by half a dozen questions that Joe had no time to answer till I finished them all.

"He's four, green broke, eight hundred pounds, pie bald with a glass eye, almost a Pinto. He was hard to handle for the other owner so I got him and a Powder River saddle for a hundred and fifty bucks. He's yours for the same amount but I have to warn you, he's got a front hoof that's white."

I peppered him with questions all through the day but that long sentence must have used up all the words he had.

The next morning, we spent trying the horse. He was small by most standards. Later I would come to realize it didn't matter, I would never become a large man.

The transaction was made. I had no money left but more would come in. Joe said he would board the horse for me free of charge if I promised to stay and work on the Gibson ranch again next summer. That was easy.

That summer started like the one before, but it was much easier, having a much better idea of what was expected.

"Our world is gonna go to shit." Joe said resignedly early one morning over coffee. "Just talked to the owners and they're shipping us five hundred head of first calf heifers next week." Not clear on what it meant exactly, I asked Joe for more. "You'll find out soon enough." It was abrupt and unlike him; he was clearly troubled.

The trucks came, one after the other they disgorged their loads, swollen bellies, ready to give birth. Joe shaking his head in disgust as he watched. "Too young, just too God damn young!" he repeated over and over to himself.

We kept them as close as possible to the main ranch. Early

the next morning we spotted the first one laying on her side. We trotted over on our horses, dismounted and hobbled them.

"Grab the chains and disinfectant." He sat behind her with both feet on the cow's ass. Two small black hooves protruded from her birth canal along with fluids and blood.

Joe grabbed the small hooves, timing his pulls with her contractions. With a gush of fluid and the sound of a wet towel landing on concrete, the calf was born. He wiped the nose clean, stood up and said, "Let's gather our stuff and back off, see what happens."

That first one went well. Mom got up, turned around and started cleaning the baby with her tongue. We stayed long enough to make sure she discharged her placenta.

We finished dinner together that evening and rode out just before dark to make another round. With no problems each round would take about one hour. We went back home, slept for three hours and made another round, this would become our schedule. Our horses stayed saddled and tied up continuously, we would rotate them with a fresh one every day.

Before sunrise the next morning another heifer was down. There were no hooves protruding this time. Joe would put his arm in her canal and pull on one leg at a time. This didn't work. The heifer was starting to bellow mournfully. He took the pulling chains and reaching inside her, Joe would wrap a chain around each small hoof. With the ends that were outside we pulled hard. Gaining very little as the heifer would bear down, this would repeat for the next hour.

"Let's use a horse to pull." Joe wasn't looking at me when he said this. "Use yours and I'll stay on the ground. Face your horse towards me and back him up slowly until I tell you to stop."

I mounted, Joe attached the end of my lariat to the chains. "Put some tension on it, when I tell you, back up and pull harder but go easy at first."

Five o-clock in the morning, it was dark and foggy, only a Coleman lantern shedding its feeble yellow light. The heifer was moaning. It looked garish and I was scared, not of the dark but that I would fail and cause her more suffering.

The rope was snug, "Pull now, back up your horse a little." With the rope dallied around my saddle horn the tension was strong. "Hold there for a minute." Joe's voice was cold and resolute.

"Now, pull hard...harder!" I pulled back on the reins, my rope so tight I took another dally. The calf moved out a fraction. "Keep pulling." My horse took a step backwards, the cow slid several inches on the grass. This young animal was moaning pitifully, I had never heard such a mournful, pain filled sound in my life.

The head appeared. One more hard pull and the calf slid to the ground. Joe quickly pulled the chains off and cleaned the nose. He put both his hands on the calf, rocking it gently. Then more firmly. Nothing. I sat on my horse, transfixed. Joe stood over the body, "It's dead, we can't do anymore here. She will make it or she won't," he dead-panned, looking down at this poor young cow. I was unable to comprehend his detachment. I was so naive, it felt like we should have done more.

"You'll get used to it soon enough." It was prophetic. "Let's drag the calf over to the gate and we'll have the guys haul it to a dry lot. There will be more before this is over."

We put my rope back on the calf's hind legs and I dragged it over to the gate from the back of my horse.

Luckily for us the owners had sent two other men to take care of the irrigating while we dealt with the cattle. Every day they had the unpleasant duty of hauling the carcasses to a dry lot. Later they dug a large hole with a backhoe and unceremoniously tossed the carcasses in, covering them with lime.

The summer wore on. It took a toll on me but more so on Joe. As the foreman, he took the losses personally. He would call the owners often, asking them to let us call a veterinarian, or better, have one stay with us to help. We weren't equipped for this. They said the losses were acceptable and to just carry on.

Sometimes there was nothing we could do. The hips of the unborn calf would lock with hips of the mother and despite our efforts we couldn't get the calf out. After hours of trying we would simply take a rifle and shoot the animal in the head, ending the misery.

I learned how to turn off my emotions, standing by her head, the cow watched as I pulled the trigger.

Through the summer I learned what the dying tremors meant. That summer I was glad when school started. Before I moved back home for the start of classes Joe asked me if I wanted to move to Visalia. It was about four hundred miles south of Sacramento.

"They need a foreman on a feedlot. It's a good job and I'll need help. Think about it and let me know. They expect me in two weeks."

"How will I get there, and what about my horse."

"I can haul you both when I go. There's plenty of room."

"Let me clear it with my folks." Joe and my father had remained drinking buddies throughout this time. I didn't see any problems getting his approval.

My mother was very quiet when I explained my plans to her. She internalized her feelings but I never doubted her affection for me. I knew she had concerns about her only son being so many miles away. She had reservations about Joe and his propensity for alcohol. One evening as the two of us sat on the back patio watching the sun disappear, my mother confided that she had the utmost faith I would always make the right decisions. This was as close to a passionate speech she had ever made to me.

We spent several hours over the weekend just sitting, drinking coffee. We would take turns uttering a sentence on occasion but mostly we were quiet, simply enjoying our short time together. I didn't smoke in front of her, out of respect.

Towards the end of the week Joe called the house early one morning. "Can you get out here before noon?" No preamble or unnecessary speech. It was Joe's character to keep it short. "I know it's sooner than expected but I can have your horse and saddle loaded and we can get out of here by twelve."

My father had left for work already so it was left to my mother. It was a half hour drive to the ranch.

"Get your stuff ready and I'll clear it with work. Oh....I'll call school and tell them you won't be back in. You'll have to let them know where you're going to be"

"Okay." I answered, walking to my room.

School had only started two days ago so I had no books at home. Packing was easy. All my clothes fit in two suitcases. A pair of work boots, cowboy boots, cowboy hat. Some reading books and winter clothes. I was on my way. I gave my two sisters very little thought. We liked each other well enough, we were just ambivalent towards one another.

Joe was ready when we arrived. I threw my stuff into the back of the pickup. My horse was in the trailer, contently munching on some hay.

"I got your rifle outta the bunk house, it's in the pickup behind the seat. Was that all you left here?" Joe asked as he walked around the pickup, checking the ropes that kept the load from spilling out.

My .22 rifle was important to me, I'd bought it that summer, used, from a man Joe knew. It was important to me to have it. "That was all." I answered him.

Joe shook hands with my mother. "He'll be fine, he's a good boy." No long speeches.

I hugged her. Maybe for the first time ever. It felt good, but a little awkward. She drove off, no need to say anything.

With one last check of the tires we jumped into the cab and left the Gibson Ranch. Excitement rapidly shoving my sadness aside. I had just turned thirteen years old a month ago, I so pitied other boys that didn't have this much joy and excitement in their lives.

The trip went without incident. I couldn't see much of the countryside after it got dark. Mostly one farming community after another. The ranch was miles out in the country. The land was flat and the smell of ammonia and manure was strong. There was a modest home and many outbuildings. It was late evening, and one of the hired hands greeted us. There were small buildings that served as homes for the hired help and families, if they had any. Mine was a typical small bunkhouse with bed, kitchen and living area all in one tiny space. The bathroom was separate.

I unloaded my horse and was shown where to put him for the night. Plenty of hay and water awaited him. Joe took the minimum gear for the night to his home as did I.

"Come over about six, we can have a cup of coffee then run to town and get breakfast and some groceries." Six was sleeping late for Joe.

My pay was eighty dollars a month with room and board. The ranch would furnish groceries and we would do our own cooking. Cigarettes, alcohol, toiletries and other personal items were our own responsibilities. A standard arrangement. We bought enough for both of us and Joe paid. I had my own money so purchased some smokes, and other things.

We took our time driving back, checking out some of the countryside. It was flat and nondescript, miles and miles of pasture and hay fields, occasionally broken by ranch buildings. It didn't matter to me a whole lot, I figured most days would be spent on the feedlot anyway.

The man who would be working under Joe, seemed genuinely happy to see us, especially to have Joe here, taking on the responsibility of a large feedlot. At any given time, there should be about twenty-five hundred to three thousand head of cattle being fattened for slaughter. Normally an animal would stay here for about eighty to ninety days. It was a typical operation but better than most. The equipment was in good shape, the corrals strong and well maintained with concrete troughs for feeding.

Curious as to my job, I asked Joe if he knew what it would be.

"Yep, follow us."

A long covered hay shed awaited me. Three hundred feet long and eighty feet wide, it was two thirds full of alfalfa hay. It has a wonderful smell like no other. There was an empty slot down the middle. A long chain conveyer ran down the slot to one end of the building where awaited a large chopper that would grind the hay into much smaller and palatable pieces. From there it would be mixed with grains and other products, then stored in huge bins until needed. I saw my future, it looked hard but smelled nice.

"Ten tons a day. Five in the morning and five in the evening." Joe was grinning. "Should take about three and a half hours each shift, maybe a little more for some others." He was still grinning, throwing me the challenge.

"I don't know; it usually took the other guy a straight eight hours to do all ten tons." Felipe had a very strong Mexican accent. "He tore his shoulder and can't do it no more."

"We'll see what happens. Let's check the rest of it." Joe led the way as he said this.

We spent the rest of the day learning the operation, and meeting the rest of the help. They were a good solid bunch. All Mexicans, friendly and hard workers we would learn.

That afternoon at four I was told to go to the hay barn and get instructions on my job. Ernesto had been doing the conveyor work with help from others when it was available. It was simple but physically demanding. Each bale of hay weighed one hundred pounds. With a hay hook you could drag a bale or carry it to the belt that was moving constantly. Laying them straight, you would clip the two wires holding the bale together, pulling them off in one motion. Folding the wires several times you would toss them into a special bin next to the belt. It was important to make sure you didn't leave any wire. If it went well the next bale would be snug against the previous one. A long line, making their way to the incredibly loud grinder, called a hammer mill. Twenty bales to a ton, five tons, one hundred bales, twice a day. With Ernesto and I both doing it we could hold a relaxed pace, alone it would be tough.

Showering that evening, then organizing my living quarters I was able to relax and have dinner. Dinner was simple, can of corned beef hash. A can of peas or string beans followed by a can of fruit cocktail. If I was still hungry another can of something would get opened. Every night was the same only the can's contents were different. I have never thought much about food, it was only necessary to fill a void and fuel me. At times it would annoy me to spend time heating even canned food. Then you would have dishes, even eating out of the pan still created some. Sometimes I would make a baloney sandwich with Velveeta cheese and lots of mayo. Simple, quick and only one knife that you could wipe off and use for weeks.

I had neither phone nor television. That was fine, I didn't have anyone to call and TV didn't interest me much. I had a radio and listened to it most evenings until bed time. I loved to read books. Every night in bed I would read till I was no longer able to stay awake. Simple, but my life was in my hands and I was very happy.

Four-thirty and my alarm went off. I enjoyed mornings and this day held lots of promise. Too early to eat a proper breakfast, I made some instant coffee, consumed a baloney sandwich, had a smoke and went to the hay barn. It was still very dark but the barn had excellent lighting. I filled two thirds of the belt with bales of hay before starting the hammer mill. It would dim the lights momentarily, the electric motor consumed a good amount of power in its starting phase. Ten feet in front of the maw of this beast there were short poles set on either side of the belt. Large, red, emergency buttons were mounted on these poles. If you got yourself hung up on the belt presumably you could hit one of these and shut the whole system down. A theory I didn't want to test.

I started the conveyor. Three hours later, drenched in sweat, my first hundred bales were done. Not too bad, but for whatever reason I felt compelled to do much better. I had no explanation for this need. All week I experimented. They left me alone but watched in some amusement, especially Ernesto.

By the end of the week I had it figured out. Filling the majority of the belt with the bales I wouldn't clip the wires until the belt was loaded, then walking down the row I would clip the wires and pull them off as I went. Folding all the wires and throwing them into the bin at one time. This saved a considerable number of steps and time. Other innovations let me achieve my goal of two hours. I was happy now.

The weekends were mine. I still helped some on the

conveyors but others took over the duty for those two days. The weather was fine, with warm days that made riding with Joe, checking the cattle very pleasurable.

That Sunday evening Joe and I were sitting on his front porch enjoying our coffee, smokes, and intermittent bouts of conversation.

"I should be thinking about school." I was searching for guidance when I voiced this. School had been open for about two weeks.

"Probably should." Joe must have thought that was considerable guidance when he answered.

"I'll check tomorrow." I said yawning. Eight o-clock and I was ready for bed, pitiful. Joe didn't offer anything further. There was never any doubt that if I needed help he would be available.

A quarter mile east of the ranch was an intersection. Having seen a school bus go by the previous week there was a chance I could get a ride to school. I got up early, did my hay work, showered, put on school clothes and walked the quarter mile. Not sure what time the bus came by I had to wait about a half hour. Not sure if this was a stop, I was the only one there, I waved my arms. He stopped and opened the doors.

"Can I get a ride to school?" I asked politely.

He studied me for a moment. "Are you a runaway?" This was not what I expected.

I gave him a brief explanation, ending with, "I really would like to go to school." I must have been convincing.

"Get in. Sure hope I don't regret this" He didn't say any more as he drove the five miles to school. More stops were made and the bus was half full when the trip was finished. They were all Mexicans; I was unable to understand what they were saying. They were polite but left me to myself.

"The office is over there." The driver offered, pointing.

Maybe trying to erase his earlier gruffness, I thought to myself. I thanked him.

"I would like to enroll in school" Standing in front of the secretary's desk I thought this would be adequate to get me in. After all, this was a school and I was a student.

For the second time that day someone looked at me as if they didn't comprehend what I meant.

"Ooookaaaay." It was drawn out slowly. "Are your parents here?" She looked behind me, as if I was hiding them until they were needed.

I explained again my circumstances. "Wait here and I'll get someone to help you." Soon she returned with another woman.

"Normally we don't do it this way. We need your parents, or at least a guardian to sign you in." For the third time that day I gave a quick rendition of my situation. I waited politely for a response.

"Let's try this." This, was thinking to herself as she spoke. "We'll have you take some tests and see what grade you fit into, we'll send some papers home and you can have your legal guardian sign them. I'm sure we can make it work."

I took the tests and it was determined that I was indeed suitable for the eighth grade, though they moved me up to advanced Algebra. I also had a note saying I had permission to ride the bus.

Things were looking good. That evening after work I took the guardian papers to have Joe sign them.

"What are these?" He asked.

"I guess they say you are responsible for me", shrugging as I handed them to him.

He sat there for several minutes studying the two papers. "I guess it's time you learn that I can't read or write worth a damn." This was a complete surprise; I didn't know what to say. "I can write my name so just show me where to sign."

I did. He wrote something that may have been his name. His inability to read or write never came up again.

The school issue was settled. My days took on a routine. Up at four-thirty, work two hours, eat a baloney sandwich for breakfast while I made two for my lunch at school. Shower, catch the bus, go to school, come home, work another two-three hours, eat my canned dinner, visit with Joe or Ernesto for a while, shower and go to bed.

Weekends would be spent riding with Joe or one of the other cowboys. One building held a community laundry facility, free for the employees. A nice feature. Usually on Sundays one of the families would invite me to have a real dinner with them. This was so kind of them. I could not have been treated any better.

It was getting onto winter and the days were cool and sometimes cold. Christmas came. Joe and I did the essential work that day and spent the evening over a jelly jar glass of Cognac and a cigar. One of my most memorable Christmas days.

This went on for another four months. I had developed an interest in girls but didn't understand why. There was no time for this pursuit but the question of their appeal became more intriguing.

The work was hard but I was extremely happy and content "Your parents are coming down this weekend." We were sitting on the porch one evening "They should be here mid Saturday." As Joe told me this a pang of loneliness went through me. Not having seen or talked to them for eight months, I suddenly realized just how much I missed them. Joe had been keeping them informed about my well-being via phone.

The excitement built over the next few days. I made sure my bunkhouse was in order and that my laundry was done. For some reason it was important not to show any failings, even on the domestic front.

They looked the same. My father was short by most standards but he was stoutly built and very strong. Greetings were made. My father handed me a grocery bag as a greeting gift. In it were a carton of Pall Mall cigarettes and a fifth of Old Crow whiskey. This was good, I felt accepted and it would save me money.

The rest of the day was spent showing them around, then evening came. My father and Joe left in the pickup, on their way to a local bar. My mother made dinner and we talked about my sisters and life back in Sacramento. She asked about my schooling and how I was being treated, they sounded like such mother questions.

My parents were staying in Joe's house, which was much bigger and had a spare bedroom.

The next morning, I took my mother riding. She loved to be on horseback. It was a beautiful April day. We spent hours riding, looking at cattle in the pastures. She smiled and laughed more than l could remember her ever doing.

Watching them leave was hard. I was very torn between wanting to go home with them and not having the responsibility of a job and school. Or.... staying and proving I was ready for adulthood. I stood there watching them drive down the road. Even when they were out of sight I stood there transfixed, as if wishing them back.

Joe left me alone that evening, he must have known what I was feeling.

My somber mood was dispelled by the next morning and my routine felt welcome. My world looked good once again. A full bottle of whiskey and all the smokes that I would need for several months. I was not much of a drinker, but on occasion it was nice to contribute to the drinking cause with my fellow workers.

"I've been trying to get your back wages from the owner and not having much luck." I could tell Joe was pissed. This was rare for him to display emotion. He continued, "I might have to go to small claims court."

He had been giving me forty dollars a month from his own account. My wages had been increased to one hundred twenty a month because of performance. I had not seen any of my wages and had been inquiring more frequently.

School had gotten out and I would start as a Freshman the next fall. My grades very high, but there was no one to show them to. Joe's mood was becoming a little withdrawn. I would find out why that evening.

"We have a hearing tomorrow with the Labor Board. It's about your wages. It'll be a binding arbitration. So whatever happens that'll be the end of it." Joe was very serious as he spoke. "The owner will be there."

I didn't understand what this all meant. I was nervous.

At the courthouse the next day Joe and I were sitting on the bench outside a room. The clerk came out and instructed Joe to go in, the arbitrator and the owner were already inside. I was told to stay seated on the bench and wait out here. For whatever reason I was not allowed in the room.

One-hour later Joe came out, angry. "Let's go. This place is a pig sty, it's full of hogs wallowing in their own shit." The clerk heard him but said nothing. This was so out of character it frightened me.

On the way back to the ranch he settled down enough and explained what had happened. "They decided that since I hired you it was up to me to pay you out of my wages. The owner said I never revealed to him how young you were. Maybe, maybe not, it shouldn't make any difference, you still did all your work." He was getting mad again.

He didn't say another word until we parked back at the ranch. "I'll make some phone calls. Go pack your stuff, we're leaving in the morning. Don't do any work, I'll explain to Ernesto."

As promised we loaded up early and left. Joe had called my parents, telling them what was happening, and to expect me home that evening. I still had the money I came down with and a little extra that Joe had given me throughout the last nine months. I still had my horse, in the trailer behind us.

Joe was ashamed, he said pointedly. He also said he would make good every penny owed me. About six hundred dollars. By now, my anger had turned to disappointment and a certain amount of disgust. This was not the way I wanted to return home. Not making sure to get a firm agreement on the money up front was a lesson that stayed with me the rest of my life.

THE DOLDRUMS

We returned to the Gibson Ranch late that afternoon. It was being leased by another large cattle rancher. Joe had worked for him in prior years and he was quite happy to have him return. I had a job if I wanted one, at one hundred fifty a month, plus the usual room and board. He assured me he had it cleared with the owners and they would be happy with the arrangements since I came recommended by Joe. I agreed, with the stipulation that I would be paid every month, no exceptions. Joe said he understood and that it was fine.

We unloaded my horse and our other belongings and together we drove to my house that evening. My family still lived in West Sacramento. It felt good to be home, even if only for a night or two.

My mom cooked a great dinner so we ate, drank a little; even my mother indulged. It was nice.

Joe left later that night. My parents said they would bring me out that weekend, two days away. I spent those two days seeing some of my friends.

Saturday I was driven out to the ranch. My mom and I rode horses all that day. Joe and my father joined us for a big part of it on some other ranch horses; there were always plenty to go around. That evening my parents went home. Joe and I settled into our routine.

It was comfortable. We had plenty of hired help. Joe and I were able to focus on the cattle, which had already calved and were doing well. The new lessees were very professional in their operation and took pride in their cattle. My check came without fail every month. I could not have been happier.

My fourteenth birthday came and went that August. I remained quiet about it, it just wasn't important to me. I needed nothing and didn't want the attention.

The ranch had twenty stalls for horses, each one having a private paddock. There were dozens of wooden corrals, and a round one, for breaking horses. It was a beautiful ranch, well thought out and impeccably maintained by the owners.

That summer they began renting the stalls to private individuals. It was a good arrangement. The owners made extra money and people were able to enjoy the miles of dirt roads and trails that were part of the ranch.

My evenings and weekends were increasingly spent riding and working with horses that gave their owners problems. The extra money that I made doing this looked good in my bank account. Joe was an excellent horseman, and would give advice to me when there were questions about a particular animal. His encouragement and enthusiasm were also greatly appreciated.

There were increasingly more young girls my own age who would come out to ride their horses. Much to my enjoyment, one girl in particular, two years my senior, spent more and more time with me. She was blonde, attractive, and a pleasure to be around. She taught me many things about maturity, but most importantly she taught me what girls had that was so important to boys.

My Freshman year in high school started that fall. I lived at home during the week and Friday nights Joe would come to our house in West Sacramento. He and my father would have a few drinks and converse. Sometimes I would join them or finish my school work if needed. He would drive me back to the ranch later that evening. I no longer worked for the ranch owners because of school, but they encouraged me to keep working with the private horse owners. It was a pleasant arrangement and the money I made was an added bonus.

The winter went by very quickly. I was fortunate and stayed on the honor roll my whole Freshman year. I had some friends in school but never developed any real close bonds.

As school ended, my parents sold the house that we had lived in for the last five years. It was in the suburbs and my father wanted to live in the country. They rented a small two-bedroom house with ten acres of pasture. It was in North Highlands, right on the north end of the runway from McClellan Air Force base. This was great for me, being only two miles from the Gibson Ranch. My oldest sister Sonja, three years my senior was in the process of getting married soon and well into her own life. My other sister, Anita, who was one year older than me would be coming with us. She was to have the second bedroom. I guess no one had given any thought to where I would live since I was gone most of the time.

Just before I was to start working at the ranch again for the summer, Joe informed me that the county was purchasing the ranch in its entirety. It would no longer be a cattle operation. They would turn it into a county park. He also said he was ready for a change and had a friend that owned a trucking company. He was going to haul cattle. I had no idea what the hell was happening.

"I talked to the county and they wanted me to stay here and show them the irrigation system and all the other things that made this ranch work." I think Joe was trying in his own way to be sensitive as he continued. "I told them I was leaving tomorrow and wasn't interested, but you might be. You know the ranch as well as anyone."

The next day I helped Joe pack his things. I was very sad to think this may be our last time together.

"You'll do well." We were leaning on the front bumper of his pickup, enjoying what may have been our last smoke together. It meant a lot when he said this to me. Without fanfare, we shook hands and said goodbye.

Later that day I met with a county official and we worked out an agreement. They would pay me for two weeks if I would show them how the systems functioned. The rest of the summer they would pay me if my services were needed. I could stay in the bunkhouse throughout the summer for free. With a slight grin he called me a "consultant."

As a bonus they encouraged me to continue working with the public and their horses. They wanted that portion of the ranch to continue being used as it was added income for them as well as good public relations. It was a nice source of income for me.

Any remnants of my dark mood from Joe's departure were quickly dispelled as I was able to salvage my summer, not to mention the attractive girl that was headed in my direction, hopefully to discuss horses with me.

We discussed horses and many other things that summer. A year older than myself, she had the poise and confidence of an adult. Very attractive, short hair, almost the same height as myself, her name was Jane. I was totally taken with her. We became inseparable that summer. She boarded her horse in one of the stalls. Having her own car, she drove to the ranch most days to ride her horse and be with me.

That August I had someone to celebrate my fifteenth birthday with. We drank a little of my whiskey and became quite giddy.

Summer ended as it surely must. I was starting my Sophomore year at school. I continued to work at the ranch on weekends but moved home. I brought my own horse home since we had such a large pasture. The bus stopped close to my house so it was convenient to get to school.

Not all things were rosy. Since the house had only two bedrooms, and my sister had one of them there wasn't any room for me inside.

My father saw no problem with this. A tent was such a simple solution to such a minor problem. With pride and a copious amount of whiskey in him he assured me one would be forthcoming tomorrow. It was such a pleasant evening I slept outside that night under the stars.

True to his word he brought a tent home the next day after work. It was used, very well used. Left to my own devices, it took me several hours to set up in the pasture behind the house. Old canvas that had many weak spots and several holes, this would be my home through the winter. A canvas cot came with it. My bed didn't warrant sheets and blankets so a sleeping bag would do. I found my dresser in the garage, moved it to my bedroom. A long extension cord that ran from the house gave me electricity for a light, but that was it, it wouldn't run a heater. So be it, my future looked cold but otherwise fine.

Jane and I continued seeing each other that fall, in and after school. She was a Junior, one year ahead of me but it was working fine. She had a hard time comprehending my living arrangements, one time commenting that it looked like I had been discarded. I assured her I was fine and quite content, which was the truth. For two months there had been no need to worry about working or the many other things that had occupied my time. Only school and Jane, life was so simple and easy. When it rained, there was some time spent covering my bed and belongings with tarps, the roof was acquiring more leaks as time and the elements wore on. Also it was a little cool on those foggy mornings that chilled all the way through a body.

My father was enamored with the ranching lifestyle. This became very apparent one evening.

"I think we may be getting a ranch in Nevada." I studied him in disbelief, as if he had vowed to stop drinking. "We applied for a homestead in Nevada from B.L.M. It got approved."

This was so new and unexpected I was at a loss for words. Finally asking who *we* were.

"Joe and me. We've been working on it for four months. They just informed me today that the application was excepted. Not sure about Joe's, we filed on different sections." His excitement was infectious. The questions started to pour out of me. "What the hell, let's have a drink." With this exclamation he got two glasses and a bottle of whiskey.

Most times I was very cautious about drinking with him, if we drank very much it could become unpleasant for me. By now my mind was conjuring up images, vast rolling plains of lush green pasture, with cows, as far as the eye could see, grazing contently. Such a pleasant vision.

"We're not sure exactly where it is yet. Somewhere in Dixie Valley." In one sentence my vision was gone. How could you not know where your ranch was, I thought to myself. My mother joined us, glass of wine in hand. She was aware that this had all transpired, but figured it was best if my father divulged it to me.

Along with another small glass of whiskey, it became more clear and foggier simultaneously.

In the early 1960's, B.L.M. opened parts of Nevada to the Homestead Act. A person applied for the ground he wanted and if approved you had to have a dwelling, a well that produced a certain flow of water, and one tenth of the acreage in cultivation. If these criteria were met in five years, a deed was given to you. If there were undue hardships, you could apply for extensions. The only fees were for filing the application.

"That's what the truck is for. We're going to start hauling stuff up there." I tried to think of what stuff he meant. He continued.

"Joe got us permission to tear down the race track at the Gibson Ranch, so we'll start this weekend."

The inside and outside of the one-mile track were fenced with 2x6 redwood boards, each one sixteen feet long. Plus, about 1500 4x6 redwood posts, eight feet long. This was a gold mine of material, at no cost. We simply had to remove thousands of nails, and pull the posts out of the ground.

This consumed every weekend and evening for two months. The truck was a 1952 International two-and-a-half ton. It came with a van, we removed that and put a twenty-foot flatbed on it. It could haul five tons easy. All the good was used out of it when my father bought it. The truck was cheap, he was happy. Over the years I would learn to hate that piece of junk.

I didn't mind the work at all. I was part of an effort that would compensate me later in life, at least that was the theory. Jane struggled with my absence, as did I. On occasion she did help weekends so we could be together at least part of the time.

By January there was a large stack of posts and lumber sitting in our pasture. My father was on a roll. He learned of a mountainous pile of used railroad ties next to the Oakland Bay. They were free to the public for the next three months, then they were to be disposed of. How my father learned of these things I haven't a clue. Any time the word free was uttered, it was like catnip, it didn't matter the object, he would take it.

There went the rest of any free time I may have enjoyed. Saturday morning, three a.m. We left the house in the truck, headed for the pile of ties, three hours away. Perfect timing, there was just enough light to start loading. Each tie weighed roughly one hundred pounds, some more, some less. We had to untangle them from the pile where they had been dozed together, carry them to the truck and get them on the flatbed. My father was not tall but he was incredibly strong, he enjoyed hard work and never left it to others. His work ethic was impeccable when sober.

He was able to lift a tie and walk to the truck quite comfortably. It was more of a struggle for me, but I managed to match him, almost. He expected no less of me and I was aware of this.

Shortly after lunch we were done loading and stacking. One hundred and twenty of those bastards, secured and ready for transport home. The truck had a six-cylinder engine and was loaded heavy. A pitiful combination. It was dark before we got home. At least I would have Sunday off.

Not so. My father had made a decision. Not wanting to waste energy unloading, then reloading them again in the future, we would simply haul them to the ranch in Nevada. I expressed some concern about the unknown location of said ranch.

"Joe and me were up there a couple months ago with maps. We kind of know where it's at." His tone left no doubt I should keep my concerns to myself. "We'll dump them close, that'll be good enough for now."

My mother fixed a quick dinner. She made some sandwiches and coffee to take along. She knew the trip might be difficult, for many reasons. Her concern was conveyed to me through her eyes. She knew better than to intervene.

We left quickly, time pressing us. Sitting on the passenger side, in the dark of the cab, premonitions and excitement took turns entering and exiting my mind. I would finally get to see my future.

We drove in the slow lane, headed towards Reno, barely able to make the speed limit. My father had been taking a nip of whiskey periodically from his flask. We didn't say anything, smoking cigarettes simultaneously, our only bond in that dark noisy cab.

The old Donner Summit highway was a nightmare. Single lane in either direction, it was a winding, switchback filled, torturous climb. Full of large trucks on their cross country routes, you got in line and stayed there, there was no passing or being passed. It must have been agony in a car, waiting for the infrequent and all too short passing lane. A bridge so narrow at the summit, you held your breath, fearful you would be sideswiped by oncoming traffic or accidentally drive off the edge. The descent to Donner Lake was every bit as harrowing as the climb.

Somehow, maybe intuitively, my father kept his drinking to a minimum. I was so relieved when we drove through Reno shortly after midnight. I didn't know anything about the remainder of the highway or the terrain, but my father had assured me it was mostly flat and uneventful.

Twenty minutes out of Reno, headed east, he pulled the truck over and simply stated, "Your turn."

We got out, stretched, and switched sides. I knew how to drive but had never driven this truck. It had a two speed rear end, the knob was on the main transmission lever. Up for a higher gear, down for a slightly lower gear. Sometimes you shifted this in conjunction with the main transmission. Once a person got the hang of it, the range of gears was doubled.

I had no driver's license or permit. It didn't matter, it was dark, the highway was deserted. The feeble headlights illuminating the desolate barren landscape. I drove on, through Fallon, Highway 50 my only focus. It became surreal, in the dark, a white carpet of craggy alkali bordered the highway on both sides. This went on for twenty miles.

I was tired, fighting sleep constantly. My father slept soundly, he had taken a few more drinks from his flask and apparently was unconcerned about my driving. There was no radio, my mind was the only source of entertainment. I kept driving east, there was nothing.

Almost fifty miles east of Fallon a small sign announced Frenchman Station, a rustic roadside bar and filling station that boasted any and all automobile repairs. Closed for the night, abandoned and wrecked cars littered the surrounding landscape, a scene suitable for some horror movie, I thought to myself. I had been told to watch for the sign to Dixie Valley several miles past the station. The sign was very small, almost inconsequential, as if to say don't go up here, there's nothing there. I felt somehow cheated, I wanted something grander, our ranch was up there somewhere.

Slowing down, I turned north onto a gravel road. It became very wash-boarded, waking my father. Not saying anything he glanced around. Satisfied all was well he leaned his head against the window, his coat as a pillow and promptly fell back asleep. In some way this reassured me. The rough road keeping me awake, I drove on for another twenty-five miles. From there it turned into a narrow single lane, winding, sometimes muddy track. Twenty miles of this and we should arrive at our questionable destination. My father's head would straighten momentarily, view the road and just as quickly go back to his slumber.

I stopped the truck in the middle of the road and announced, "I have no idea where the hell I am."

This woke my father. He took a long look. It was still dark but the eastern sky was acquiring a gray tint. "I'm not sure, let's have a cup of coffee and wait for it to get lighter."

Stopping the engine and turning the lights off helped our vision. Drinking the coffee, stretching, the cold morning air felt good.

"I know where we are." With this he took over driving. After two more miles on the rough road that we had come so far on, he turned left onto a barely discernible jeep track, the truck's frame groaning in protest at the rough treatment. Another mile and we arrived at half a dozen concrete slabs of varying sizes with nothing on them. We were at the base of a mountain range that rose to the west. It ran north and south for endless miles.

The slabs of concrete were remnants of an abandoned mine, long deserted. Several abandoned mine portals, neglected and crumbling.

Feeling the pressures of time, we threw the ties off the side of the truck, leaving them jumbled.

The sun was bright but had little warmth. We stood, side by side as my father pointed in a general direction down the slope. "That's where the property is."

I had no way to distinguish exactly what made our land different from the half million acres of sagebrush that stretched for forty miles, in a north and south direction. The valley did have a certain allure. Twenty miles wide and eighty miles long, it was bordered on both sides by tall, rugged mountain ranges. Down the middle, ten miles wide and twenty miles long was a wet salt marsh.

"Should be right there, a couple miles from here." His pointing still very vague. "They should be done surveying in another month and set the corners." His pride and enthusiasm were infectious. Even tired and dirty, I was excited.

We took turns driving back home. I had several naps while he drove, but they were short and didn't help much. My mind in constant turmoil, how this whole undertaking would affect my life. So many possibilities and none that I could control.

The next several weekends were a repeat of that first one. My father would drink a little more, trusting my driving as more miles rolled under the truck. Maybe he thought it was better to get a ticket as an unlicensed driver than as a drunk driver, I was never sure how his mind worked. He may even have thought if I got the ticket, I would be responsible for the fine.

One trip we left Sacramento knowing a storm was raging in the Sierras. A large sign announced Donner Summit was closed, due to a major winter snowfall. I was driving, my father didn't see a problem with snow. He directed me off Interstate 80 and said to take the Feather River canyon, it was lower and shouldn't be closed. The rain was coming in sheets, our wipers making a pathetic attempt, the wind, howling, seemed somehow evil. My father content, taking his nap, the alcohol salving any concerns he may have had.

The rain was slowly turning to snow. The absence of hardly any other traffic worried me. Slowly my vision out the windshield was reduced, the heater on the inside was on full defrost, it had little if no affect. The wiper blades, fully encased in ice were helpless. I had to make a decision. The road was covered in snow but my traction held firm. It was after midnight and there hadn't been another car for half an hour, I stopped in the middle of the road. Ice scrapper in hand I leaned out the door and cleaned my half of the windshield. This was so much better. The blast of frigid air must have woken my father. "What's the matter?" He was gruff.

"Had to clean the windshield, the snow was sticking." I answered him tersely. I wanted to scream at him that I was scared shitless, and tired of having a fucking drunk for a father. I didn't say this, I couldn't.

I started the truck moving, praying I had enough traction. After spinning a moment, the rear tires took hold and I drove on.

The snow was getting heavier and deeper. When I stopped again it was at a wide spot and I started to put on the chains. My father got out to help, I was glad, it was a cold, dark, miserable and wet night.

He didn't offer to drive and I didn't ask him to, feeling so much better now that the chains were on.

We made it over the hill without incident. Pulled the chains off on the other side. Past Reno my father took over driving. I was relieved. The rest of the trip went without any problems.

These hauling trips were made until the end of March. School was hard, I was tired all the time but managed to stay on the honor roll, that was important to me.

The largest hurt was Jane. We felt very deeply about each other, we may have been in love. It withered. Then it died from neglect, much like a plant left laying on its side, unable to take firm root.

Many times that last two months I lay in my tent, cursing the rain that made its way inside, cold and alone, wishing for something different. It came soon enough.

Damn, I Shot My Horse

LONELINESS

The next Friday morning, before spring break was to start at school, I was instructed by my father to notify the school office, I would not be returning after the break was over. Also, bring all my stuff home from my locker. This was characteristic for him, no preamble, no explanation. I stood there, not moving, hearing the words but not comprehending.

"We're going to Dixie tomorrow to start working on the ranch." The expression on his face told me that's all I was getting. My mother was standing in the kitchen with us. They must have been discussing me some time during the night. She looked mad, really mad.

My sister Anita, coming into the room must have felt the tension. She left immediately, under some pretense. Only one year older, she was so much smarter than me.

I looked at my mother, her eyes said so much. She had done all she could on my behalf. I was fifteen, I told my mother I was ready.

My father was not a mean person. He rarely raised his voice, sometimes he was quite jovial. When he spoke it was in such an authoritarian manner it never crossed my mind to contest him, whether I agreed or not.

I went to school. Between classes I searched for Jane, wanting to tell her, explain what was happening. She wasn't there that day. I couldn't even say goodbye. Several of my friends asked what was wrong. I didn't want to go into long explanations, I simply said nothing was wrong. They left it alone, l was very withdrawn.

At the end of the day I stopped at the office and told them I was leaving for the rest of the year. They asked where they should send my transcripts. I had no answers, telling them only that we would contact them. I added that I would be back that fall. This seemed to placate them.

I had no idea that I would never see school or any of my friends again.

The next morning was Saturday. My father said to pack my stuff including my tent. He and my mother were going to get groceries. This struck me as odd, my father never went to a grocery store.

"How much stuff should I pack?" I didn't have that much.

"Everything, it's going to be a while." Such a simple statement.

My belongings were in a pile by the driveway when they returned from shopping. My father had a blue Volkswagen bus that he used to commute to work. I opened the side door to put my clothes in, the tent, also my bedroll and .22 rifle. The back of the bus was filled with case after case of canned food. Hand tools, including shovels, picks, buckets and a six-foot steel bar for digging. I had no idea what to expect when the door opened but it wasn't this. It appeared as if we were going on a major expedition. A chill went through me.

For the second time in my life that I could remember, my mother hugged me. She pulled back to arm's length, her hands on my shoulders. Her eyes, penetrating mine deeply, were slowly misting. "Take care of yourself." It was a mother's plea.

She turned around and walked into the house, wanting to be alone.

"Let's go." My father was anxious. We were on an adventure; emotions were for other people.

My somber mood lifted with each mile. Late March, a beautiful spring day. The new freeway was completed over Donner Pass. The snow, meters high on each side.

Through Reno, then stopping in Fallon for gas. This was the last grocery store or gas station. From here it was almost a hundred miles to our property, one way. Forty-five miles east on Highway 50, which was designated the "Loneliest Highway in America." Then north for another 50 miles on dirt road.

Leaving Fallon, the first ten miles were acres of farm ground. From there it turned into the most barren, inhospitable place in the country. Crossing miles of salt flats, it had a stark, appealing beauty.

Traveling north on the dirt road it became rolling miles of sagebrush. Between two mountain ranges, the Clan Alpine on the east and the Stillwater Range on the west. They were high, with some pockets of pine and juniper, very few places to cross them.

Twenty-five miles after leaving the pavement several dirt roads led to the east. A loose scattering of ranches, about a dozen, was called the Dixie Settlement. A small single room building served as a school for all grades, at any given time maybe six students with one teacher. The few high school students were bused to Fallon, the longest bus route in the U.S.

These were not large prosperous ranches. Some were viable, some were in varying stages of decay. The owners and their families were hearty, tenacious people.

We continued north for another twenty-five miles, bordering a wet salt flat on our east side. The Humboldt Salt Marsh, 25 miles long was sometimes a lake, sometimes a long quagmire of bottomless, sticky mud, totally devoid of any vegetation. As the water receded sometimes in the fall, a one-inch thick crust of white salt and alkaline replaced it. No one ever went on it.

The trip was enjoyable. We had made some conversation, but mostly we were lost in the drive. I could tell my father was in good spirits. He had drunk very little, explaining the valley as we drove past the different parts.

It had a beauty that was slowly beginning to register on me. The stark white-blue of the marsh, the endless miles of purple sage, leading to the multiple colored mountain ranges. The colors varied between soft hues and vivid, brilliant hints of underlying minerals. It was feral and serene at the same time. That day I fell in love with this valley.

We came to the property. The survey was done, the corners marked. A mile between each corner, a full square section, 640 acres, the east side bordered on the salt flat. It inclined gradually to the west. Two miles west of the line you ran into the buttress of the mountain range.

He pulled off the main road onto a set of tire tracks that led to the base of the mountains. Half way there we stopped. There was about two hours of daylight left, so we found a level spot and set up our beds for the night. That was simple enough, we put a tarp on the ground and put bags on it. I gathered some sage brush so we could have a fire later. My father grabbed some wooden stakes he had brought, along with a hammer.

We walked to the mouth of a canyon, following a nearly non-existing road. There was a nice, clear stream flowing. It followed the main wash, ending in the salt flat, three miles east and several hundred feet lower.

"This canyon is called White Rock; I was told this road will take you to Lovelock eventually." I was never sure from where he got all his information, usually he was correct. I filed the name in my memory bank. We followed the stream down the wash for half a mile. He stopped, looked around and declared, "This should do it." I was uncertain what "this" should do.

"We'll dig a ditch from here to the upper corner of our property. We can build a reservoir and use it to irrigate with." He made it sound so simple. It was over one and a half miles to the corner he indicated. There were many ravines and rises to go around. Plus, it wouldn't be easy to get it out of this wash. The surrounding level was three feet higher. One good thing, it was all downhill from there. We put stakes into the ground to mark the path of the ditch for the first half mile.

The sun was setting, so we made our way back to camp. I started a fire while he heated some canned food on the Coleman stove. Our stomachs full, we sat by the fire, having our after dinner smoke, taking small sips of whiskey from a bottle. The moon was full and brilliant, so bright a person could almost read by it. A thought crept into my mind, I didn't like it, I didn't want to face it.

"You're not staying; you're leaving in the morning." It was a statement, not a question. He sat in silence for a long time but I knew he'd heard me. I didn't want a response, knowing what it would be. I had such a hollow feeling in my stomach I was almost sick. I was scared of my future.

"I have to be at work Monday. You'll be all right, there's plenty of food." He said it so simply, he didn't understand why it should be a problem. I wasn't ready for this; it was too much. I wanted to argue, explain, cajole, but I didn't, knowing it was useless. But I wouldn't plead, I remained silent, stoic.

We left it that way, going to our respective sleeping bags. So many emotions were going through my head that night I was unable to stop them long enough to dwell on any one in particular. I got very little sleep, dreading the morning. It came too soon.

There was enough light to see. We both got up. I started a fire, the air was cold. We unloaded the canned goods and tools, not a word said. My father put his stuff in the bus, looked at me and said, "I'll be back in two weeks, get as much done as you can." No slap on the back, no handshake, no well wishes, no encouragement. I waited in vain for more, some assurance, it would never come. He simply drove off.

I stood there. I stood there some more, not moving. I would look at the large pile of canned food, then at the trail of dust. I stood there transfixed, watching that trail of dust disappear, I could see it for fifteen miles, each mile of watching tearing me apart, but I couldn't stop. I simply sat down, not able to do anything. I wanted to cry, I couldn't. I took solace in a cigarette.

My empty stomach forced me to get up. A good part of the morning had been wasted, waiting in vain for the dust cloud to come back, announcing a reprieve. It never came. I went to my store of canned goods. Ravioli, spaghetti, Spaghettios, tamales, beans, pork and beans, case after case of canned fruit. Boxes of crackers, Vienna sausages, jam. Cases of corn, string beans, peas and pickled beets. I came across a case of corned beef hash, taking out a can. My utensils were in a black metal lunch pail. I took out a can opener and spoon. Opening the can, I ate it cold, right from the can, I didn't care, my mood was so desultory. Setting the can down I wiped the spoon on my shirt after licking it clean, so much for dishes. I opened a jar of jam and ate two spoonsful of raspberry preserves, that helped the taste in my mouth. I cleaned my spoon for the second time.

I walked around my sorry camp, aimlessly, I couldn't deal with it yet. I walked over to the stream, preparing how I would deal with building a diversion dam to start the ditch. My mind refused to deal with this also. Returning to camp, I sat once again on my upside down five-gallon metal bucket. I stared at the cold ashes of the fire, lost.

Late that afternoon I was able to pull myself from this wallow of self-pity. I erected my tent, it was sorry at best. It would have to do, I just didn't know for how long. Putting my clothes and sleeping bag inside I was surprised how little I had. I got my .22 and case of hollow point bullets, the bullets went in the tent, the rifle always stayed close to me, maybe I had read too many westerns. I found a cardboard box with two tins of tobacco and papers to make my cigarettes, a pint of Jim Beam whiskey, half full, no idea who put it there, but I would save it for later. Best of all, there were about two dozen assorted paperback books. I looked through them, no romance, that was good. The books helped, they helped a lot. I knew they were from my mother, I pictured her smile as I discovered this treasure, this brought a swift, intense pang of homesickness, but it was fleeting. I was feeling so much better, such a little thing as a book could work such wonders. I finished preparing my camp, arranging the canned food in some semblance of order. Set the stove up on some rocks, pumped the reservoir and set an empty pot on it, ready for dinner. I gathered some more sagebrush for a fire, walked to the stream and brought back water in another bucket.

I cooked and ate dinner. Made a pot of coffee and sat, watching the sun set. It was lonely, so lonely but tranquil. I thought, two weeks, I can handle this. I tried in vain to make an adventure of this mess, but I wasn't ready for that much optimism.

I didn't have any lights so I went to bed before it got too dark to see. Through the holes in the tent's roof the moonlight was visible. I lay there, my rifle at my side, it was eerily quiet. I even wanted the reassurance of my father's snoring. Waiting for sleep, eyes wide open, scared, not only of the dark but of the sheer desolation of my situation. Twenty miles from the next human being, no way to get there other than my feet. I missed Jane a lot that night, she was so easy to talk to, so nice to be around. I missed my horse, Pinto. He was an undemanding companion, I hoped to have him with me soon. Damn, I even missed my sister, not too much, but I would have welcomed even her sharp tongue for a little while. With these thoughts I began to realize how lonely I was. Sleep finally took possession of my troubled mind, thankfully.

I awoke as the darkness gave way to light. It was cold, much colder than the previous night. There was a thin coating of ice on my bucket of water outside. Starting a fire, I put a pot of coffee on to boil. I put my coat on to ward off the chill. Hunger rumbled in my belly, so I opened a can of hash, setting this on the grate, next to the coffee pot over the fire. It's a poor way to heat a can of food, the bottom and the outside start to boil long before the center gets warm, unless a person stirs it often. Tired of waiting, I retrieved it with a pair of pliers, cautiously sampling the contents. Some was hot, some was cool, it didn't matter, it was food, I was hungry and I wouldn't have to wash a pot.

Second can of hash in two days. This would work to keep track of the days, I had no calendar or watch with day/date. I rinsed yesterdays and today's cans so they wouldn't attract animals, filled them with gravel and set them in a row off to the side. When there were thirteen cans someone would show up. Somehow this made me feel better.

After my coffee and smoke, I walked over to the stream with my tools. It didn't take much of a plan to start. Build a dirt dam across the wash at the narrowest point until it was high enough for the water to exit into the ditch. Even after all the years of hard work my hands were blistered in three hours, even with gloves. I went much slower. By noon the blisters had broken and were bleeding, but only slightly. I surveyed my work, estimating three, maybe four more days. This would have to do, until my hands got better, it was too painful to continue.

I went back to camp, opened a can of something, eating it cold, a can of fruit cocktail for desert. The temperature was very

[54]

pleasant, a brilliant, blue day. I took my rifle, removed my shirt and went exploring. I wanted to check the abandoned mines, close to where all our ties were. It was about a mile cross country, visible on a slight rise. The walk felt good but my hands were tender, hard to carry my gun, annoying but not too painful.

Some of the concrete slabs still had bolts sticking out, they must have held the buildings down. Some of the slabs were in bad shape, cracked and crumbling, others, still very serviceable. Old dried lumber, scattered everywhere, the remnants of the structures. A lot of good firewood, this was filed in my brain. Wood for fires was hard to come by, sagebrush burned fine, just not very long. Old rusty nails littered the ground, some straight, but mostly bent.

It must have been a very old mine. The main tunnel started into the mountain about a quarter of a mile away. The portal was the size of a house, with very little wooden shoring. Some cave-ins having occurred in the past, the entrance was a jumble of boulders, still, plenty of room to enter. I didn't, standing outside, looking in, was enough. A long way in, it narrowed to a proper tunnel. There were many more portals spread along the base of the hillside, some higher, some at the base of the mountain, all normal size. The ones that started immediately into solid rock seemed very solid. Some of these I entered, going as far as I dared without a light, a strong odor present in several of them, I assumed it was bat droppings.

I found two shafts that went straight down, about a quarter mile from each other, large piles of dirt accompanying each one. No lids on them, just gaping holes in the earth. I approached each one cautiously in turn. The first having the remnants of a wooden ladder leading down. It disappeared into the dark. Throwing a fist sized rock, I counted to five before a sound returned. I had no idea of the formula to figure the depth but it sounded deep regardless. The other shaft had no ladder, throwing a rock into this hole produced similar results. Good place to stay away from

I thought to myself.

I explored some more. Piles of empty cans that once held food lay in a wash. Empty five gallon buckets scattered haphazardly. Rusty fifty-five gallon drums also scattered randomly. Pieces of corrugated tin, some mangled some still surprisingly straight. The sun, having fallen behind the mountains lent a strange eerie feeling to the place. With a slight chill I took a quick glance around and started back to camp, looking behind me several times, holding my gun securely in my sore, blistered hands.

My dinner was identical to the night before, canned food, heated on a fire, straight from the tin. I bathed in the stream just as darkness was encroaching, the water cool but the evening air still warm. The soap hurt my hands but my body felt so much better. That evening as I sat by the fire, a tiny sliver of contentment took hold. Sleeping was much easier that night. I still kept my rifle next to the bed.

No ice the next morning, temperature cool but pleasant. Another can of hash, another day marked by the empty. My hands still hurt, the blisters covered by a slight glaze. Working on the dam was hard with my hands so tender. I continued cautiously, trying in vain to protect them. Traces of blood covered the handles of all the tools. I worked slowly, methodically, able to disregard the discomfort most of the time. It took the focus off my loneliness, I think the pain was preferable. By midafternoon I stopped, pleased with my progress. Returned to camp and had a late lunch, several cans of food this time, I was hungry.

That afternoon I followed the stream for several miles up into the canyon. Cutting up an old t-shirt, I wrapped my hands, this helped considerably, also much easier to carry my rifle. The hike was comforting, following the stream. At one time a bulldozer had carved a crude road, following the bottom of the canyon. The road crossed the stream countless times, large boulders pushed to the side, it must have been an arduous job. A person might still be able to negotiate the faint remnants in a four-wheel drive truck, if careful. I was happy, exploring such a pleasant respite.

I returned back to camp, leaving plenty of time before dark and repeated the routine of the previous evening. Sleep came easy that night.

Each day my hands improved, the dam grew and I hiked into and up a different canyon. Some were craggy and impassible; others simply went on much further than I could travel in one afternoon.

Eventually the dam was complete, a small pond behind the earth works. A rock spillway, so the overflow wouldn't erode all my work. I was very pleased with my progress. Starting the ditch was a different challenge. Mostly pick and shovel, loosening the ground with the pick for ten feet, then shoveling the trench, most of the dirt and rocks going on the downhill side. Repeating this two, sometimes three times in the same length, until I was satisfied of containment and gradient. Digging the connecting foot to the previous portion, I would watch the small stream flow, fixing any trouble spots. It was slow and tedious, sometimes encountering a rock so large I would spend half a day removing it. Then filling the hole back up with dirt so the ditch would flow uninterrupted. Going through gravel beds, I would make the trench larger, then haul some dirt, I preferred clay, in a bucket, lining the ditch. This worked well to stop water loss, sometimes finding the right dirt was a pain in the ass.

Each morning, walking and planning my route for the day, I made a mental map then marked it with stakes. Way too often, I would stare at the distance remaining, wishing it closer. Checking what had already been completed, I would constantly be disappointed at my feeble efforts so far. Every morning I walked the finished portion that had water flowing down it.

Digging some trouble spots was much easier once it was wet. Some of the undisturbed ground was so hard I would scratch a small channel then let the water soften it for a day. This caused more back and forth work, but made my life easier and made for a much better job.

Each day a repeat of the day before. My life was hard but simple. Several times a day I would search the road for a dust trail coming towards me, always in vain. Every day as my calendar of cans grew, so did my spirits. My hands were healed, I was getting stronger, I worked harder, wanting to impress, searching for validation maybe, I don't know why, I just did.

My empty cans told me it was Saturday morning. I was excited. Two weeks without another human voice, another face, a smile, just someone to look at would be enough. I picked up my dry laundry, having washed it the evening before. It was draped over several sagebrush to dry, a clothes line would not have helped, with no poles for attachment. I didn't want my home to resemble a refugee camp, at best it still looked very sad.

All morning I watched for the telltale sign of a dust plume, mentally trying to gauge departure time with arrival time, it was pointless. I couldn't get much work done, I couldn't help myself, I became a victim of my own excitement.

The sun made its relentless arc across the sky with no regard for my feelings. I willed it not to set, I didn't want the darkness to come, but it did. As the light faded, so did my hopes, consoling myself by thinking they may have gotten a late start. I sat by my meager fire, looking south for headlights, too dark now to see any dust. I was very hungry, opening a can of something, I didn't care what it was, the contents were consumed without recognition, my eyes never wavering, searching in vain for approaching lights. Sitting on my bucket, hour after hour, my only interruption, rolling a cigarette. The fire long out, I got cold but sat there some more, the cold keeping me awake so I could continue watching, hoping. Several times I nodded off, jerking awake, chastising myself for maybe having missed them. That was a stupid thought my brain said as I sat shivering, gloom replacing any hope. The night was wasting, bringing my sleeping bag outside, arranging it so I could watch for any hint of lights.

The light woke me; it was the sun creeping over the mountains to the east. I became despondent, knowing somehow there would be no arrivals that day. The trip was too long for a one-day drive, deep inside I knew my father wouldn't waste time on something so unproductive. With resignation I started my day with its normal routine, another day another can, so be it. I continued looking south, stupidly trying to keep my glances covert as if somehow I could deny it was happening.

I worked, my efforts desultory, mere motions with little success. That evening, admitting finally it would be another week, I felt betrayed.

The next week took on a monotonous repetition, broken one night by soft gentle rain, some of it making its way into my tent but for the most part I remained dry. What did get wet was quickly dried the next day in the sun. Digging the ditch was becoming my prison and my release at the same time, I didn't understand how or why, it just did.

I watched a trail of dust across the salt flat slowly making its way to the north. There must be a dirt road at the base of the mountain range across the valley. I was unable to see the vehicle but the long trail of dust marked its passage. I watched it for a half hour wondering who it was and where they were going. That lone symbol gave hope there were still other humans out there, it also reinforced just how alone and isolated I was. I kept digging.

The next weekend was identical to the previous one. Excitement then despair followed by a slow lifting of my spirits.

The weeks themselves became repetitious, much like an endless roller coaster, with each decent I would go lower, forcing myself to claw back up mentally, never as high as the week before.

One mid-afternoon a trail of dust was making its way from the south, still miles distant but on the right road. I watched, shovel in hand, heart beginning to beat wildly. It was my parents, I had no doubt. I ran back to my camp, picking something up to move it, only to set it back down in the same spot, only to move on to something else. It was a frantic activity that accomplished nothing.

I stopped all movement, mesmerized, as the vehicle approached the turn that would lead it to me. It didn't turn, it didn't even slow down. I willed it to stop, to turn around, it continued on its journey with total disregard at the agony it was causing. I ran after it, sprinting, cursing, screaming. I stopped, hands on knees, out of breath. Watching it disappear into a low spot, thinking it would surely comprehend its mistake and return. It didn't. I turned away, a new low, anger and bitterness creeping into the deepest recesses of my soul, what a cruel irony. I made my way slowly back to camp, refusing to do anything but wallow in self-pity the rest of the day, I succeeded. I didn't get out of bed until the next morning.

Another day just like so many before, another can of hash. Filling it full of dirt after eating the contents I placed it in line amongst the others. I studied them, thirty cans now mocked me, I was beginning to hate them. They no longer promised respite or better things to come, they tormented me, as if testing to see how many I would place in line before giving up. I rearranged them into a square, this little act made me feel better, I went to work, feeling I still had some control.

Digging the ditch was becoming so familiar I no longer had to think, my body doing the work with very little input from my brain. My physical actions were robotic, my mind was free to wander, and wander it did. Sometimes the thoughts were pleasant, remembering happier times, sometimes dark, taking me places I didn't want to be, so difficult to escape. More and more often throughout these days a pervasive fear was taking hold. What if my parents were both killed in a traffic accident on the way to see me? No one else knew I was here, I was unable to think of one person, my sister maybe, but she didn't have a clue that I was aware of.

It was impossible not to continuously check the road for traffic. I forced myself to focus, stop looking at the damn road, there was nothing there for me, only disappointment.

Late that afternoon it got increasingly warmer, too warm it felt like. Gnats were driving me crazy, swarming around my face and sweat drenched body. The air was very still, not a whisper of movement. Unusual, every afternoon brought a refreshing breeze. Setting my tools down I headed back to camp for the evening. One more glance south, only one more I promised myself.

My eyes didn't make it to the road, something ominous, some portent of evil, something totally unknown was coming. Far distant, thirty miles to the south, just becoming visible, a wall of dust was marching up the valley. I remained rooted, my feet unable to move, my eyes unable to turn away, transfixed, my brain told me to breath, I needed air, my diaphragm took over, sucking in several lungs full.

My mind couldn't process the signals my eyes were sending. A rolling wall of dust, several thousand feet high, encompassing the whole width of the valley, almost reaching to the tops of the mountains on either side. Obscuring everything behind it, relentless in its advance. It looked apocalyptic, so dark behind this encroaching horror it simply looked black. For the first time in my short life I was afraid, a fear deep in my gut. It was coming. Like a slap to the back of my head I knew, wind... a wind like I had never experienced.

It became a race. My coffee pot was first, taking the lid off and throwing the contents out, I put it into a five gallon can that was my stool, grabbed the other two buckets, stacking them one inside the other. Filling them with dirt, coffee pot and all, quickly dug a hole and buried them half way, standing upright. It didn't take long; I was desperate to save as much as possible. The metal grate and tools should be alright, they were heavy.

Surveying the tent, I knew there wasn't much hope for it if the winds were as strong as foretold by the dark mass rolling up the valley. Doing a check on the poles and ropes that held my home upright and together, I felt confident there was nothing to be done that would help. Like myself the tent would have to take its chances. The zipper on the entrance panel had long since quit working, it was tied back with wire. I was uncertain what to do next, mainly wondering how to protect myself.

Several dozen cases of food were at one end of the tent. I set about stacking them two high in two separate rows, there was enough room between them for my bedroll with a couple feet at the end left over. I used this space for my duffel bags that contained my clothes and anything else that was loose. I set another case of canned goods on top of this pile to hold it down. The rest went along the inside of the perimeter of the tent to hold the floor down. I was grateful these cases were heavy. With an afterthought I moved two of them to the upper end, where my head would be as protection. I looked around, knowing I should be doing more but there was nothing else to be done. I went outside to wait, wanting to see what was coming.

I should have stayed inside. It was terrifying and exciting. I thought about making a run for one of the mine tunnels, not sure if they would be any safer, but there wasn't enough time by now. I also felt a need to stay here and protect my things as much as possible.

I stood there in awe, watching, paralyzed momentarily by the power and magnitude of this spectacle, a total feeling of insignificance. A faint roar was beginning to announce its arrival. With each passing second it became louder, all matter of debris being flung up and down the monstrous face of blackness that now darkened the whole southern sky.

Two steps brought me into my tent, hurriedly I crawled into my bedroll, leaving my boots on in case I needed to run, it came to me there was no place to go, I still left them on.

My straw cowboy hat and rifle went into my bedroll with me, I crawled far enough down to cover my head, holding tight to the blankets and waited.

The noise wasn't just loud, it was a physical presence, all around me, as if consuming me. The wind, when it came several seconds later, didn't slowly build, it hit like a wall. Light to dark instantly, I huddled in my bag, sneaking a glance out a corner, quickly retreating, too dark to see anything.

With the first blast my tent was being ripped apart, the tearing, ripping, and flapping, barely audible above the tremendous roar that was shredding me mentally as well as my surroundings. There was no doubt about my tent, it would be gone. I wondered if a body could be rolled across the dessert, endlessly rolling like a tumble weed, coming to rest in some deep washout, mangled and broken. Each new gust stronger than the one before, I didn't think it was possible but it was. Hour after hour, it may have been minutes, I had no concept of time. This constant roaring and buffeting by the wind was slowly removing my capacity for any coherent thoughts. Dust was making its way into my cocoon, breathing was miserable, I could feel the grit working its way into my mouth, eyes and nose. Small bits of gravel sometimes pelting my bag.

It went on. There was no sleep, fear and apprehension making it mentally impossible. Somehow during that dark howling night, rational thought began to make feeble attempts at repairing my tormented mind. I would survive. Somehow I would survive stronger than before. My fear was slowly being replaced by frustration. The wind had diminished slightly, the roar lessening as well. I tried shaking the loose sand and dirt off my bag before sticking my head out slightly, still a cascade of the stuff fell onto me. I tried brushing the grit off my face, mostly irritating my eyes. They opened tearfully, stung by the dirt. It was spooky, dark and light simultaneously. The faint light had no source, a pitiful attempt at illumination. The darkness was everywhere, looking upward, there were no stars visible, there air was thick with dust.

The wind diminished slowly, more gusting with a stiff breeze in between. There was enough light to see, but the air held so much floating dirt I could only see for several hundred feet. I could see more than I wanted too. I got up, trying in vain to get the sand off me. I retrieved my hat, boots and gun. Checking the latter, the action had a gritty sound but still functioned well enough. With my hat and boots on I walked around surveying the destruction. The tent was completely gone, nothing left but the floor panel. The parts of the floor that weren't covered with canned goods were also shredded and gone. Looking further, my buckets and tools were still there.

My watch said mid-morning, but a gloomy dark pall made it feel like a predawn lightness, my mood was becoming as dark as my surroundings. I had so little, only one thing for protection, my tent, even that was mostly an illusion. Now I had nothing, no refuge from the rain or the sun. My anger was building, it seemed so unjust, what the hell could I have done in my short life to deserve this. The more I looked at my pathetic shambles of a home, the more I thought about the long weeks that I spent here all alone, watching vehicles go by, no human contact, living out of cans, sleeping on the ground like an animal, listening to coyotes, sometimes so close I could hear them walking around outside my tent that had no door. Rattlesnakes were next, I knew it was time for them to come out, joined by scorpions and maybe tarantulas.

I let my anger build, no way could I stop it, I wanted it, I wanted it to consume me. It did. I found the half bottle of whiskey and sat on the ground. Smoking and drinking, the foulest language coming from me. I shouted my anger, my frustration, my fears, I drank and smoked some more, sitting in the dirt. I was caught in a torrent, I shouted, I screamed, I ranted, I cussed, most of this must have been directed at God, for I was looking up, I screamed at Him with all that was left, "I don't fucking need you anymore." It was clear I had crossed a line, it was okay, that was the last time I would ever acknowledge Him.

I woke up with a bad headache, I felt like shit sitting on the ground. I must have fallen asleep or passed out sitting there. It made little difference. I got up stiffly, noticing the bottle laying in the dirt, empty. Good riddance I thought. The sky was clearing, almost some blue straight above me, no wind. I wanted some food, I was hungry. Pork and beans sounded good. I decided not to eat my hash that day, the need to count the days had left, it felt good. As long as there was food, things would be okay, I could build another shelter somehow.

I went to work getting things back together, there wasn't much, most of my time and effort spent getting the dirt out of my belongings. Moving all the cases and my bedroll off the floor, I shook the dirt from it and secured the perimeter with a ring of rocks, replaced my belongings after cleaning them. The sky was clear now, so clear and blue I wondered how it could have been so ugly such a short time ago. The water felt refreshing as I stood in it naked, washing away the grime. I must have washed more than simply dirt, I felt good, cleansed, I felt a new resolve, mostly I felt mentally strong. There was no doubt my need for protection from the environment needed to be dealt with. Tomorrow was soon enough, I would enjoy this evening, watching the sun set as I drank my coffee. Maybe the coyotes would keep me company tonight, I no longer feared them. All my fears were gone; somehow the wind had taken them.

A LONG SUMMER

I felt good the next day. Sleeping under that bright, moon-filled sky the previous night was thought provoking. Nothing deep, mostly about the future, it seemed like such a long hard task, building a ranch from nothing. It made sense to get water for irrigation a priority. What followed was not certain to me, someone else would determine that. That was fine, most things would probably fall in order just by necessity, I knew money would also play a role.

Having my morning coffee, I focused on my sleeping arrangements, there were no problems if the weather held. I did feel a little apprehensive about things that crawled on the ground, there was nothing available as a defense. Finally, I removed my bedroll from between the two rows of canned food, sliding them together gave me a raised platform, barely large enough for my sleeping bag. I understood my safety was mostly an illusion, things could still crawl up the boxes, so be it. I chuckled as a thought became clear, it would only be a short time before I literally ate my way to a problem once again.

The weather looked good so I made the decision to sleep here for another day or two, then make some kind of a better provision for myself, not having any desire to get caught in a desert rain storm.

My bedroll did have a covering of oiled canvas which would

repel some water, but like most things, the water would eventually find a way in.

I worked on the ditch the rest of the day. My shirt off, the temperature was perfect. I didn't attack the ditch with a frenzy, my efforts were methodical, the results giving a sense of accomplishment as the progress went forward. It seemed so slow, forty feet in one day was at the upper limit, some days much less. I was fine with that, by days end my body was done, sore back, tired arms and shoulders. I bathed in the pond created by the dam every evening, the water a pleasant temperature from the day's sun. Laundry was done by hand every five, maybe six days. It became a soothing monotony.

My head was down and my ass up in the air, rolling a rock out of the way. A deep roar became more audible every second. Checking for the source, my vision caught movement between myself and the salt flat. Two Navy jets were streaking at an incredible speed down the valley toward the south, less than half a mile from me. Maybe two hundred feet off the ground, they must have been on the same level as me, the pilots outline faint in the cockpit. The air rumbled as the pilots stood the jets on their tails and went into a vertical climb. The noise and vibrations were primordial, breathtaking. The sheer, raw power of their afterburners shook the very earth, black smoke pouring from their exhaust. F-4 Phantoms, a fearsome all-purpose jet. It was said they were proof, if you put enough power on an anvil, it would fly. It was awesome, I watched as they disappeared, wishing them back to entertain me longer. For some reason I didn't understand, that all too brief interlude gave me comfort. I loved airplanes. Years ago, when younger, most evenings I would tediously build plastic models of most airplanes made. From World War II prop-driven fighters and bombers, to modern jets, I had them all hanging from my ceiling, once upon a time when I had a ceiling, I thought, grinning.

That evening, sitting at my meager fire, I dreamt endlessly of what it must be like to sit in the cockpit with so much power and destruction at your command. They were great dreams. I saved the earth and mankind so many times.

More excitement the next day, not so pleasant, my first rattlesnake. No great fanfare, walking along the ditch, it was crawling alongside a large sagebrush. It must have sensed me, coiling, it rattled a warning. I didn't want to kill it, but it was too close to my camp to suit me. Maybe only two feet long, it was buried without ceremony after killing it with my shovel. This forced the issue about my camp. Something had to be done.

I took my rifle and a canteen of water and walked to where we had all the railroad ties. An idea was forming. The concrete slab adjacent to the pile was fairly smooth and intact. Selecting only some of the better ties I laid out a grid, using six. One side wall had two laying end to end, the other side the same, the ends had one. Roughly six by sixteen feet inside. On what would be the front I lapped the two ties, side by side about two feet in the middle, this would give me an entrance, next to the end wall. Happy with the outline I put another row on the bottom one, it was hard work, carrying them the twenty feet before setting them in place. By late afternoon I had four rows up. Satisfied this could turn out well I went back to camp for my dinner and to wash the sweat off my body. One more night here, it would work out well. Tomorrow I would spend the day working on my shack, the ditch would keep.

After eating my cold breakfast, I gathered my gun, hammer and a canteen of water. It felt good to have such a clear purpose. I knew packing my water over a mile would be more effort, but the nights would cause me much less worry.

That day saw considerable progress, as the walls rose so did the effort to get the heavy ties higher.

Eventually I would set one end on the wall and then lift the other end into place. There was no way to lock the corners by staggering them, I had no saw. There was plenty of lumber laying around and plenty of nails, most would have to be straightened. Finding what I needed took a while, finally there was enough material to reinforce the corners and my butt joint. It became quite sturdy. The walls were four feet high but I wanted two more feet before putting the roof on, six feet inside would be plenty of headroom.

Contentment filled me as I made my way back to my camp. After eating and bathing, I gathered my bedroll, put some cans of food into it for later that evening and for breakfast. Several times I had to stop, resting my arms from the load. On one stop a vehicle was making its way up the dirt road on my side of the valley, only three maybe four miles distant. Watching, I was dispassionate, they would either turn up my road or they wouldn't. I didn't have any idea what day it was, that precluded me from having any real expectations. It went by. Picking up the things that lay at my feet, my walk to the new camp continued, it felt curious not to care one way or the other.

Once my bed was spread on the slab of concrete, I went in search of something to make a door. Walking around, eyes on the ground, a piece of sheet metal caught my attention. Removing the debris that covered it, I was glad to see it was in okay shape and might work. On the way back to my tie house I gathered a hand full of nails as I walked along. The tin was about eight feet long and two feet wide. I nailed it across my doorway, laying on its side, butting one end against a wall. Two feet high was easy to step over, it fit fairly tight so I hoped it would keep most things out, as I nailed it into place.

Standing inside, I could see over the walls, but at least I had walls, of a sort, and a door, of a sort.

No shortage of wood around my new home, tonight I splurged but still my fire seemed extravagant that evening. It was such a pleasant evening, nice fire, coffee, a good cigarette, full belly, stars overhead, and a home, of sorts. For the first time since the storm, loneliness was creeping back in. I shoved it back out, there was no room anymore for self-indulgence, somebody would come. My new confidence made things so much easier for me.

The next day I finished the walls, it was hard work getting the last few rows of ties that high. Nailing things together made the whole thing feel pretty stable. Later that afternoon I walked down to the ditch and did my evening ritual. Taking two of the buckets, filling them with cans of food they were much easier to carry to my new home. There was enough time so I made another trip, but my rifle stayed behind, not enough hands, for everything.

Getting the ties onto the roof of my new home was difficult for one person, it took two days to cover the whole thing. Many holes, I thought to myself, looking up through my ceiling. There may be enough chunks of plywood, or some tin, flying around.

I went back to working on my ditch project. One evening I moved the remaining cases of food off the floor of my abandoned tent. It was made of rubberized canvas, some weak spots were beginning to appear, a couple of small holes already present. I could fold it several times and use it for a sleeping pad, or nail it over my roof. Judging by its remaining size it should cover about two thirds of my home.

It was heavy and awkward to carry, but determination was becoming a constant companion of mine. The next morning was spent nailing it down on the roof, but it only covered a little more than two thirds. The rest was done in salvaged pieces of tin. I nailed the shit out these, then put a few ties on top of the whole mess. I felt confident it could withstand a storm equal to the other night.

The days took on serene monotony. Every day, walk my mile to the ditch, work until late afternoon, then head back, carrying half a bucket of water, and a full bucket of canned goods. The remaining pile was down to about half of what needed to be carried, plenty of time. My abandoned camp looked pretty sad and forlorn, with only the remaining cases and my hand tools for digging.

Walking up to my new home I reflected that it had all the appearances of a third world slum building, much like National Geographic had shown.

Late one afternoon as I was loading my bucket with cans in preparation for the walk home, a plume of dust announced someone coming up the valley. Surprised it hadn't gotten my attention earlier since it was only about a mile from making the decision of whether or not to turn off the main road. It was slowing, I recognized the vehicle, the blue Volkswagen bus. I watched it bounce its way to me, now only a quarter mile away.

I stood there leaning on my shovel, uncertain what to do, the bus stopped ten feet from where I was.

Through the windshield it was clear my father was by himself. I was torn it two directions, one of me wanted to run to him in greeting, but there was a small, nagging voice telling me not to, should I or shouldn't I. I stood there, feeling it was important not to display too much emotion, why such a stupid notion would take hold at this time I didn't understand.

"Where the hell is your tent?" He was searching, his head turning back and forth in a small arc. After not hearing another human voice for six weeks these were the first words I heard. Standing by the open front door, of the bus, this was his greeting, his face had a questioning look, as if he was surprised at the bareness of my former camp.

"A huge windstorm came about ten days ago. The whole thing blew away except the floor. I salvaged it and moved up to the ties. Took a bunch of them and built a hut. I think it turned out pretty good." I pointed in the direction of the rise where the hut was barely visible. That is enough detail I thought, so much wanting to be like my father, detached, but it was so hard, this was not the greeting I had expected, or wanted. I so desperately wanted him to ask if I was okay, if it was hard being alone here all these weeks, if the storm had scared me, if I was tired of eating from cans endlessly, mostly, I guess it was important to know someone gave a damn.

"Let's see how the ditch is doing." Walking to what was clearly the end of the ditch.

"I expected more done. Guess it'll take all summer at this rate." It was said so accusingly, so like him, but it stung deeply. It was so hard for me to understand him, countless times he would say something to me, directly, or indirectly, it didn't matter, I was never sure if it was a criticism or not.

Holding my tongue was hard, not barking at him for the shit I had been through, because of his doing. I dropped it.

"Do you want the rest of this stuff hauled up.?" I nodded yes. "You can show me what you built." This was said with genuine interest, as we loaded the few cases left. I could tell he'd been drinking, not by his actions, simply by his breath when we got close. I wasn't even slightly surprised; no smell of whiskey would have startled me.

We followed the old track up, it was rough but not difficult, several times stopping so I could move a rock that might damage the undercarriage. It felt strange to ride and not be walking.

"It's not too bad." He walked around my new home, looking in my almost door. This was high praise. I expected to have some shortcomings pointed out. It would unnerve me if it ended on a good note. I was ready with an explanation for several things he might find fault with. No need. I felt good, prideful of my accomplishment, as he checked the inside, shaking his head back and forth, there was no way to tell what he was thinking.

We unloaded the bus, putting more cases of food inside at the end of my hut. There was a surprise for me. A new canvas cot, no longer would concrete be my mattress, plus, if it rained and leaked onto my floor, it wouldn't matter.

Bread, a real loaf of bread, it was like Christmas. A small cooler held a package of bologna, cheese and a small jar of mayonnaise, some tomatoes and fresh peaches. I damn near became giddy.

"I knew your other cot wouldn't hold longer than a week or two, the canvas was rotten when we brought it up. Your mom sent the other stuff in the cooler, the ice should last for a couple more days."

My dad set up another cot in the bus for himself, before it got dark. Another great surprise, two folding chairs. Finally, I could sit and rest my back. So much comfort was added in such a short time. My father was smiling as he set them next to the fire that would be perfect for our bratwurst roast. It was a great evening, as we sat there smoking, sitting in our chairs, having just finished our dinner.

"If you're wondering why it took me so long to get back, it's..."

"It doesn't matter." It was an interruption, which I rarely did. "It really doesn't. Let's have a drink." It was extremely rare for me to make that suggestion. He took me at face value. Not asking if there was any left of the bottle he left behind so long ago, he brought another from his stash under the front seat. We both took a healthy dose in our empty coffee cups.

We made very little small talk. Maybe father and sons don't have much to say to each other when by themselves. We talked some about Joe, still driving truck. Joe was pissed because his homestead application was denied on grounds of "Unsuitable for Agriculture."

The evening went on in a very pleasant manner. Surprising

me, my father gave me a little background on his part of World War Two. In the German Navy, he was on a P.T. boat stationed on the coast of France. No details of any specific actions. My understanding of the war was vague, just what was taught in school and in reading books. This was a side of him that had remained hidden until now, at least to me, his emotions private. Another drink for us both, he no longer talked to me, he was talking to himself, staring into the fire, long pauses broken by a sentence faintly spoken, unheard by me. I watched him, I watched him reflect on his own life. It was sad, he always seemed so stalwart, so full of strong purpose. I wasn't sad for him, that night, under that star filled sky, it came to me, my father had his own demons. I couldn't begin to understand what the war had done to him, or my mother, or the countless millions of others. That night I had an inkling, maybe I didn't understand shit. I saw my father in a different light after that. It wasn't a lightning bolt slapping me alongside the head that night, it started as a dim, faint realization, that became more clear with age, other people also have problems.

I would have sat there all night, comfortable with his company, comfortable with life in general. Hours may have gone by, he stood up, making his way to his bed, mumbling something that sounded like goodnight.

The next morning, we walked around the old mine, my father was very curious about mining. After two hours, checking some of the tunnels with a flashlight my father always carried in the bus, we both came away thinking, what a crap way to make a living, being a miner.

"Your mom's coming up with me in two weeks. It's Memorial weekend, we've both got three days off. I'll borrow a trailer and we'll bring your horse." He handed me paper and pencil, "Make a list, we'll bring what we can."

The list was short, sack of grain, horse shoes, my shoeing

equipment, saddle and related items. All my stuff was together in a shed. The grain he would have to buy.

He checked the list, satisfied, got into his bus. Starting the engine, looking at me, he voiced, "Be back in two weeks." Raising his arm in farewell he drove off.

So much different than last time. I began to appreciate his method of departure, no endless stream of warnings, be careful, wash your hands, change your underwear, all the other mindless things that men have ignored forever. Watching the dust fade, I had a pang of guilt, it felt good to be alone again. That thought bothered me a little, why, I didn't understand. For six weeks I waited for him to come back, scared and lonely. Now two days and I was ready to be by myself again. Maybe I wanted him to hurry, so he could return with my horse. Whatever the reasons, I had a ditch to dig.

The next two weeks were so tranquil it was a little spooky. Several times a vehicle would pass on the main road, I barely gave them a thought. The Navy jets came back to play one afternoon, I barely saw them, two sonic booms hit me so hard it compressed my chest, one after the other, I only saw their red exhausts, right over the top of me they had flown, silently, no idea what kind, their rumble shaking the valley, they disappeared before my breath came back. Scared the hell out of me, but I still loved it.

The weather was perfect. Cool nights, the days warming to a pleasant temperature. Several times it was quite warm, a promise, a glimpse into my future, I'll take it. The air was the clearest I had ever seen, in the cool mornings, mountains fifty miles away weren't just visible, they were clear enough to make out some details. The stars at night filled the sky, so bright were they. The Milky Way, so prominent it mimicked a thin hazy band of clouds across the sky. Sometimes I would sit outside without a fire, smoking and gazing at the sky for hours.

One more rattler and several scorpions were dispatched the second week, a stark reminder not all things are pleasant in the desert.

The ditch was going slow, sometimes painstakingly so. The earth was being baked harder every day by the sun, but so was I. The time of trying to predict a finish date had long since passed, I simply dug. Daylight was too long now, by late afternoon, my body spent for the day, I had to stop. This gave me plenty of time for chores and reading, which I came to love more and more.

I saw them arrive just in time, so focused on my digging I didn't see the tell-tale dust cloud, just a pickup with horse trailer. They parked on the main dirt road, not wanting to drag the horse trailer across the rough road to my camp. I dropped my shovel, making my way as quickly as was possible cross country, weaving around sagebrush, sometimes jumping them in my haste.

We greeted, smiles all around, my mother hugged me with a huge smile on her face, telling me I looked too thin. Unloading my horse, we unhooked the trailer and left it on the shoulder. They drove together while I rode my horse bareback with just a halter to my camp. It felt so good to be on my horse, a gelding, he was well behaved and dependable, his ears back and forth and head looking around, he must be wondering what the hell happened to his world. He quenched his thirst from a five-gallon bucket, drinking two thirds before finally stopping, water running from his mouth as his head came up.

Tying the lead rope to the pickup, I got some grain, grateful they brought it, this would help keep him around since there was no corral to confine him. Taking his halter off I fed him a can full, pouring the contents on a small piece of plywood.

Meanwhile my father was showing my mom around, there wasn't much to see. She had a pained expression on her face after looking inside my home. She looked at me hard, trying to read something from my face as her head moved slightly back and forth. I grinned at her, saying it was quite comfortable. She smiled, still shaking her head.

After unloading the pickup and putting things away, they wanted to take a walk over to see how the ditch was going, and stretch their legs. My poor horse, he didn't know what to make of this situation, he was free to go anywhere he wanted, probably hundreds of miles in any direction before coming to a fence. He chose to follow, walking behind the three of us. I thought he might, horses being a herd animal and we were as close to a herd as it would ever get. Also, he would learn where water was and I wouldn't have to pack it for him.

I think there was genuine appreciation at the amount of effort being put into constructing this ditch. They both voiced that they were impressed. This didn't sound like my father, rarely given to platitudes, maybe it was for my mother's sake.

We walked the mile back to camp, my horse staying behind, contently feeding on some grass alongside the creek.

Such a small pleasure, having your dinner prepared by another person. We sat around afterwords, my mother asking some questions about my daily life. I tried to keep my answers positive, not wanting her to worry. It was easy to be that way, I was naturally a positive person, and for the most part my life was pretty good.

The three days went quickly, putting stakes into the ground between the corner posts to mark our property lines took a full day. Marking where the reservoir would be and setting those dimensions gave me a much clearer goal for my ditch. We determined where the house would sit, along with several out-buildings. We also defined where a corral would be located. These activities used up what time they had to spend with me. I was anxious to start some other projects but we didn't have the material or money to do anything else yet. Plus, water to our property was a high priority and it didn't cost anything to dig the ditch, this struck me as humorous, so like my father, something for nothing. There was no mention of helping me with the ditch project, I found that curious but somehow relieved, for some reason I was possessive and wanted it to be mine.

The morning of departure my mother cut my hair with hand clippers, how she could think of these small things, like bringing clippers along amazed me. She had always cut my hair, it was a simple process, take it all, right down to the scalp. I was happy with this, when my hair would get longer it became annoying. During the cutting, my father busy with something else, she stood in front of me and said in a somber tone, "You've changed, you're different." Patting my shoulder with one hand as if to reassure me it was a good change. I waited for some kind of explanation, but that was it.

Their departure was bittersweet. "Two, maybe three weeks." My father's departing words. My mother seemed sad and didn't say much, only the cautionary things that mothers have given to sons since the beginning. Nodding my head in earnest, I promised to heed everything she said. Watching the cloud of dust once again disappear into the horizon became less depressing each time.

No desire for digging this afternoon. My horse was a half mile away, working on a patch of bunch grass. I whistled loudly, repeating several times before his head came up. Over the years this was a signal that I wanted him to come to me. Whenever he did, I rewarded him with some grain, most times just petting him or brushing him down, sometimes going for a ride, work or just pleasure, he never seemed to mind. I didn't have the illusion that my horse loved me, he loved grain. He slowly made his way in my direction, stopping for a quick bite of grass several times. As he got closer I held the can of grain aloft, shaking it. This inspired him to quicken his pace. It may have been quicker to just go get him, he was a very easy horse to catch, never running from me. I have watched people spend hours trying to catch some worthless piece of shit, shaking my head in disgust as I watched, thinking, just can that worthless bastard.

I saddled him, aware I wouldn't be able to go for a long ride until I put shoes on him, maybe in a couple of days. The next couple of hours were so enjoyable it was hard to stop. We rode to the mouth of several canyons, just exploring, happier than I had a right to be, having just watched my parents drive off, knowing I would be alone again for a while.

Back at camp I removed my saddle. Taking a can of water from a bucket I rinsed the salt from his back. Joe had insisted it was important to keep the salts from abrading his skin, ultimately leading to saddle sores. It was good advice and served me and my horse well. He would usually find a patch of dirt and roll on his back afterward.

Some days would bring a surprise, like the Navy jets playing in the sky above me, someone driving by, no idea I was there, an afternoon thunderstorm, brief but wicked. One day, working on the ditch, a pair of open top Jeeps came up the road leading to the mouth of White Rock canyon. I was in a low spot; they must not have seen me. I hunkered down, watching them slowly make their way up the rough road. A couple in each vehicle, they were laughing at something, happily rolling over the bumps before entering the mouth of the canyon. They must have made it through, or come back sometime during the night, I never saw them again.

My father came and went. Returning in two weeks, sometimes three. More canned food, plenty of Prince Albert tobacco in a tin along with papers. A new pair of work boots, a new pair of Levi's, books. These last must have come from my mother's influence.

My mother came every other time as a rule. I think it was hard for her to sit in a vehicle for so long with my father. He could become very gruff and cranky when drinking, and drink he did, as he drove from Sacramento to Dixie Valley. Many Saturdays as he arrived, it was obvious. He could continue as normal, no staggering or any overt display of drunkenness. His German brogue was so heavy it covered a lot of his speech, until he was too far gone. Sometimes he could be quite jovial, laughing and telling jokes. One evening as he and I sat around the fire having a drink, he much further along than myself, my father leaned towards me in a conspiratorial manner, "Don't ever sit on bare concrete, it'll give you piles." I had no idea what piles were, but I knew he was serious, taking on the aura of a wise sage he came forth with more wisdom, "And whatever you do, don't marry a Portuguese woman, they'll get a fat ass right after the wedding." I had no idea where the hell these came from; we weren't even talking. Out of the blue, with great emphasis, my father must have thought we finally had the father son discussion, almost sixteen, never too late, sound advice I would heed forever.

The days became very hot now. Picking up any metal that had lain on the ground would burn your hands immediately, this was a quick, one-time lesson. The summer wore on, heedless of my discomfort. The nights stayed hot also, I took to sleeping outside, my hut was too hot and began to stink of creosote by late afternoon. I must have gotten used to the high temperatures, the heat seemed to bother me less.

After putting shoes on my horse, we sometimes spent the afternoon in the cool of the canyons, checking every little draw that was passable. On occasion we would scatter a band of chukar. If things went well I could take my .22 from its scabbard and shoot one or two from the back of my horse, careful to shoot from his side and not over his ears. The meat was very tasty and a nice addition to my canned food. A cottontail would meet the same fate when I had an opportunity. Jack rabbits were safe from eating, too full of ticks, but they were fun to shoot from the back of my horse.

I had no idea what the date was, but I was sure August 21 was behind me, so my 16 birthday had come and gone, it didn't matter. I took sixteen cans, set them in a row and shot each one in turn, I was close to them so it was easy not to miss.

For several months I had been requesting a radio, craving music and just human voices at night. My father finally relented and brought me a transistor that worked marginally at best. Some evenings after the sun set I would be able to pick up a station from some distant, large city, usually L.A. It was a comfort to hear other humans speaking and music would be so welcome when I could get it. I would hear references to Vietnam on occasion, but it didn't mean much. The batteries lasted about six weeks, my request for new ones were ignored or deemed not essential. My father never brought me anymore, for reasons I couldn't fathom. I nursed and coddled the damn batteries, warming them in my hands, sometimes coaxing another hour of entertainment once they were warm and rested. In frustration I eventually gave up, put the radio away in a box somewhere and forgot about it, my connection to the outside world once again severed.

The days were getting slightly cooler and shorter, which was a nice change. On one of his trips my father brought a sledge hammer and four steel wedges. These tools were for splitting the railroad ties in half, length wise. This would give us many more fence posts for the three miles of fence that would be built in the future. It was hard work, but broke the tedium of ditch digging. Every afternoon I would spend a couple hours splitting posts.

The ditch was going well, over half way done but I had reservations about finishing before winter. The water volume was less than half but still adequate for all my needs. I did get a little tired of packing my water in five gallon buckets to my camp every other evening. Normally I would use two buckets, filling each one half way and carry them the mile to my home.

Vehicles would come and go, the occupants unaware they

were being observed. No longer did I want them to stop. My parents were the only humans I had contact with for the last six months. Surprisingly even their visits began to feel somehow less pleasurable, as if their presence was an interruption. Always glad to see them come, I was equally glad to see them leave. More and more I wanted my solitude. My work filled the days, my mind free to dream, filled my nights. My horse filled my need for an audience, and my cans filled my belly. At sixteen I began to think people were overrated. Solitude was becoming not only pleasurable but desirable.

A thin coating of ice on my bucket of water began to greet me in the morning. Still plenty warm during the day, it was ideal weather for my work. Down to about a half mile of ditch still to dig made it certain I wouldn't quite finish this fall. I wasn't disappointed, this was a huge undertaking for one person.

Resting on my shovel momentarily, gazing at the mountains, a very strange sight caught my attention. A man was making his way toward me on horseback. Not in a hurry, his horse walking. I watched with interest, stealing a glance at my rifle leaning on a rock not too far off. He stopped about twenty feet from where I was standing, still leaning on my shovel. Looking at me then the ditch, he leaned on his saddle horn, resting both arms.

"Looks like a tough job." He was thin, tall and looked gaunt with a dark weather beaten face. He looked very comfortable on his horse.

"It has been, but I'm gaining on it."

"Are you here alone?" Tilting his hat back on his head he looked around for others.

"Have been all summer, working on this ditch."

"Where the hell you going with it?" Half smiling with a puzzled look.

"We have a ranch, right down there." I was pointing in the

direction of our property. I was enthusiastic with that pronouncement. He looked at me as if the sun had cooked my brain. I gave him a brief explanation. It must have satisfied him.

"I'm camped about a mile from here. You're more than welcome to come and have coffee with me. Dinner if you want, there's plenty."

He looked at the sun, checking how much daylight was left. About two hours. "Is there a place to throw my bedroll and spend the night?"

"Plenty of room if you don't mind sleeping outside. There's only room for one inside to sleep. You'll have to water your horse here, there's not enough at camp."

"Sounds good." He dismounted, took the bridle off his horse and let him drink his fill from the small stream. He didn't get back on his horse but chose to walk with me, leading the animal.

Looking at my tie house he seemed relieved to be sleeping outside as he spread his bedroll on a flat spot. I gave him a can full of grain for his horse which was hobbled for the night a short distance off. Answering his puzzled look, I said, "I've got a horse somewhere, he's running loose but comes around every couple of days." He thanked me for the grain, grateful his horse would have something extra.

Building a fire and heating some canned food didn't take long so we sat around talking about how I came to be here. "This gets more interesting the longer I sit here." Saying this as he shook his head.

He asked me questions. "Do you know how to shoe a horse.?"

"Know how, and have been for several years." I answered with pride.

"What about school?"

"That's up to my parents, but I really want to finish."

Mostly they were questions born out of a true curiosity. He was extremely polite and easy to be around. I found myself liking this stranger.

The next morning was cool with the usual skim of ice. I gave the stranger another can of grain for his horse. We got a morning fire going and had a nice warm breakfast of hash and some canned peaches. My horse must have seen his, he was making his way quickly to us. Ignoring us humans he went over to the other animal and they did the usual horse greeting antics. Necks bowed, nostrils flared, they sniffed and snorted, then that was the end of it. I caught my horse, put a halter on him and fed him some grain.

The stranger's name was Chase. He came over, leading his saddled horse getting ready to leave. He looked at my horse's feet, checking something. "Is that your shoeing job?" Chase continued looking at the horse's feet as he asked.

"Yes, about three weeks ago."

"What are you doing this winter?"

"I don't know; it hasn't come up yet." It felt like this was leading somewhere.

"Do you want a job, at least for the winter? You'll be a buckaroo. It pays one fifty a month, room and board." Before I could respond he added, "Probably you'll need to check with your folks."

"Not really, won't be much to do here this winter. I'll just answer you now." He seemed surprised. "Yeah, I would like a job. When would I start."

"Two weeks from today, roughly. Middle of November. If you can make that. Can you get someone to haul you and your horse up to our main ranch.?"

I asked how far and where it was.

"Should be about seventy miles north east of here." He

pointed at the base of a prominent mountain about thirty-five miles to the north. "Go to the base of that mountain. You'll run into a dirt road, it's rough but passable. Follow it for twenty miles to the top of a rise. The road forks, take the left, stay on it, you'll be able to see the ranch from the forks, should be about fifteen miles."

"I can ride that. How about if I'm there in two weeks. What do I need to bring.?"

"Horse, bedroll, chaps, lariat, one change of clothes. Don't bring shoeing stuff, we'll furnish that. Oh and some heavy winter clothes, you'll be on a horse every day, regardless of weather."

"Good enough, I've got all that stuff." I shook his hand. "See you in two weeks."

"You sure your parents are going to be okay with this." He seemed a little skeptical.

I nodded my head yes. "They'll be fine." Holding onto my horse so he wouldn't follow, I watched Chase ride off, looking so comfortable on his horse. I knew he had a short ride of six miles to his stock truck. I thought about riding along with him but there was work to do.

I was excited, and as each day passed became more so. I used my can method again to keep track of the days. On the eleventh can I started making preparations. Digging a hole in some soft dirt close to my hut I buried all my leftover canned food, keeping enough for several days. As I back-filled I left a post protruding to mark the spot. I was hoping my parents would arrive before I had to leave, they didn't. I was a little relieved, fearful my father would have other plans. I nailed a Prince Albert tin upside down on the post marking my food cache. Early the next morning, excitement hastening my actions, I saddled my horse, having kept him hobbled from the previous day. I left a note in the tin on the post marking my food:

I didn't want to make it a long explanation. There wasn't really much to say anyway so I kept it short and to the point.

I stuffed the note into the tin, careful not to push it too far into the can, closed the lid carefully and tightly.

Have job for winter on ranch seventy miles north.
All is well, be back in spring.

Damn, I Shot My Horse

BUCKAROOS AND PROSTITUTES

The first few miles I was possessed with a feeling of guilt, not for leaving without telling anyone, but for leaving without finishing my job. There wasn't enough time left before winter came on hard and I had no desire to be sitting in my hut or anywhere else without heat while it was zero degrees outside. I consoled myself, thinking my actions were a matter of self-preservation. I knew the note that was left in the can was a little short on details but I felt it said all that was needed to say. A sudden fear sent a chill up my spine, shit, I'm turning into my father.

Several times I turned around in my saddle gazing back at my tie hut, it saddened me to be leaving. It wasn't much but had given me many nights of comfort and protection, until the damn creosote smell became overwhelming. Riding by the ditch terminus I stopped and surveyed my summer's work. Surprisingly I didn't hate it, it was my test of will, administered by my father. Why I thought this, was a puzzle to me, maybe it made my circumstances tolerable.

Too much thinking I chided myself. I was filled with excitement and some fear. Seventy miles seemed such a long way cross country, would I get lost, what if my horse got hurt, did I have enough food if something went wrong? These questions had no answers I thought, it didn't help.

I told myself to enjoy the ride, forcing myself to look at the surrounding mountains, it helped. This would be the first time I had traveled more than five miles north of my hut. Staying on the main road that traveled north made it easy to gain some distance. Keeping my horse in a walk would make it easier on him, being loaded heavy with me and all my gear. He was a good walker, this could be taught somewhat by tapping with my heels or spurs, encouraging him to go faster until he broke into a trot, then gently pulling on the reins, putting him back into a walk. This was repeated constantly on a young horse until he naturally developed a fast walk. It didn't work on all horses; some were natural slugs, which were gotten rid of quickly.

The ride became more enjoyable as the miles gave way. I was even with the north end of the wet salt marsh, sage brush beginning to replace the white crust. Riding halfway between the mountains and salt flat I was surprised to come across another ranch about ten miles north of my place. Approaching it slowly it was soon apparent the occupants had long since left. Deserted, screen doors on hinges swinging in the slight breeze, a large two-story farmhouse sat desolate. Cottonwoods, huge, overshadowed the front yard and sides. The dirt track that was called a road went within twenty feet of the front door. A creek flowing nicely about ten feet from the north side, made its way from the canyon visible about a mile to the west, up slope.

Sitting there on my horse, his ears worked back and forth as if hearing something I couldn't. Looking around, I started to get a little spooked. It's not a house I would want to spend a stormy night in alone. Leaving the road and heading straight to the mountain that was my beacon. It loomed much larger but still presented a formidable distance, even cross country. Losing elevation over the next several miles I began to cross some bizarre terrain. Now only several feet higher than the salt flat, the ground was still covered in a white crust, sometimes several inches thick. Mounds of dirt two to three feet high, were home to clumps of sagebrush but between them the crust with mud hidden underneath. My horse began to sink deeper and deeper into the mud. He stopped, ankle deep, waiting for a sign from me. There were miles of this shit, I had no stomach for this, neither did my horse, now laboring to get his front feet out, having sunk another six inches in the few seconds of my indecision. Smarter than me, I thought, as he got them out with large sucking sounds, turning quickly he began to lunge, the only method now available to get his hind feet out, it was a violent motion. Now heading back in the direction we had come, firmer ground felt welcome. Looking back, some of the holes were filling with water. I had no idea how far we would have sunk, maybe out of sight, but this was a great lesson in caution of the unknown. We stayed in a northerly direction for about six miles, giving this sucking bog a wide berth, judging by my horses' action, he was fine with this decision.

Feeling comfortable we would be long past any problems, I began heading in a northeasterly direction once more, the large mountain taking on the appearance similar to the Rock of Gibraltar.

It would become a land mark that served me well indeed over the years, so prominent and distinct.

The ride was so enjoyable, such a release from the days, weeks, and months of being bent over, working mindlessly. Working itself didn't bother me, the emptiness, the mental vacuum, never knowing what my future held, had weighed on me occasionally throughout the summer.

My horse needed no guidance, once headed in a general direction he would follow it unerringly, any small corrections needed only a slight knee pressure from me. He was such a pleasure to ride, thanks in part to Joe, having unstintingly given me advice over the years on how to take a horse from average to exceptional, assuming the horse had the right material to begin with.

This gave my mind ample time to wander and wander it did. For hours my mind would occupy itself, no conscious input required. Later I would learn there is an actual term for this called "Trail Dreaming" A way for the mind to amuse itself when there is no outside stimulus. It worked well, a pleasant time filler that became my companion throughout the long summer, filling hour after hour.

In this state, awareness came back. The sun was dropping over the western mountains, the shadow catching, then passing me hurriedly making its way east. An hour of daylight left, thinking this I began to watch for a place to sleep for the night. Chase had informed me there was a small stream coming from a canyon on the north end of the mountain, this would be about half way and fine for camping. Spotting a ribbon of willows, I felt more confident I was on the right track. Soon the creek made its appearance, knowing the water was fine for drinking, I followed it for a suitable campsite, mainly some grazing for my horse and hopefully a little firewood. Finding both was easy enough, a nice level spot with plenty of feed for Pinto. Spotting a large dead sagebrush several hundred feet distant, I rode over shaking a loop from my lariat I simply roped it, my horse pulling it out and over to the camp spot with no strain, giving me plenty of wood for tonight and morning.

After hobbling my horse and removing his saddle I fed him a little grain, made my camp, started a fire and had dinner. Smoking a cigarette as twilight turned to dark I listened to Pinto munching on the grass, a tranquil, soothing sound. Sometime during the night coyotes woke me, their yipping sounded close, my hand rested on the rifle that lay next to me outside my bedroll, the silhouette of my horse a faint but reassuring outline. I fell asleep gazing at the stars.

I awoke just as it was getting light enough to see, checking to make sure my horse was still there. All was well, but there was a good frost on the ground and I had to force myself out from under the warm blankets. My excitement for the new day and all the promises it held prompted me to forgo breakfast and a morning fire. It didn't take long; we were on our way again. It was colder than any previous mornings so I rode with my hands inside my pockets for the first hour, bringing them out long enough only to roll a cigarette. Finding the road I was to follow proved easy. Everything was as it should be.

By noon we topped a ridge into a whole new valley, the road forking, I took the left hand and in another mile my destination became visible, a cluster of trees and buildings sitting snugly at the base of a large mountain. I was excited and quite apprehensive, so many new things awaited me. I knew no one except Chase, would I appear a fool if he wasn't there, what if he had changed his mind. There was a chance I would be unable to do the work required of me. I had enough confidence in myself so the thought of turning back was not an option.

The sun continued its relentless journey, promising to touch the mountain tops towards the west in another two hours, plenty of time, the buildings becoming more distinct with each closing mile. I could see a canyon full of cottonwoods, with groves of aspen marking a plentiful source of water for the ranch.

The last mile, cresting a gentle rise began to reveal a fair sized operation, dozens of corrals, some holding horses, Pinto seeing them gave a knicker that went unanswered. Close to a dozen outbuildings of varying descriptions. A large farm house that I assumed to be the owners' residence. Everything was very well maintained, the fences intact and sound, the gates hanging properly, paint and roofs in good order. It was the kind of place that said we take pride in ourselves, it was a good omen.

I stopped in a graveled courtyard, sitting on my horse, waiting for a sign of a human. It wasn't long before a man came out of long shed carrying a bucket full of milk.

"Just as well get off your horse and plan on spending the night, too late to get anywhere else before dark." Short, a little thick in the middle, clad in farmer's overalls, late forties as a guess, he was so welcoming it eased my nervousness greatly. I dismounted gingerly, knees and legs so tender it was several moments before I could straighten up properly.

"Must have come a long way, judging by how you got off." Moving his bucket of milk to his left hand he stuck out his right. Name's Pete, actually Peter, but haven't used that in years." We shook, I told him my name and why I was here, asking if Chase was around.

"Let me take the milk up to the cook and I'll be right back to get you settled. You'll like it here, son. Chase should be here shortly." Walking away he stopped and added, "That's the bunk house, use any bed that's empty."

A hitching rack conveniently located in front of the bunk house made it simple to unload my bedroll and other personnel things. A long building, four metal cots on a side, spaced well apart, with a wood stove on one end, apparently used for heating. Three of the cots had bedrolls on them with an empty one furthest from the stove. This would work fine, an empty next to me gave some separation. A chest with a lid sat on the floor of each bed. An uncomplicated process to put my roll on the cot, unrolling it I put my spare clothes, tobacco, and remaining cans of food in the chest. Went outside and waited for Pete to return.

As I waited Chase and three other cowboys rode up on their horses. "Figured you were good for your word, glad you made it." Smiling as Chase shook my hand, introductions were made. Two of them were undoubtedly full Indians, short, stocky and somewhere between forty and sixty years of age, they were both quick to smile. The third, his name Rob, was tall and thin, maybe some Mexican in his blood, about forty with a twinkle in his eye and a mischievous grin. He must have sensed some uncertainty and apprehension in me. He was very gracious and well spoken, not what a person would expect of a buckaroo. He did a lot to ease my mind that first hour and we would become close friends, riding endless miles through the desert, side by side.

I followed them to the corral with Pinto behind me. We unsaddled all the horses, turned them into a corral, gave them some grain and watched to make sure they didn't gang up on my horse, he was fine. After eating the grain, they rolled in the dirt on their backs, stood up and shook the dust off then trotted over to start on the sweet alfalfa hay that was generously spread out in the manger.

"In the morning you can pick out several more horses, we all have four." Rob and I were leaning on the corral fence, rolling a smoke, watching the horses eat. "They're all pretty good horses, they get rid of the worthless ones before somebody gets hurt. Let's get ready for dinner, it's at six."

The bunkhouse had a sink with only cold running water. No toilet, there was an outhouse, and for bathing, a nice natural hot water spring ran through a bath house, it was a good set up. A separate small building held a washing machine and dryer.

After bathing, Rob, the two Indians named George and Benson and I went to the main house for dinner. A large table with ten chairs for seating, was piled with food. Beef stew, mashed potatoes and gravy, corn, peas and pie for dessert. I would have worked just for the food, it looked and smelled so good. Chase, who was the ranch foreman, ate with us, but had his own private bunkhouse. The cook was of some Indian heritage, she was very short and round, no way to guess her age. Very stoic and not given any need for conversation, she nodded her head at me and went back to her kitchen. Pete, the handyman, also ate dinner with us.

I was in heaven, more food than I could imagine, and it didn't come out of a can and was warm all way through. The others all asked questions of me, their interest genuine, a little perplexed at how I had spent the summer and was able to discuss it without anger. I tried to impress upon them it was also in my interest, I too would see benefits in the future. Not sure if I was successful, but they were fun to talk with, having been so long since I had engaged in just normal conversation.

After dinner, we all sat on the porch and rolled a smoke, it was a large porch with plenty of seating for all. Such a nice change from the last six months.

"How old are you?" one of the Indians asked.

"Sixteen." Proud of how old I was, damn near a man.

"Christ, we're getting them younger all the time." He said this good naturedly, smiling, poking the other Indian in the rib with his elbow, "Pretty soon they'll be so young they're going to need little ponies to ride." Laughing at his joke he waited to see how I would take it, so were the others.

"You can laugh all you want, I'm still taking my pillow, if I don't get a nap after lunch I get cranky." This must have satisfied something in them, it started a winter of back and forth ribbing and poking fun. They never did use my name, either calling me boy or son. I was fine with all of this, being the youngest and new to the ranch there was no doubt what it would entail.

We retired to the bunkhouse, taking care of personal needs then each of us going to our respective space. We each had a private reading light above our bed, so I followed their lead and stayed to myself, reading, conversation done for the day. Soon all the lights were off.

Breakfast at six, exactly six. They didn't wake me, expecting I would hear them and arise on my own accord. I did, years of early rising making it a natural event.

The breakfast was big and plentiful, pancakes, ham, eggs,

potatoes, and apple pie, what a feast. So much better than a can of lukewarm hash.

After breakfast we all rolled a smoke and Chase gave instructions for the day. I would ride with him. It would be a day ride along the base of a mountain range picking up cattle as we rode along. Taking turns riding up a canyon, looking for cows that had made their way towards the valley, pushing them into the main herd that was slowly being worked towards the winter range. Small bunches sometimes only one pair at a time would be hazed into the main herd, letting them graze as Chase and I kept them bunched loosely. Rob and the Indians taking turns scouting canyons.

It was easy work, exactly what buckaroos did, I thought to myself. The sky was such a brilliant blue a person would have to experience it to understand. The horse I was riding was a good one, dependable, even tempered, not given to acts of stupidity. He did the work mostly by himself, spotting an animal that was lagging behind he would take it upon himself to send her back into the bunch. If a parcular animal continued to cause him problems he would trot towards her, ears back on his head and threaten to bite her on the ass. It was effective.

The cook had packed us all sandwiches, that were eaten as we rode, no need to stop. I was extremely happy. Plenty of food, well mounted, other humans even though they didn't talk much it was comforting to know I wasn't all alone, country so big and open you could see into tomorrow.

We stopped the cattle that evening at a small stream emerging from a gravel bed, at the entrance to one of the many canyons. A flatbed pickup with hay was waiting, having been driven here by the ranch hand. We scattered a dozen bales to hold the cattle for the night, hobbled our horses a little distance from each other and gave them each a generous helping of hay with a can full of grain on top of the flakes. The day done we jumped into the pickup, rode back to the ranch, about ten miles away, Chase sitting in the front seat with the driver and the rest of us sitting on the flatbed. The ride was welcome, my ass was sore, not used to so many hours in the saddle.

The next morning, we hauled fresh horses in a stock truck, trading them for our tired mounts of the previous day. The ranch hand hauling them back. The same pattern as the day before, they would send me alone into some of the canyons today, apparently having earned their trust, it felt good, I hoped these days would never end.

By the end of the day the herd was about three hundred head of cows with about two thirds having calves of various ages but most of them being of weaning size. We stayed with the herd that night, sleeping under the stars. That morning we had packed our bedrolls, leaving them on the porch of the bunkhouse to be brought to us by the ranch hand. The cook sent plenty of food, heated by Scotty in cast iron pots over the fire.

Sitting around the fire that evening having a smoke, Chase made a short speech, surprising us. "You're doing a good job and I'm glad to have you." this was directed at me. "I won't fill your head with crap, just remember if I'm not saying anything to you, I'm happy. That's all you need to know."

I nodded my head at him, accepting and appreciating the praise, something I rarely received from home.

"What about me boss, I have feelings too." This from Rob, grinning.

"Us too, we try to make you really happy. Do you even care about us?" The Indians weren't going to let an opportunity pass by.

Chase looked at them, deadpan, not rising to the bait.

More talk about the next day finished the evening, the fire turning to embers, we went to our bedrolls. I lay there, waiting for sleep, the stars so bright I couldn't help but wonder how many held some form of life. The coyotes were close and very vocal that night. I felt very fortunate, not many people would ever have this kind of experience.

The weather was kind to us, cool nights with warm fall days. They became a succession of searching for cattle, bunching them and slowly making our way along the foothills, the herd growing larger every day.

Our final destination was reached one day. A satellite ranch, owned by my employers with corrals and large fenced pastures with tall grass. We stayed here for a week, separating the larger calves from their mothers. It was hard work, roping the calves one at a time, branding, castrating the males, ear marking and waddling. Each ranch had a distinctive ear mark; some, a crop or swallow fork, under bit or over bit, others had a combination of several on both ears. The waddle was a flap of skin, about five inches long, cut with a knife to hang loose, some having two waddles, usually on the brisket or other parts were there was loose skin. Each ranch had a State registered earmark and waddle, along with the brand, these made it easy to identify ownership at a distance, these animals were very wild and hard to get close enough to see the brands.

When this was done we separated the calves from their mothers to wean them, putting them in separate corrals for about a week to dry the mother's bags. The nights were filled with a cacophony of bawling cows and calves, trying desperately to get together again. The thin walls of the bunkhouse did little to diminish the noise. I learned to sleep through it.

When the cows were dry we took the cattle and some calves to winter pasture. The steer calves and half the heifers were held back, to be hauled at a later date back to the main ranch for more intense feeding in preparation for a feedlot, to be fattened and eventually slaughtered. Not much of a future.

All the haying and general work was done by two ranch hands who stayed here permanently. They were good men, hard working. One had his wife there, she did the cooking for all of us. I was happy not to be involved with general ranch work, being a buckaroo had its privileges, if we couldn't do it from horseback we didn't do it. It was a constant internal struggle not to develop a superior attitude, not sure if I was successful but it didn't matter, there was no one to be smug for. Much like flying first class on a plane, but you are the only passenger, I suppose no one gives a damn.

This whole process was repeated for the next month in another valley. The weather becoming increasingly colder. This removed some of the gloss of being a buckaroo, zero degrees sitting on a horse was damn cold. Long underwear, chaps, rubber over-boots, along with heavy shirts and coat did little to ward off the cold. After hours of sitting on your horse the cold would permeate so deeply you would be forced to get off and walk, your feet having no feeling, stumbling along until a semblance of warmth would return way too slowly. The only way to warm your hands, put them between your horse's hind legs with gloves off. The warmth hurting momentarily, needless to say the animal took very unkindly to this intrusion, ears back, moving away skittishly, sometimes raising his hind foot as a warning. You took your chances, the only way of getting them warm enough to roll a smoke. This act would be repeated a dozen times daily, your mind filled with thoughts of a nice warm bunkhouse. Nobody complained, we were buckaroos.

After ten weeks of constant riding and working cattle we made our way back to the main ranch. It felt good to be back, mainly to take my first real bath since leaving. This was something that was given very little attention. Ten weeks with nothing but a sponge bath, and this only rarely. We wore the same pair of Levi's for the whole duration with no washing. Hand washing one pair of socks and underwear weekly did little for personal hygiene, the only thing consistent was brushing my teeth daily, but I was the only one who did this on a regular basis. The whole thing made for some interesting aromas in a small line shack at night. So be it, we were buckaroos and our horses didn't care.

The main ranch had a bath house fed by a natural hot springs, more like a hot tub with a constant flow of warm water running through it. You could stay in it as long as a person wanted, it was a luxury unequaled, especially on cold days. I took complete advantage of this on our return.

The next morning after breakfast, while having a smoke, Chase told us we had a week off and could catch a ride to town.

"We can go to the bank and I'll pay you what's owed, then take you wherever you want to spend your days off." This was directed at me, from Chase.

"What's there to do?" I hadn't a clue how big town was and what was available.

"Have you ever been to a whorehouse?" he asked, grinning.

"No" I had only a vague idea what a whorehouse was, and that only from reading so many western novels.

"Hell, let's just drop him off for a week, he'll get a real education and maybe we can get some work out of him." This from one of the Indians.

"We can wait outside for five minutes, that's all the time he'll need." This from the other Indian, both of them laughing now, happy with themselves.

"Shit, he'll just fall in love and we'll never see him again. Even if he does come back his head will be full of just one thing." Of course Rob wasn't to be left out.

"Yeah, that'll be perfect." I said, with a lot more bravado then I felt, ignoring the ribbing from the others. Now I was really nervous, not sure what to expect.

"Be ready in an hour. Make sure you've had a bath and wear clean clothes or they won't let you in."

Chase spoke directly to me, his eyes twinkling with humor.

Nodding my understanding, I hurried to take my second bath in as many days. I was done and dressed way too quickly, giving me too much time to think. A pervasive fear being that I was only sixteen, what if I was arrested for impersonating an adult, I had no idea if that was even a crime, or for that matter how old you even had to be for a whore house. What if things didn't work and they laughed me out of the place. Shit, maybe I should just stay here and do something else. Luckily Chase came and saved me from myself. I was on my way.

Sixty miles of gravel road, it took forever but was over way too soon. My nerves fraying with each passing mile. The two Indians and Rob making things worse, constant ribbing, good natured but increasing my apprehension.

"First time he sees that thing he's going to run like a rabbit that just saw a coyote." One of the Indians again.

"Best leave the door open so you don't run into it." The other one.

"I've heard that's how a priest is made; they never return to normal." Laughing and guffawing, slapping their knees, they were having a great time at my expense. It helped the time pass but didn't help my confidence.

First stop was the bank. We all went in and cashed our checks. The two Indians were dropped at a casino. Rob and I dropped off at the whore house. It looked like any other large house, a red light next to the front door distinguishing it from all the others. All the curtains were drawn closed. Walking up to the front door I almost bolted and ran.

"Let me do the talking, and just follow my lead for a while." That sentence from Rob calmed me down a little.

The doorbell was answered by a large woman, middle aged, seventy-five extra pounds, a neck waddle to make a turkey jealous. The blue makeup around her eyes must have been put on with a four-inch brush, I was reminded of a clown face. Hope she's not the only one here, I thought to myself, this was not at all what I expected.

"Well Rob, it's been a while." She looked at me, "Looks like he needs a mother more than one of my girls. How old is he?" Her scrutiny didn't help my anxiety.

"He's been riding with us a long time, he's old enough, just got a baby face that's all."

She may have known this was a lie, but left it alone. We entered into a parlor, low lighting, walls covered in red velvet wallpaper, a bar along one wall, several tables with chairs. Two girls, maybe late twenties reclining and talking to each other on a huge couch. Stealing a glance in their direction they let it be obvious they were watching me, smiling, I looked away quickly.

"Let's sit down and have a drink." Rob pulled out a chair indicating which table.

"I don't have any idea what to offer him." The madam, bringing a bottle of whiskey set a glass in front of me hesitantly. "You guys sure this is okay. You don't by any chance have some I.D.?" She picked the glass back up, head cocked, she was looking at me.

"I know how to drink." I tried in vain to make it sound authoritative, it came out as a squeak. "I didn't bring my wallet, but I do have money." This sounded a little better.

Maybe the word money convinced her. She set my glass on the table, pouring Rob and I both a generous amount. "I think we have just the girl for you, honey. I'll go get her in a minute and you can see what you think." She smiled at me and left us alone. She would call me honey forever more.

"What the hell happens next." I needed some advice.

"Did you bring all your money or did Chase keep half for you."

"He kept half, saying he'd give it to me back at the ranch." I would be grateful later.

"If you want, they might let you stay here till Chase comes and picks us up. Let me talk to her, see if I can set it up. There's not much to do here in town." Rob continued, grinning. "Just as well get your fill."

Ten minutes later a very attractive lady came and sat down at our table, introducing herself as Judy. Maybe early thirties, very cute, short blonde hair, trim and wearing very little clothes. Most of her attention was directed at me. Five minutes and I was in love, deeply. I drank my glass of whiskey way too quickly, feeling better but still nervous. She was very sweet, I began to relax, could have been the drink but more likely just her personality. Trying not to stare at her body as she sat there, I knew she was talking but nothing was penetrating my brain. It's hard to make a coherent sentence when you're mentally trying to undress someone that's damn near naked already.

"Let's go upstairs to my room honey, it'll be easier to talk there." She took my hand and led me away. I looked at Rob over my shoulder, wanting to say some kind of farewell. He waved me off, grinning like a dumb shit.

Her room was very clean, a bed, neatly made, dresser and two chairs. A door led to a bathroom with shower and tub. A simple room, warm and inviting, the lights muted, a radio playing some kind of music. No doubt this was a female room. Looking at the bed it dawned on me, I had not been in a proper bed with sheets for about two years,

"Business first, this may be new for you so just trust me and we'll go from there." She was smiling and so seductive, I could not have withheld anything from her.

"I've got three days in town and I don't know anyone or have any place to go. Would it possible to stay here if I pay.?" I knew what I wanted, it was standing in front of me, almost naked, so damn teasing.

"This is a new one, most guys only stay as long as it takes, then leave. Let's start with how much you want to spend."

Taking my cash from my pocket we sat on the bed. Two hundred twenty dollars in twenties. I looked hard at my money, thinking how many freezing days had been spent on a horse to earn this. I went to look at Judy, my eyes stopping at her bosom, so close and inviting. I would have given her twice that, with my horse thrown in, I was so damn weak.

She took two of the twenties, giving them to me, "Keep these for yourself." She took the rest. "Let me go downstairs and I'll see what this gets you, maybe we can make it work. Don't you dare run off." She shook her finger at me, emphasizing the last. That was a wasted threat, they would have to remove me in pieces.

Ten minutes later she burst back into the room, downright giddy.

"You are good to go, buckaroo!" Her excitement infectious.

So began three days of intense, blissful education. I learned many things under her tutelage. The obvious of course, but also table manners, decorum, bathroom etiquette, respect for females, but most of all just how complicated the female mind is.

At some point we discussed my stay. Three days, one fifth of whiskey per day, to be shared with Judy, two meals per day. A simple arrangement, very much to my liking. I would be free to sample some of the other talent if so inspired. "You could stay with me the whole time, if you want." Judy whispered to me coyly. I did, by then so deeply in love I was beyond hope.

As I lay in bed, thoughts of my friends in school, by now Juniors, caused me to chuckle. I felt sorry for them, struggling with school work as I lay here, bottle of whiskey on the nightstand, naked woman next to me in bed, my only care that it would end too soon, which it did.

Three days, true to his word, Chase came to pick me up. It was a poignant farewell. I didn't want to leave, life was good here and like any young man under the care of such a wise and effervescent woman as Judy, I was irretrievably in love. Those three days were etched in my mind forever. But, not unlike too much time spent at a buffet, satiated to the point of gluttony it was time to move on.

We picked Rob up at a hotel, and left town. One of the Indians was in the hospital from alcohol poisoning, which I learned later was not uncommon for him, and the other still on the reservation, unavailable that day.

Rob and I spent the next several days shoeing our horses and doing cattle work around the ranch until the Indians came back.

We spent the next ten weeks moving cattle, checking canyons for strays and all the other things required of us. Far and wide we rode, sometimes staying in line shacks sometimes sleeping in the open. On occasion I would be sent alone to check a row of canyons by myself for several weeks. The others splitting up, doing likewise. The solitude was welcome, mental confidence adding to my maturity, content in the knowledge I was equipped to handle any surprises thrown at me. My mind would often return to the three days spent with Judy, how it had changed me, given me such a positive view of life. By now I had no idea what was normal any more, especially for a male of sixteen. These men that I had spent five months with were so instrumental in making me believe I could accomplish anything. They never spoke bullshit, didn't give compliments, when the instruction was given it was assumed I would do it. They were easy to work with, never mean, never churlish, I enjoyed and valued them. I never complained, no matter the conditions or the job. They wouldn't tolerate it. They did it and expected you to carry your end. Several times we would go a couple days without food, getting stuck in some canyon after dark unable to return, no food or bedrolls, sleeping on the ground with only saddle blankets to cover us. We didn't make light of the situation; we just did it without complaint.

Chase rode with us off and on. Returning to the main ranch for supplies and other reasons, then riding with us for several weeks. The weather was getting warm again, an occasional storm bringing rain now instead of snow. Our rain gear consisted of oiled canvas overcoats, split in the back to drape on either side of the rider and saddle, still covering your legs. For most cases it worked well, except if really windy, then it was miserable.

My thoughts were starting to drift towards home and my own ranch with the coming warm weather. Chase must have sensed this. On one of his returns he said, "Let's go have a smoke." We walked over to some rocks and sat.

"I know you're thinking about heading back to your place. Three days will be the end of March. I've got money on me to pay you through then. You can stay if you want, we can use you here but you should go and tell your folks what's happening. If you were my kid that's what I'd want. If you decide to go home and stay, I want you back next winter again if there's any way you can make it." It was a long speech for him.

We sat there, finishing our smoke while I thought. "It feels like I should go back for the summer and help my parents. No reason I can't come back again next fall. I would like that. It's been a hell of a winter, in more ways than one."

"That's the right thing to do. Hate to lose you, but so be it." Three days later I said my goodbyes. Not a big production. Simply a handshake and a goodbye.

"Here's your money. There's an extra hundred, you earned it. Hope to see you next fall." Chase shook my hand and we rode off in separate directions. Mine was a three-day ride over two mountain ranges, a different direction than five months previous. I was starting in a different valley. I didn't care, I felt hardened, like a piece of metal that had been forged. Enough food for three days, I was ready to go home.

THE TRIP HOME

It was sad to be leaving. I sat on my horse and watched Chase and the others ride off, there were no backward glances from them. My horse also wanted to join them, taking several steps in their direction. I turned him to the west, somewhat reluctantly he obliged, this was normal, horses being herd animals. In several minutes he was fine, resigned to his fate of solitude once again, I felt the same.

I knew by afternoon a mountain range would stand in my way, visible in the distance, it looked imposing. Chase was uncertain which canyon would be the quickest and easiest to navigate. Having ridden each of them at one time or another looking for cattle, he had never traveled them far enough to crest the high ridge that would mark my summit, his advice had been to follow my gut instinct. This was very little to go on but the best he could do. My immediate future looked formidable, rocky crags dotted the horizon, patches of Juniper and other scrub trees stood out under the rock outcroppings.

Pinto was walking along at a good clip, we ate up the miles across the valley floor, each hour bringing me closer to decision. There was enough food with me for two, maybe three days if I ate sparingly, weight was such a consideration. The trip back would take three days if all went well, eighty miles, half of which was unfamiliar, over this wall of mountains. I was ready for this challenge, for some strange reason I welcomed it, another character test, as long as my horse stayed sound I would be fine. I had the utmost confidence in Pinto, he was very focused in rough conditions, stopping on his own when necessary, his own self-preservation instincts were deep rooted, I trusted his judgment.

By late afternoon, approaching what appeared to be the least onerous of the many draws falling down from the high escarpment, my choice was made. The grade was easy, following along the bottom of the small canyon. New spring grass was abundant on the side of the ravine facing south. Another quarter mile a small rivulet of water gave promise of a good source should I choose to camp and summit the next day. A wider expanse with a cool clear spring made the decision of where to stop for the night. Early evening, the sun, long since gone, dropping to the west and leaving me in shade. There was ample grass for my horse, enough sagebrush for a decent fire and a flat spot to sleep.

I followed the same routine as so many times before, remove my stuff from the saddle, throw out the bedroll, take the rifle from the scabbard, unsaddle. Before I put his hobbles on I turned him loose so he could roll. It gave me pleasure to watch, he would walk around looking for the perfect place. When he found the ideal spot his front legs would bend halfway at the knees, maybe another turn in that position until he was oriented properly in his mind, then with a grunt he would bend all the way on his front knees, ass still in the air, the hind legs would fold and he would be on his side. Most times he was able to roll from one side to the other then back, maybe repeating it, his head and ass moving side to side like a rope whipped back and forth. Every cowboy I knew watched his horse do that, don't know why, we just did. Standing up he'd shake vigorously, a cloud of dust and dirt coming off him. His bath over, he took several bites of the young spring grass and made his way to a pool in the stream and drank until full.

It was very narrow in the bottom with steep sides, being up canyon from me, I left him loose to graze while I made my camp and heated a can of something for my dinner. It didn't matter what was in the can, anything to keep the stomach rumbles away for a while. I had found a new luxury that winter, Raspberry Jam. The ranch purchased it from some store that I had no knowledge of. Made by Empress, it came in a good sized can with a tight lid that had to be pried off. Of the finest quality, a can would fit perfectly in my saddlebag. The only source of sugar other than canned fruit, this one item became my constant traveling companion. Waiting for my coffee to boil I took my spoon, popped open the lid and put a spoonful in my mouth. So simple but so much pleasure, letting it melt, not wanting to swallow, fighting that urge until it was unavoidable. My water came to a boil in the small coffee pot, taking the same spoon I put my ground coffee into the water and waited for the grounds to release their magic flavor before mostly settling to the bottom. I rolled a fat cigarette from my pouch of Bull Durham and pissed away the last hour of daylight, watching my horse graze contently, puffing on my nice fat smoke, burning my bottom lip on the metal enamel coated cup just as I had done a thousand times before, happier than I had any right to be. My life is good; I couldn't help but think. So damn good I stole another spoon of jam. Just before dark I put hobbles on Pinto, draped my arms over his back while he grazed and watched the sky go from orange to pink, then fade into that gray just before darkness. I patted him on his ass several times and crawled into my bedroll, dreaming of Judy, endless cans of Empress Jam and unlimited sacks of Bull Durham, what a life.

The morning looked ugly, promising of rain, so much for my good life. The sun didn't rise, just going from dark to a gray dismal pall, cold and misty. I got up and gathered my stuff, a quick cup of coffee so I could burn my lip once more. Horse saddled, one spoon of jam and I was on my way, forgoing breakfast, hungry but saving my meager supply of food.

We climbed out of the draw and followed a small ridge, climbing ever higher, hoping I wouldn't get rimmed in. A few tricky spots causing me to back track around small outcroppings of rock. I was in the clouds now, making it very difficult to see the terrain, cold wind blowing the mist into my face. My luck held as we crested the main ridge, the rain was now large wet snow flakes blowing horizontal, making our lives damn miserable. Tricky decision, which spur ridge to take down, my instinct telling me to avoid the bottoms of a draw.

I chose one for no other reason than to get off this high windy ridge. Visibility was so limited, I was focused on the hundred feet immediately in front of me, reminding myself not to go down something I couldn't get back up, a Cardinal rule unless you were absolutely sure of the terrain. My luck was holding, Pinto picking his way carefully, we made our way down the ridge. The snow, now again rain, was coming down hard, I was cold and miserable, hunger constantly reminding me it was past lunch, and I hadn't eaten anything since my meager dinner the previous evening. Nothing to do but continue, my wide brimmed hat protecting my face from the worst of the driving rain as long as I kept my head down. Thinking I should be about half a mile from the valley floor and things would look better, my world went to hell.

I felt my horse fall out from under me. Still half way in the saddle, instinctively kicking my uphill leg out of the stirrup. We were both on our right-hand side, sliding down a steep rock face towards the bottom of the ravine. Hitting bottom, my horse scrambled and got his feet under himself, dumping me unceremoniously on my ass. I sat there for a minute, waiting for pain to come, indicating some injury.

Nothing came, I took a few tentative steps, legs shaking but fine, I had been lucky. Walking over to Pinto I checked him, a few patches of hair gone from his hip and shoulder, his head already down, taking this opportunity to grab a few mouthfuls of grass, apparently unconcerned. For some stupid reason I checked my can of jam. It was fine, still snug in my saddle bag.

Looking up the slab of rock it was obvious what happened. We had been crossing at the upper part, about twenty feet above where I stood, the rain soaked dirt had given way under the added weight of our crossing. It was steep, too steep to go back up, smooth and slick. We were somewhat protected from the wind so that helped a little. Taking the free end of the mecate that led to Pinto's bosal off the saddle horn, we went exploring for an escape route, I stayed on foot, leading him.

We walked down along the bottom, both sides impossible for an exit, shear vertical walls of dirt and rock. Several hundred yards down, the canyon floor dropped over a rock waterfall. Impossible, twenty-five feet of nothing but air to the bottom. Discouraged we headed back up past the spot that started this crap. It got worse, the walls on both sides just got higher, still vertical. Fifty yards farther, the bottom ended again, another wall of solid rock ten feet high. It might as well have been a hundred, no way could I climb this, let alone take a horse up it. I stood there, lost in thinking, watching a small rivulet of water falling down the face, ending in a pool that disappeared immediately. At least I won't die of thirst.

We walked the same circuit again, looking more carefully for anything that may be an escape route.

Nothing, no way would I get out except the way we got in. I had a problem, a real problem. Too late to try anything that evening I scouted for a place to camp for the night. There was plenty of grass for Pinto in the bottom, and water was available. Finding a place to throw my bedroll for the night, I made preparations. The rain was over, that helped considerably, although cold and somewhat wet I was able to start a fire, this helped to lift my gloom a little. I didn't hobble my horse that night, where the hell could he go, I thought.

Hunger forced me to eat my second to last can of chili. Taking the time to heat it was difficult, I couldn't face a cold dinner. Some dead cottonwoods gave me plenty of wood so I built a large fire, getting warm and drying some of my clothes, that helped. I sat there for hours, staring into the fire, warming myself, running possibilities through my mind. Nothing came. I went to sleep thinking how quickly my life had gone to shit, twenty-four hours, what a difference.

I lay there the next morning, waiting for enough light to start the day. I didn't want it to start, knowing the problems I faced. The weather at least was better, the sun just starting to highlight the bottoms of white cumulus clouds, remnants of yesterday's rain. I got up and went through the morning's ritual methodically.

My belongings back on my horse, with empty belly except for two spoonful's of jam I made the decision to try going back up the way we had come down. Approaching the bottom, I stood and studied the slab of rock, not having much faith. I started up, leading Pinto, my cowboy boots barely able to make a purchase. As soon as all four feet were on the slab he would slide back down, scrambling for footing, like a fawn on a sheet of ice. We tried several more times, each time he became a little more hesitant. I gave it up and walked once again down the bottom, checking both sides carefully, anything to give me hope, there was nothing. Back up to the other end, as if something would magically appear. This met with the same result, nothing.

Going back for another attempt, I stood there, studying, thinking of options. They were few and unappealing. Leave my horse and walking home, forty miles, maybe more. This was doable but then should I leave him there, probably to die, or would I have the courage to shoot him. That would be my last option and I wouldn't think about it until that ugly situation presented itself.

I unsaddled my horse, deciding to haul all my possessions to the top of the slab. Starting up with my saddle on one arm I only got several feet before sliding back down, my boots too slick for traction. Taking them off helped, I was able to climb out in stocking feet, depositing my saddle on a level spot and making two more trips, leaving only my horse down below. This gave me an idea, maybe if I removed my horse's shoes he might be able to climb out. I had a pair of fencing pliers, an all-purpose tool. That presented a problem, difficult to remove shoes even with the proper tools, I had no rasp to file the nail heads, which are turned over at the ends to prevent the nails from pulling out. With only fencing pliers it would shred the outside walls of the hoof when the shoe was pulled off, with nails attached. Another possibility but an ugly one, and I wasn't convinced it would give him enough traction anyway.

A glimmer of an idea was coming, one with real possibilities, I acted on it. Taking my lariat, I looped it around a small juniper at the top of the rock and threw both ends toward the bottom. Taking my saddle blanket, (I still had a heavy saddle pad,) with me to the bottom. I cut it into quarters with my pocketknife. Sacrificing about four feet off the end of my mecate, I made socks for him from the heavy wool saddle blanket. Each quarter was sufficient to cover his hoof and I secured them with the unbraided strands from the mecate, tying them tight above his ankles. It looked funny, but gave promise. I took one end of the lariat and secured it around Pinto's neck with a bowline knot so he wouldn't choke. The other end was several feet up slope. Taking a strong hold of the free end I pulled, putting tension and starting him up. He was apprehensive, his steps cautious. The moment of truth, all four feet on the steep rocky slope, his feet held. I kept tension on the rope, his neck stretched slightly.

Each step bringing him closer to the top. I was nervous, hoping and wishing my luck to hold. I let him take his time, testing each step. Several more steps one foot slid out from under him and he landed on his side, neck and head stretched tight from the lariat that I held fast. He looked uncomfortable, I let him lay there, giving him no slack. Slowly he got his feet under him and stood up on all fours still stretched stiff as a board. Another step, then several more, in haste I pulled the slack, in one last burst he made it to the top, it was unglamorous, feet flying in every direction.

Elated, I led him away from any danger of sliding back down. Removing his socks and putting my boots back on I saddled him, loaded my stuff and got the hell out of there.

The remaining descent went without incident, the valley floor a welcome relief. We trotted for a while, alternating with walking, the terrain familiar now. Hoping to make the stream where I had camped on my first night when I came north five months ago, it seemed like years since that trip was made.

We made good time, reaching the stream with an hour of daylight left. Making camp I decided to heat my last can of food, it felt like I was starving but forced myself to wait. As I enjoyed my meal, reflections ran through my mind. I could have been injured or crippled when we slid into the wash. It struck me how tenuous this remote life was. No one had any idea where I was, or worse when I should show up, let alone when or where to start looking. I had a much better understanding of self- preservation, I became a little less cavalier about life and its responsibilities.

Hungry still, or again, it didn't matter, it was my constant companion I awoke the next morning. Anxious to get under way, I was in the saddle just as the light went from a promise to reality. The weather held, cool in the morning, giving way to a very pleasant temperature as the sun climbed its slow arc. Trotting along, I was struck just how remarkable these valleys, full of their purple hued sagebrush were. I felt so fortunate, the smell of sage intoxicating at times, sweet and pungent. Spring time brought the desert to life, washing the dust and dryness with the rains that came and went rapidly. I felt good, happy. I patted my horse several times on the neck, wanting to share this spontaneous exuberance, I don't think he really gave a damn.

Home, such as it is, beckoned me. I couldn't give a reason, it just did. I was in Dixie Valley again, home of my future ranch. I wanted to see my parents, tell them of my experience being a real buckaroo. All the things that were seen and done throughout the winter, minus the whorehouse. Each mile increased my impatience but I had my horse to consider. Fifteen more miles, the mountains becoming very familiar.

Mid-afternoon, home. Things were different. Where my tie hut had once stood there now was an enclosed van, about eighteen feet long, two swinging doors at the end, unlocked. Still holding Pinto's lead rope, I opened the doors and looked in. A foldout couch at the far end, made into a bed, table and two chairs for eating, a refrigerator and cabinets. Counter top with a sink, bucket underneath to catch water. Canned food on shelves, immediately bringing a rumble in my stomach, soon enough, a full belly.

Outside, a Ford tractor, diesel motor with front loader and box scraper on the three-point hitch in back. A solid looking tractor, industrial grade. Key in the ignition. A fifty-gallon drum laying in a cradle with a spigot in the small bung. I cracked the valve, a trickle of water fell into my palm, it tasted fine. My gaze fell across the post with the attached tobacco can, where so many months ago my note was left for my parents, also marking my cache of canned goods. I walked over and opened the can, a simple note from my father.

Finish Ditch

Damn, I Shot My Horse

THE DITCH AND THE WELL

This wasn't what I expected. I chuckled to myself but it was a chuckle borne of disappointment. Two words, they seemed terse, as if I was being chastised. Not sure what I had expected, I knew it wasn't these two words, finish ditch. Gratefully, hunger and duty to my horse removed any more thoughts along this line.

After removing my saddle and other belongings from Pinto I took several cans of water and washed his back, removing salt while also checking for any saddle sores. These are raw spots under the saddle that only grew larger and more painful for the horse if not addressed. He was fine. I turned him loose so he could roll on his back in the dirt, which he did immediately. He was thin, so I gave him a double helping of grain, grateful that half a sack was stored securely in a drum with a tight lid.

My horse taken care of, I focused on my own needs. The van had a two burner stove hooked to an outside propane tank. After opening the valve, I used the stove to heat a can of something, my hunger by now making me impatient. I found a box of crackers and dove into them while dinner heated. I ate from the pot too quickly, my stomach cramping momentarily.

Leaving the pan dirty in case I got hungry again I went out, gathered some firewood and built a fire while my coffee made. I sat there, having a smoke, burning my lip from the damn cup but overall enjoying the last couple hours of light. It was strange,

I felt a little as though I were trespassing, as if I should have permission to use all these conveniences. I became melancholy sitting there, feeling sad as I gazed into the fire. I was lonely, I didn't want to be alone anymore. I craved, deeply craved another human, someone to laugh with, talk to, share my apprehensions, put their arms around me and tell me I had some value. These were strange feelings and I didn't have any idea what to do or how to deal with them, my mood keeping time with the setting sun, darkening as the gray of evening disappeared. I sat there and watched as my fire dwindled. There were no tears, I had no recollection of ever having shed a tear, though I surely must have as a child. I was despondent but didn't know why.

I rolled another smoke, seeking comfort in tobacco. Getting up I walked over to my horse. He was just standing there, not twenty feet from me, maybe he was lonely also. I draped my arms over his back and stood there with him, his chest slowly, rhythmically expanding and contracting with each breath. His head came around and he nuzzled me with his upper lip. I laughed, a real laugh, the darkness was gone, just like that. I understood this was no magical bond between man and horse, as if there was some deep cosmic connection, it was only his way of asking for more grain, what a little beggar shit. I obliged him with a little more grain, so grateful to have a purpose, as little as it was.

I slept outside that night, under the stars, I was home, I was happy.

My eyes opened before daylight, looking to the east, a hint of grayness but the sky still rich with stars. Not wanting to get up, with no pressing reason to get out of my warm bedroll I fumbled for my sack of tobacco and rolled a smoke in the dark. I lay there, enjoying my first taste of tobacco for the day. I was hungry, but still didn't get up. I threw the butt onto a piece of barren ground away from my bed. I knew I was stalling, not wanting to get up, the day promising many decisions and little enjoyment.

My bladder forcing my decision, I crawled out of my bedroll just as there was enough light to see silhouettes. As with countless times before, my morning routine was mechanical.

The sun, fully over the mountains to the east, was beginning to radiate its warmth. I walked around slowly, so much was different. So many things had been hauled up here throughout the winter. A large offset disk, about twelve feet wide, used for turning soil over lightly and cutting stubble or other field debris. A 500-amp welder, so huge it was on its own trailer. Several pallets of Portland cement, covered under canvas and waterproof tarps. Several small utility sheds that must have been hauled in one piece, and unloaded here, they looked pretty rough, like you wouldn't want to store anything valuable in them.

Fifty-gallon drums, five-gallon buckets everywhere, all empty. Used rolls of barb wire. Some lengths of well casing that looked to be about sixteen inches in diameter, anywhere from ten to twenty feet in length. A sixteen-inch gate screw valve with a ten-foot rise, this I figured would be for the reservoir outlet, the long screw had a sizable bend that would have to straightened. It had the look of a small junk yard. Everything looked old and tired, used up and wore out.

I looked at the disk again, a quarter of the blades were broken or had chunks missing, plus it looked way too big for the tractor. Perhaps there was a large field tractor in the future. No way to make any plans until my father showed, my immediate concern only to finish the ditch.

I knew the tractor would make finishing the ditch somewhat easier, but I was hesitant to use it without permission. It was strange for me to be indecisive, such as not sleeping on the bed that was in the van, it would feel somehow invasive. My winter's absence, along with the vast array of foreign materials and equipment made me feel as a stranger might, somehow I felt as if I were a trespasser.

I gathered my pick, shovel and steel digging bar, they felt so familiar. Thinking how many endless hours had been spent using them last summer I tossed them into the tractor bucket. Starting the diesel motor, waiting for the oil pressure to build I made the decision to deal with any guilt feelings in the future. I followed an old Jeep trail cross country to the terminus of last year's digging.

All was as I had left it so many months before. Pulling the kill switch on the tractor I leaned over the steering wheel and rolled a smoke. It felt good to be here, I knew what to do, I had a purpose, a job to finish. The tractor made the digging much easier, I was able to do most of the rough work with the bucket, using my hand tools to smooth and do the finish work. Some of the larger rocks still required hand work but I didn't mind.

The weather was kind to me over the next several days, clear skies with moderate temperatures. The occasional spring rain warm and soft, like a heavy mist. One heavy downpour came and went during the night but it caused me no grief, only made the stream run heavier which was good.

It was well over a week and the ditch was right at the finishing point so I started clearing the brush where the reservoir would be, careful not to puncture the tires as I pushed huge piles of the nasty, tire piercing bushes.

I had no idea what day it was, only that it should be the first or second week of April. My mind would jump from bouts of loneliness to feelings of anger that someone would come and intrude on my solitude. I didn't understand these feelings, they would come and go much like hunger but most days were filled with pleasant memories of my whorehouse days, Judy foremost. Also the months spent buckarooing, filled so many hours with happy memories. Bouncing between quick moments of frustration at not having any control over my destiny, and just as quick, moments of smug satisfaction. The nights spent with a naked woman laying her head on my shoulder, snuggled next to me, drawing circles on my bare stomach. A bottle of whiskey on the nightstand available at any time without recriminations or guilt. The endless hours sitting on a horse, doing your job, with men that treated you like any other man, no more, no less. I would reflect often on that winter, so heady and grateful.

Several days later I had an area of land cleared. Two hundred feet on the downhill side with about seventy foot wings on both ends, terminating to nothing. It would be a three-sided reservoir, taking advantage of the natural slope. As I sat there that evening having made a rough outline with a bank of dirt, I had no idea just how large of a project this would be with only a small tractor to move the rocky, hard packed dirt. I was eager, looking forward to long days on the tractor, mindless, back and forth the sound of the engine was my music to fill the days. I started the drive back to the van and my camp on the hill. Checking the road to the south for the hundredth time that day I was rewarded by a plume of dust making its way up the valley. I recognized the old truck grinding uphill in low gear, getting to camp slightly ahead of myself. I realized I was nervous, not sure how to act or what to say. I had no idea who was coming, my father for sure, maybe my mother, soon enough I would know. All of a sudden I didn't want this meeting.

Twenty feet separated us as the truck came to a stop, both doors opening, my father exiting the driver's side. Frank, his hod carrier of many years, stepping down from the passenger side. I killed the engine on the tractor and started walking towards them.

"Glad to see you made it back. Bring the tractor over here and let's get some of this stuff unloaded while there's still enough light." No preamble, just like my father, no questions about my work or my winter. He was already loosening the straps that secured the load as he spoke.

I didn't say a word as I got back on the tractor. I was half pissy, surely the unloading would keep until morning. I wanted a handshake, a slap on the back, anything to let me know things were good between us. It was not to be. As I drove the tractor over to the truck, raising the loader to unload a cement mixer, my father and Frank both took long pulls from a bottle of whiskey. It hit me that they had most likely been drinking all the way from Sacramento. Nothing changes I thought to myself. At that age I didn't understand the insidious and destructive hold that alcohol had on some people.

We finished with a half hour of daylight left, my father having not said another word to me. We ate dinner together, sitting outside on chairs, plates on our laps. Frank and I having some dialogue about nothing important. I had known him for almost five years and got along well with him. Tall and thin, with deep crags outlining the features of his face. Dark complexion, a felt cowboy hat resting on his head. My father and he had been drinking buddies along with working together for years.

My father was plainly withdrawn that evening but I had no idea why. A few declaratory sentences spoken at odd moments. They didn't seem to call for a response so Frank and I left him alone with his thoughts. I lay in my bedroll that night, mentally bouncing between anger and confusion at the coldness from my father. Drifting off to sleep the realization finally took hold that he had been indifferent and aloof towards me for as long as I could remember.

We awoke the next day just as the sky was light enough to see. A hasty breakfast. I felt good that morning, understanding my father made dealing with him much easier. Or maybe I just didn't give a shit. It didn't matter, a new day with the sun shining always lifted my spirits.

I rode on the back of the two ton flat-bed as we drove to the future sight of the house. Measuring the dimensions and staking the corners, seventy by twenty-eight feet. A house and a shop joined together for ease of building. Doing this seemed to lift my father's mood, smiling on occasion he would draw a diagram of the building in the dirt with a stick.

"Your mother will come up with me in two weeks. She's going to stay here for several weeks and help pour the slab for the shop and house." My father's arm was making a huge arc over the future slab as he said this, as if it would be that simple.

"What about the reservoir?" I asked

"Work on that when you get time. You need to move some sand and gravel down here and get it screened so when your Mom comes you won't have to waste time doing that."

With that we walked a quarter mile to a wash that held plenty of sand and gravel, though there were many large rocks throughout the material. Without a doubt it would have to be screened.

While we were doing this Frank was walking around in a circle with a bent coat hanger in each hand. I had no idea what the hell he was doing.

"He's going to find us water so we can dig a well." My dad answered my unspoken question.

We watched as Frank made a X in the dirt with the heel of his boot. Then crossed the same spot from different directions. Each time he crossed the X the coat hangers would swivel and cross each other.

"That's the spot. No doubt you'll hit water there." Frank acted so certain I expected water to come shooting out of the ground at any moment. I was skeptical. I'd never heard of water witching before.

"How deep is it?" My skepticism must have shown.

"Feels like a little over twenty feet." Once again no reservation or doubt. He might as well have said the sun will set this evening.

"How can you tell?" I tried to temper my doubt as I asked.

"It doesn't work for most people. Has something to do with magnetic attraction to water. When you move over a source the wire will cross. You can tell how deep by how strong the pull is, it wants to pull the wires to the ground. You have to develop a feel for it."

"He's done a lot of wells and he's never been wrong." My dad added this to Frank's answer.

I shook my head in mock wonderment. It was hard for me to accept so easily, so I didn't. I knew better than to let my doubt show, particularly as they were so steadfast in their convictions. Plus, I knew the whiskey bottle had been sampled a few times this morning. It would serve me well to keep my mouth shut and let the well driller test his theory.

"Let's get going. We have a long drive back to Sacramento and we have to work tomorrow." This was directed to Frank as my father started to open the door of the truck. "I'll leave all the food here and be back in two weeks with your mother." This at me.

"What about the well? Is the driller coming?" I was hoping for some company, even if only for a short while.

"What the hell are you talking about. Who said anything about a driller. You're going to dig it. Right where Frank said." I was standing five feet from him as he sat in the truck with the door open. I could detect some anger in his response.

"I don't know anything about digging a well. What do I do? How should I do it?" I had so many questions.

He looked at me for several moments, his face was getting darker with each passing second, his brows coming closer together. I felt as if I was a moron and had just asked the most stupid question of all time.

"You dig a hole. When there's water in the bottom, it's a

fucking well." Such a simple statement It caused me to grin at him.

He was really pissed now.

I didn't know what had set him off so bad. I was mad too. Not about the well, but his treatment of me. It was nothing new.

I watched as they drove away. I didn't even rate a ride back to camp.

"Fucker!" I screamed to the cloud of dust. The one- mile walk back in the heat adding to my anger.

I made myself a late lunch at camp. I didn't feel like working at the moment, but I didn't see my horse around anywhere so a ride was out of the question. I walked around camp aimlessly, looking at all the stuff scattered about. I was in a funk, half pissed at my father but also mad at myself for accepting his treatment of me.

I made a cup of coffee and had a smoke, trying to focus on the future. It helped to look at the bigger picture, making a ranch was the goal. I understood money was always in short supply and many things would have to be done by hand.

I greased the tractor, filled the fuel tank and drove down to the home site. I was in a much better mood. I worked on the site for the future home, finishing leveling the ground. Midafternoon I was finished with that business and turned my attention to starting the well.

I marked a three-foot circle with the x in the middle. Started with pick, first strike penetrated about half an inch. The ground was dry, rocky and hard. I knew it would be, so resolved myself to a test of endurance. There was no doubt I would continue until I hit water, whenever that would be. I had little faith in this whole water-witching crap. If there was no water, I wondered how far my father would have me dig. I thought if there was no water would I just keep going, becoming more possessed the deeper I went? I had no idea how far a person could dig before it became impossible to go any deeper? What was the limiting factor?

These thoughts bounced around in my head as I struggled to dig a lousy six inches in the next three hours. Hot, tired and thirsty I called it a day with an hour of daylight left and headed up to my camp for the night.

For the next two weeks it was a matter of mindless work. Move the aggregate down to the building site and screen several loads with a shovel. Work on the reservoir for five or six hours, then finish the day working on the well. Each day just like the one before.

The two weeks went fast enough. Though I was still only sixteen, I was honing my ability to let my mind wander anywhere it wanted. It gave me hours of entertainment and moved the days along in a quick succession.

Sure enough, in two weeks a dust plume heralded the arrival of my parents late on a Friday afternoon. I was pulling a bucket of dirt from the well as they drove up.

My mother quickly came to me and gave me a hug, so unlike her. She seemed happy to see me, the smile on her face even more rare.

My dad walked over to the well without a word. Looking in he stated the patently obvious, "No water." It almost sounded like an accusation, as if I were deliberately preventing water from gushing in. I wanted to make some smart ass remark but held my tongue. All in all, that evening was very enjoyable. My mother and I making small talk as she prepared dinner. She asked so many questions about my winter spent working on a real cattle ranch. I enjoyed it, telling her in great detail about my winter. I did leave out my stay at the whorehouse. For the most part my dad stayed quiet, content to listen, sipping his whiskey.

The next day was busy. Moving the mixer to the pile of

aggregate, bringing the Portland cement down and setting it next to the mixer. Getting the water supply from the ditch that was nearby. Forming the perimeter of the slab that the house and shop would sit on, with lumber. Fortunately, we had metal stakes as the ground was like concrete itself. We used a transit to ensure the forms were level.

The next day we awoke early and my father helped us mix the first batch and showed my mother and myself the proper consistency of concrete. He wheeled it over and poured our first load. Several hours later we had a section ten feet by fifteen done. He showed us how to trowel a finish and set the perimeter bolts on the outside edge that would hold the walls.

"After it hardens a little spray it with water so it stays wet." After several more instructions, he headed back to Sacramento. My mother and I watched the dust as it hung in the late morning stillness.

"Not much for good-byes. Course he never has been." My mother uttered quietly but loud enough to hear. I looked at her and shook my head in acknowledgment, no need to say anything. We cleaned up all the tools, wet the slab and had lunch. That afternoon I would spend working between the reservoir and the well. My mother stayed at the site for a while then walked back to camp.

The days were identical. The slab growing larger and the well getting deeper, just not fast enough. I put a tripod over the well with a pulley system. I had a bell on the tripod that I could ring from down in the hole with a small twine. When my mother heard the bell she would know that several bucket loads of dirt would need to be hauled up as they were filled. I couldn't load them very heavy as my mom was small and didn't weigh very much. It was slow but worked well. By now it was getting harder to get up and down into the well. The depth being about fifteen feet, I would pull myself up the bucket rope, using foot holes that I had dug into the sides for my feet. Crude but effective.

The two weeks flashed by, every day like the one before. The concrete slab was finished, thirty feet by seventy, big enough for the house and shop. We were tired and proud.

My father showed in two weeks as promised. He came alone this trip and expressed disappointment that the well was only twenty-five feet deep and there was still no water. He gave reluctant approval of the slab, which was better than his normal criticism.

That Sunday morning, he left with my mother and once again I watched the dust plume fade into the distance. I was melancholy, it was so much nicer to have my mother there. Not just to help with work but for the companionship, plus I was a deplorable cook. I ate only as a source of fuel with little regard to taste. Most times heating a can of something that was quick and easy. My mother took special delight in baking rolls and bread and I took a greater delight in consuming them. I would miss her and them.

I worked on the reservoir with the tractor for several hours until the sun was high overhead. Early June and the days were starting to heat up into the low/mid-nineties. After lunch I lowered myself into the hole/well and started digging. I used three buckets to remove the dirt. Filling one, taking another from the hook that I had suspended six feet above me I would set it on top of the full bucket filling it and do the same with the third. The end of the rope had a three-pronged grapple hook and I would secure this onto the bucket on top of the others. After pulling myself up I could pull each successive bucket to the top, using the hook to snag the bail. Very slow, frustratingly slow but it was all I could manage alone.

Several rain storms came and went without incident, one was heavy but brief. The desert, with all its sage has a pungent fragrance that is like no other after a cleansing rain. A heady aroma that is unique and impossible to describe, very thick and always welcome.

The banks on the reservoir got higher and the hole/well got deeper. Back and forth on the tractor, up and down into my hole, digging and emptying my buckets. The monotony both frustrating and soothing.

No one came after two weeks but it didn't matter. I had plenty of work and food. I enjoyed the solitude except for the rare bout of loneliness. The third week I was down to forty-five feet in the hole/well. Digging was much easier, damp sand and gravel replacing the extremely hard packed layers of rock and clay. Hope began to replace pessimism, each foot of digging getting more moisture than the previous foot. As I got deeper, removing the dirt became slower and more difficult.

After the third week, both parents along with Frank arrived late Friday evening. That Saturday was spent moving the van, which was still up by the concrete slabs. We loaded it on the two-ton truck and hauled it to the home-site, this made life much easier. My father expressed frustration with my progress in the well department, stating it should be done by now. I didn't argue or plead that I had spent the last twenty days with my head down and my ass up, digging until my back begged for relief. It was becoming increasingly clear, no matter how hard or long I worked, how much was accomplished it would never satisfy him. I understood some of it was the whiskey and some was his need to force me into some form of submission, which I didn't understand. At times he was tyrannical but occasionally there were glimmers of kindness, though these were rare and fleeting. I knew better than to engage him in an argument, sixteen years of German patriarchal dominance was more than I was capable of confronting. I simply let him vent.

They left that Sunday morning. My mother, sad at leaving me alone once more. She tried hard to be a buffer between my father and myself.

I went to work in the well immediately, resolving to have water in the bottom upon their return, if there was water to be had. After the third day six inches of water awaited me in the bottom that morning. I wanted someone to share the happiness with. The water was cold, having no rubber boots I worked in my leather boots, cold wet feet damping my enthusiasm. Going deeper was problematic, the sand gravel mixture difficult to load on a shovel. I would scoop with the bucket, pouring out the water until it was mostly full of material. It was cold wet work even in the heat of the day. I persevered over the next several days until the water was waist high, and I was unable to extract any more.

That afternoon a man drove up to the home-site. Medium height, normal build with a fedora on his head. Middle-aged he had the same dark craggy face that was so common in the desert, his smile infectious.

"My name's Hank, I came up from the settlement to see how you're doing." He introduced himself. "Heard you were up here alone mostly, working your ass off."

I shook his hand, introducing myself, nodding my head in agreement.

"How's the well going?"

"Good, I answered." Not sure how he knew so much.

"I know your mom and dad; they stop at the settlement on their way home some times." He elaborated, then went on to explain most of the people in the small gathering of ranches had a good idea what was happening at our place.

Hank was the owner of an old cable tool well-drilling machine. It had no motor to propel itself but if I would come down with the tractor and pull it up to our place he would be happy to set the casing and maybe drill a few more feet if needed.

"Thanks for the offer but I can't agree to spending any money."

I declined, shaking my head.

"I'll do it just to help." The offer seemed sincere and without guile. "I've got plenty of time and the rig needs to be worked anyway. It'll only take a day."

We agreed I would drive the tractor to his place the following morning and pull the old well rig up to our place that same day. We sat around for another hour and talked about the difficulties living so remote, trying to get things done.

Though it was twenty miles one way the trip down and back went without problems. He followed me home in his pickup, spending the night so we could get an early start.

We brought sixty feet of six-inch casing from his place with us. I still had plenty of money left from working at the ranch that winter and offered to pay him. He assured me not to worry, he would work it out with my father.

I had dug the well fifty-five feet from top to the bottom. There was now sixteen feet of standing water. It was good water, cold with no taste to it. We set the casing, the bottom twenty feet having perforations with the rest being solid. Frank drove the casing another five feet. The old well-rig was a sight. No paint left anywhere, solid rust. The radiator leaked badly, we had to add water constantly. The motor was an old four cylinder that died for no reason at times. The cable was frayed and kinked. Half the day was spent tending to the rig but we got the job done.

"All you need now is a windmill and a tank, you'll be in business." We stood there gazing at the three-foot hole with the casing in the middle. "I still can't believe you dug that all by yourself." He shook his head in disbelief.

We pulled the old rig several hundred yards off to the side. Hank wanted to leave it here until it was needed again here or elsewhere. With a handshake and thanks from me he drove home. Hank had invited me to come down on my horse and have dinner with his family, I would be more than welcome to spend the night at his place. I declined, but would in the future.

The next day was spent filling in the hole around the casing that I had spent countless hours digging. It was bittersweet and somehow anticlimactic, but at least we had a well.

Another weekend came along with my parents. This time another car followed with four other friends of my father. They were construction men, here for a week to help him frame the house as much as possible. Introductions were made, then I was largely ignored. I took great pride in showing my father the foot of casing that protruded from the ground. I removed the bucket that covered it, dropping a small pebble to hear the rewarding sound of it hitting water. I waited for a slap on the back from my father.

"Where the hell did you get the casing?" He asked gruffly. I explained to him the arrangement with Hank. He never said a word, just walked off, grumbling.

It didn't matter too much. My mother thought it was great when she came over to see the well. She was excited, she showed me four books from a correspondence school in Chicago. "You can finish High School and get your diploma. Your dad didn't really want to but I insisted until he agreed. These will finish your Sophomore year." I was happy, but it was because she was so excited at the prospect of her son finishing school. I hadn't thought of school in many months and then it was only to wonder how my friends were doing. I would not have traded places with any of them, in spite of my father being tough, my life was damn good. I gave her a hug and thanked her, vowing to make an honest effort to complete the school work.

The house and shop were going up very quickly. All the walls were already standing. The rafters going up next. My mom did the cooking and I was just a gopher, keeping the generator running and making sure they all had plenty of material on hand.

That Thursday a nice new pickup came driving up, two men in well pressed shirts and khaki pants waited by the hood of the truck. My father introduced himself and there were a few moments of conversation. I heard my name and saw him waving to come over.

"They want some tractor work done at the mine, I told them you could do it." I introduced myself, they looked skeptical but held any comment about my age to themselves.

"We can drive up to the mine and show you what we need."

They asked a few questions as we drove to the mine, the same one close to the concrete slab that had been my home for some time. They were going to do some exploration drilling and needed level pads for the drilling rig. They showed me several sites, explaining how large they needed to be. We agreed on a price per hour, they were somewhat surprised I was able to negotiate without any parental input.

"Can you start tomorrow; the rig will be here in two days?" The man who appeared to be the boss asked.

"Shouldn't be a problem." I answered, having no idea if it would be a problem.

Damn, I Shot My Horse

Fred Hauptmann

MINES AND WINDMILLS

They drove me back to the home site. A step up from what my father would have done. The two men left in their dusty new pickup, they must have been confident in my abilities and felt no need to discuss things further with anyone else.

A brief explanation to my father, who didn't seem to care, intent on the house construction. Feeling liberated from my menial labors of the last few days I serviced the tractor and left for my new job. I was happy, very happy. This was my kind of work, a little challenging, making a hundred by hundred-foot level pad on a slope. I worked several long days and finished the first pad in plenty of time for the rig, already well into the second pad when they arrived. They expressed their satisfaction with my promptness and quality of work. Such a difference from my father who most likely would have complained about my slowness, and excessive fuel consumption.

That Sunday morning my parents along with the other four men were getting ready to leave. My father had yet to express any interest in what I had been doing at the mine.

"How are we going to get the water out of the well?" I was so unprepared for this question from him I just stood there with a blank look on my face.

"The water's not gonna do any good sitting in the bottom of the damn hole." He must have thought his former question needed elaboration.

"I'll take care of it." With firmness and a smile. I was learning that the more confident I became the easier it was to deal with him. I was also learning my confidence rankled my father. It wasn't my intent but it felt good.

"Don't forget about your schoolwork." This from my mother as she gave me a slight hug, knowing I was sensitive about showing affection in front of other people, especially men.

They left and I drove the tractor to the mine, my mind working on the problem of extracting the water from the well. I had a vague idea of how windmills worked, but not sure about what went on in the well, or exactly how I could even get any of the components. I left it for a later date, focusing on the work at hand.

Two weeks went by and my father came with one of his drinking friends and worked on the house for the weekend. Saturday evening, we sat around a small fire and I joined them for a drink of whiskey. This always pleased my father but he still had no interest in what I was doing at the mine. They left the next day while I was working at the mine.

Five weeks later the tractor work was finished. The foreman of the mine asked if I had any interest in learning how to mine underground. I answered yes, so I had another job for about six to eight weeks helping to drive a tunnel to what may be an ore deposit. The foreman brought me a sum of cash for all the tractor work, knowing a check would do me little good. I did sign a receipt for tax reasons. The pay for the mining would also pay very well.

It was great work, learning how to drill holes with a jackleg. Loading the holes with dynamite and shooting them off with a burning fuse, I was only a helper but right in the thick of things. Twenty-six holes, eight feet deep, we would shoot at the end of the day, then a couple of muckers would clean out the rubble and we would repeat it again the next day. So the summer went.

Many evenings I would sit around my fire alone, reflecting on my good fortune. Whiskey, cigarettes, dynamite and whores, what a life so far, and not quite seventeen.

The miners along with the foreman took a keen interest in my life and had little good to say about my father, especially with his treatment of me. Most evenings were spent by myself, though they invited me often enough to stay with them at their camp. They were generous and always treated me well, even loaning me one of their pickups to drive back and forth to the mine. It was a good pickup, three quarter ton Chevy about ten years old. One day the foreman asked if I was interested in taking the pickup as part wages, though there wouldn't be much money left. I agreed readily, keen to have my own vehicle.

The tunnel was completed, the pickup title handed over to me by the foreman. He also gave me a young dog, part black Lab and some other breed, along with a large bag of dog food.

"Don't know much about him, somebody gave him to us a month ago but my wife didn't want a dog. He might be good company for you." There was no leash, so I tied a string around his neck and held him next to me. "If he doesn't work out just get rid of him."

"That's a little bonus for being so dependable and a hard worker. If you ever want a job look me up." The foreman shook my hand and handed me an envelope that held two hundred dollars. Without the need for any more conversation they left, finished with their contract. This bonus along with the one I had received from Chase, the ranch foreman, instilled a good work ethic that lasted a lifetime and served me well indeed.

I watched them leave that morning, a little saddened. Taking the twine off my new dog I named him Smoky for his gray color. I took the tractor and resumed working on the reservoir, which was taking good shape and would be completed by the end of summer. That afternoon I quit early and studied the well, standing over it I was not sure how to proceed. I put my dog in the back of the pickup and drove to the settlement twenty miles away, in hopes of some advice.

I was in luck, Hank, the driller who had helped me finish the well was home and invited me to stay for dinner. His wife Teresa, a robust woman was so kind and gracious I felt right at home that evening.

It was so enjoyable to sit at a table and have a normal meal with conversation. They had a foster boy about my age who was full blooded Indian. He was so gregarious and outgoing we became friends that evening, and remained friends for years.

Hank was full of information about getting water from the well, in fact he would become a good source of knowledge for more questions as time went on. He knew of an old windmill that was in pieces and scattered on the ground but with the tower still standing. Also a five-thousand-gallon water tank that seemed to be intact the last time he had driven by, which was many years ago. It had been abandoned for so many decades' no one knew why it was there or to whom it belonged. He gave me a rough idea where it was located and told me it would be worth checking out. He also drew me a rough illustration of all the components and how they functioned.

I left that evening, thanking them all. Driving home, I was a little apprehensive to start a project of this scope but felt confident in my abilities.

I worked on the reservoir once again to fill in the next day, knowing it was a Friday. I was just about finished building the banks on three sides and felt confident it would hold sufficient water for our fields but I would let my father make the final determination.

Late that evening my father arrived in a cloud of dust. It was mid-August and there had been no rain for months, the road was a ribbon of dust and the temperature was still very hot at night.

Another man had come with him whom I didn't know and they were both slightly drunk, but luckily for me they were in good spirits.

"Who's truck?" The first words from my father's mouth, as he walked around my new pickup, under the light of a full moon.

"It's mine." I proudly explained how I came to own it. Adding I still had hundreds of dollars left from working with the tractor which I would give him the next day. This cheered him further. We sat around for a while and I joined them in drink and conversation, though mostly I listened since nobody seemed to care what I had to say.

The next morning all the good cheer seemed to have evaporated. I tried to explain my plans about getting the water from the well with a windmill. He was a little surly, pretty much saying it was my idea so it was my problem and he had plenty of other things to think about. I walked off in disappointment, not really surprised but nonetheless feeling somehow rejected. I unloaded the two barrels of fuel from my father's pickup with the tractor then proceeded to load the tractor on the two-ton truck, knowing I would need it to load the tank and windmill. I gathered all the tools I thought I would need along with my sleeping bag, a canteen of water and a few cans of food. My father was working on some plumbing in the house and his friend was doing some wiring.

"I'm taking off to get the windmill, don't know how long it'll take." I was speaking to my father's back as he worked on some fitting.

"Better take your dog." He didn't bother turning around as he dispensed his advice.

With nothing more to say I walked to the loaded truck, put Smoky on the back and left. The truck barely started, I knew the battery was old and tired but figured it would last for a while longer. It was futile to ask for a new battery anyway; my father would always answer that I only drove one thing at a time so one battery was all that was needed.

It was about twenty miles to the north over a rough Jeep track so the drive took about three hours. The temperature was about one hundred and ten and it was extremely hot in the cab of the truck while going that slow.

I spotted the windmill off in the distance and wound my way tortuously to it, the truck with the heavy tractor groaning in protest. Arriving I found a sizable ditch and backed the truck's rear wheels into it so I could unload the tractor.

It was a sad-looking sight, the tower was still standing and the gear-head was still attached at the top but the blade circle was laying on the ground with several of the blades bent at ridiculous angles. The tail was about twenty yards away in some brush. The sucker rod hung listlessly down the middle of the tower, two feet from the ground, attached to nothing at its bottom. I dropped a pebble down the well but heard no sound of water as it struck the bottom, simply the sound of rock hitting dirt. The five-thousand-gallon water tank was sitting on its two concrete rests and looked to be intact. I spotted a watering trough in a ravine several hundred yards off and walked to it. A one-inch pipe extended from a hill-side with a small trickle of water running into the trough which was full of water. It was good clear water and tasted fine, this explained the abandoned windmill. There was no sign of any cattle having used the trough recently.

With nothing else to do I unloaded the tractor, this was touchy since it was a sizable drop from the bed of the truck to the ground. It went fine so I drove to the tank with the tractor and rolled it off its rest and loaded them on the truck towards the front, leaving room for the tower. Almost dark now I left the rest for the next day. I ate a can of food, fed Smoky and slept on the seat of the truck with the doors open, still hot. The coyotes were close and very vocal that night, they didn't bother me, being so used to them by now.

I woke early the next morning, stiff from sleeping on the front seat. I looked for my dog but he must have been out exploring so I didn't give him another thought. I ate my last can of food as I sat waiting for enough light to start the day. It was still very warm, promising to be another hot one. After starting the tractor, I drove to the windmill tower and raised the bucket as high as it would go and chained it loosely to the tower.

All four legs were embedded in concrete so I would have to cut them. All I had was a hack saw so I started cutting one of the legs about four inches from the bottom. It was four-inch angle iron, galvanized. Slow and tedious but my blade was sharp and I had several more. I stayed with it, resting several times to roll a smoke, giving my arm a break. It took an hour for each leg. I tipped the tower over with the tractor and lowered it to the ground without damage. Loading it along with all the other components took several more hours. Mid-afternoon and I was ready to leave.

My dog still hadn't appeared. I was hot, sweaty and hungry, anxious to get under way, I set some food out for him, knowing he could get water from the trough. I started the truck and left, confident I would return the next day to retrieve the five-thousand-gallon tank.

The horizon was shimmering with heat, sun glaring as I drove home slowly. It was dark when I arrived so I didn't unload. I ate something and poured water over myself to wash away the sweat and grime, then went to bed.

It was hard unloading by myself with no tractor. The tower I pulled off with my pick-up and the rest were man-handled as best as possible, accompanied by a lot of swearing and sweating. Too late to drive back that afternoon I spent another night at home.

I left early the next morning, the truck barely starting, motor turning over so slowly I wasn't sure it would catch, but it did. My plan was to load the tank and get home again by afternoon, so I only took one can of something to eat and a gallon of water, plenty I thought.

Mid-morning and two miles from my destination the motor coughed several times and died. I sat there, cussing and thinking, opened the door and rolled a smoke. Finishing that, I went into a routine that was normal for most backyard mechanics, gas or electrical, the two most common engine failures. I started with gas, opening one side of the hood then the other I let the hot air escape, enveloping me in heat and oil fumes. After gathering some tools, I checked the carburetor, no gas. Breaking the fuel line, I put it to my lips and cautiously sucked, once again no gas, only air. I checked the fuel tank that was hanging outside the frame behind the cab on the driver's side, satisfied, I had a half tank. Two hours of searching I found the problem. After exiting the tank, the fuel line went through the frame on its way to the engine. Over the years a hole was worn into the line at the frame, small, but enough to allow the pump to suck air instead of gas. Finding some electrical tape, I removed the line, taped the hole with many tight wraps and reinstalled it, hoping this would suffice. I found an empty beer can under the seat, broke the fuel line at a low point and sucked until gas came out freely. There is no way one can do this without getting that shit in your mouth, the best you can hope for is not to get it into your lungs or stomach, luckily I avoided that. After filling my can half full of gas while I spit continuously, I poured some into the carburetor and hurried to the cab. Pushing the starter button it gave momentary promise, then the battery went dead, the engine refusing to turn over. I leaned over the steering wheel, sweat pouring off me only to dissipate immediately into the insufferable heat. Still a glimmer of hope though.

There was a hand crank that a person could use to start the engine. It was under the seat along with a two by four to balance the handle, ungainly but I had used it several times with success. Cautiously I slid it under the radiator into the front of the motor, the ears caught, I put the board under the handle, balancing it very carefully and pushed down on the crank with all my weight. The engine almost started, the crank slid off the motor dumping me on my ass and poking a hole into the bottom of the radiator. I sat there on my ass, in the floury alkaline dirt momentarily stunned, my body covered in a layer of dirt, my eyes barely able to see they were so choked with dust.

Vision and hearing simultaneously giving rise to panic, I rolled/crawled through the four inches of desert floor to staunch the flow of fluid escaping through the hole in the radiator. Knocking my head on the front axle hard enough to stun me again, I put my thumb over the hole, stopping most of the leak. I lay there for a while, under the truck, a tiny rivulet of green radiator fluid coursing down my arm through the thick layer of dirt into my armpit, around my shoulder, then finally running into the dirt. With fatalism I removed my thumb, it was a tiny stream, slightly bigger than a pencil lead but I began to realize it was fatal. There was nothing to be done, no sticks, no containers, no one to help me in this god forsaken, hot fucking desert.

I lay under the truck, watching as the last of the green fluid fell to the ground. At least I was in the shade. There was no doubt in my mind I had to do something. I reviewed my options, walk home, that would be quitting, walk to my tractor and drive it home, that would also be quitting. Wait here until some-one came along, never happen. I could lay under the truck and feel sorry for myself, but I was done with that already. Sliding out from underneath the truck, I decided to eat my one and only can of food, pork and beans. I ate it slowly, cold and out of the can, watching as the sun slid behind the mountains to the west.

I felt much better but nowhere near full. One hour of daylight left, and a plan was formulating. I found a punch in the tool box and a hammer. Crawling back under the truck I used the punch to make the hole perfectly round, taking pains to keep it small as possible. Taking my knife, I whittled on a hard piece of grease-wood about two inches long until it fit into the hole about halfway. I removed it several times and worked on it until it was as round as possible. Finally, I put it into the hole and tapped it with the hammer until it felt very secure. It was all I could do.

Almost dark now I lay on the front seat with both doors open. I had about a quart of water left in my canteen, enough to get me to the spring in the morning, about two miles away. I was still hungry, thirsty, caked in dirt with no way to wash off. It might have been my seventeenth birthday today, or it might have come and gone already, perhaps still a few days in the future. It didn't matter, just another day, except the next day or two were going to be pure shit. It seemed like I was hungry most of the time. At least I had plenty of Bull Durham for smokes, yep, could be a lot worse as I finished my last cigarette of the day. I fell asleep wondering about my dog Smoky, was he waiting for me at the windmill site?

I was already walking as the dark gave way to light, the last star disappearing, one moment it was there, the next gone. It promised to be hot again, already sweating as the sun came over the mountains to the east.

Early morning I arrived at the site and first thing was to call for my dog. No response, there was no evidence he had been there, no dog food was gone. So be it. Probably the coyotes had got him.

Starting the tractor, I drove it over to the water tank. First thing was to clean myself up, I stripped my clothes and poured water over myself, rinsing off the accumulated grime. I filled my canteen and drank until I could hold no more of the cool clear water. Feeling much better I took the air cleaner off the tractor, holding my finger over the hole in the middle I used it to pour water into the tractor bucket. Naked, with only my boots on I was glad no one was around to see me. Occasionally pouring water over myself I continued putting water into the bucket until I had about twenty gallons, this took considerable time but I wanted plenty, knowing some would be spilled on the way back to the truck. Filling my canteen, getting dressed, then putting a few chunks of old wooden posts into the bucket I started the slow drive back.

Going that slow it took several hours, every time I hit a rough patch of road a little more water would spill. The chunks of wood kept it from sloshing. I still had about two thirds of the water when I arrived at the truck.

I used the air cleaner again to pour the water into the radiator, checking my plug often. No leaks, it was swollen tight enough to hold water, a good sign. I tried wiggling the plug when I was done filling but there was no give.

Leaving the rest of the water in the bucket I parked the tractor. Very cautiously I prepared to start the truck with the crank again. It took several tries but I was rewarded with the sound of a running motor. I checked my plug, no leaks. Feeling confident I drove back to the windmill site. Things were going my way, no problems.

Taking my rifle and canteen with me once more, I looked at the dry chunks of dog food and decided I wasn't hungry enough yet. Walking back to get the tractor was simply a hot, hungry slog but I had no choice, I needed it to load the five thousand-gallon tank. I made it back just as it was turning dusk. No more I could do that day so I resolved myself to another hungry night sleeping in the cab.

The next morning my hunger was constant but not acute. I looked at the dog food once again with the same result, not hungry enough yet but it was looking more appealing.

Loading the tank was pretty easy, after digging a trench with the tractor I cautiously started the truck and backed it in, lowering the bed by several feet. I left the truck idling while I rolled the tank on and secured it. All went well and I glanced at the dog food one more time, decided not to try it and left with the loaded truck. I would come back and get the tractor in a day or two.

By now I knew my dog was no more, I was a little saddened but hunger occupied my thoughts mostly on the way home. Thinking over and over again what I would eat when I got there.

The trip was hot but without incident. Getting home, I ate two cans of food, almost threw up but didn't. I knew I would need the tractor to unload the truck so I went looking for my horse that afternoon. He wasn't far, so I led him home, grained him and tied him up for the night. My stomach was grumbling again, so I ate two more cans of food.

Early the next morning I fed him more grain and a little hay before daylight. After watering him we rode to where the tractor was. Taking the saddle off and putting it into the bucket of the tractor it was simple to lead him home as I drove. It was a long day for Pinto but he was tough.

The next couple of days were spent building a mound for the water tank, setting the rests and rolling the tank onto them. Straight forward just time consuming, of which I had plenty.

Now for the windmill. This was more challenging, no manuals to go by so I wasn't sure what I had and didn't have. I spent the day straightening the blades as much as possible, figuring out how it went together. It was frustrating but I was getting a clearer picture. I knew there were some parts missing and some were broken so a trip to town was necessary. I loaded some questionable parts onto the pickup and got things ready to go to Fallon the next day, a hundred-mile trip one way. The next morning, I was full of excitement, I put on my best Levi's and a clean shirt and headed to town. I had about four hundred and fifty dollars, some of this was from my buckarooing and the rest from mining, I felt rich. My first trip to Fallon, my first trip to any town in seven months, I was eager.

A long drive, fifty miles of gravel road and about fifty of pavement, a two-and-a-half-hour trip through some very desolate country but I felt at home in the solitude. I listened to a local radio station on AM, music and other people's voices, what a luxury that was.

First thing I needed was a Nevada driver's license. They required insurance so I found an agent, got the minimum and went back to the DMV. Took the written then the practical, passed and I was good to go. While there I also transferred the title in my name. Next, to a hardware store, they directed me to a salvage yard where I might have better luck. This was a blessing, the man was so knowledgeable and helpful. He spent several hours going over parts and I went away with almost a complete windmill set. More than enough to totally restore what I had, along with the pumping cylinder for the bottom of the well. All together this cost much less than I had anticipated, seemed like it was almost too cheap but he assured me that it was fair and he was glad to sell some stuff. He was a valuable resource for many years to come.

I went to a farm supply store and bought some galvanized pipe and other materials to make sure I had plenty of supplies to complete my project. I still had plenty of money and room in my pickup so I went to the bulk plant and bought one barrel of gas and one barrel of diesel. The bed of my pickup was now very full but I still had about two hundred dollars. Next I found a clothing store and purchased a new pair of Levi's and work boots. Then a grocery store to get some things that I really enjoyed, like Vienna sausage and canned peaches, plus my favorite jam. My biggest indulgence was store-bought cigarettes, three packs of Lucky Strikes, I felt like a King.

My last stop was a hamburger joint on Main Street. A double

cheeseburger with fries and a large Coke. Damn it was good. Some kids my age started to appear and I soon came to realize this was a local hangout for high school kids. Most of them were ranch kids and very friendly. They took a keen interest in me and what I was doing. One girl named Brea, was exceptionally interested and we sat together on a bench outside, she was cute and flirtatious. Most of them knew about Dixie Valley and its remoteness. Two of the boys were brothers, both in high school and lived in Dixie Valley. They spent the week in town either with relatives or a boarding house and rode the school bus home on Fridays. There were four high school kids from the valley that used this method, the lesser grades went to a small one-room school at the settlement with one teacher, there were six students at the time. I met the brothers and we had a mutual liking, having so much in common, they already knew a little about me and how isolated I was.

We all went our separate ways having used up the better part of two hours. I didn't want to leave; I didn't want to leave town or my new friends. Brea kissed me goodbye, giving me her phone number, insisting I call her next trip in. There were no phones or electricity in all of Dixie Valley, but I promised I would as soon as I got to town again. Damn it was hard to drive away, so happy but depressed at the same time. This encounter had driven home just how alone I had been for the last year and a half. But go home I must.

The memories of town began to fade as I occupied myself with the windmill over the next several days. I poured concrete for the four legs of the tower, leaving about six inches of angle iron sticking up to bolt the legs of the tower onto once it was erect, with a lot of measuring I could only hope it would fit together. I built a cradle to elevate the top end of the thirty-foot tower so I could mount the blades, tail, and all the other heavy parts before I stood it upright. Plus. I needed to get under it with the tractor to do this, a crane would sure have been handy.

It must have been the weekend, my father and two of his friends showed that evening. By now we had established a routine, he would express a slight interest, I would give him a quick rundown, then go our separate ways. I didn't say anything about the difficulties in getting all the stuff here, figuring it would be a waste of breath. I was never clear if he just didn't give a damn about me, or if he disliked me, or, as I would like to think he had so much confidence he figured there wasn't much to say. I would ponder this for many years, never arriving at a conclusion and never wanting to ask. They worked on the house and I continued on the windmill. My father never offered assistance and I was too stubborn to ask, intent on doing it myself. He was fixated on the house it seemed, like a horse going down a road with blinders, content and oblivious.

As they were ready to leave I said to my father, "You better get the house plumbed, you'll have water the next time you come." I meant it as a jest, maybe I said it wrong. He took it as an affront, a challenge from the pup.

"Don't get smart with me." His face red, eyes locked on mine. I didn't say anymore, the other two men sitting next to him suddenly having a keen interest in their feet. They drove off. I was saddened by this little episode; I knew this wasn't how it was supposed to be. We were in this together, trying to build a future, a ranch. Maybe this was how fathers and sons were supposed to act, I didn't know, I had no reference points. But I had plenty of shit to do besides thinking so much.

The days were still warm, not so hot you couldn't touch any metal but still plenty warm. The stream that was to fill the reservoir was dry now, only coming out as far as the canyon mouth, about two miles away. I would have to take the tractor with two fifty gallon drums in the bucket and drive there. Filling them and coming back would eat half a day and the water would be red from rust for several days. It was tedious but necessary, it gave me more impetus to get the windmill done. The evenings were getting long enough now that I would try doing some school work, without much success. My mind would drift often, mostly back to the whorehouse and Judy. Hunched over my make shift desk, kerosene lamp smoking or on the verge, I would give up and just let my mind dream. School work didn't seem all that important.

I started back to the windmill as daylight came the next morning, anxious to get it working. It used up the better part of four days to put the top end together and build the cat walk, this gave a person a place to stand and service the top end. Satisfied that all was in order I chained two of the legs to the protruding pieces of angle iron, moved the tractor underneath the tower and slowly raised it, nervously waiting for things to go to hell. They didn't, I had chained the tower to the bucket with some slack, as it went past center the chain tightened and I let the tower settle into place. The legs aligned well enough to suit me. With some bars I twisted and moved the legs so they were close enough to drill holes and bolt it securely. The welder also had a generator so I used it to drill holes, finally getting it all fastened. I breathed a huge sigh of relief, that was its most vulnerable position, standing free, a small gust of wind could have toppled it easily. I was no engineer but four half inch bolts on each leg looked to be more than enough. It was almost dark, I was tired and hungry but proud of myself. I made sure the brake was on, it wasn't really a brake, only a lever at shoulder height, pulling this down would pivot the tail so the blades would no longer point into the wind, simple but effective. The stronger the wind, the more you would angle the tail.

The next morning was much cooler, with clouds that gave false promise of rain and a slight breeze, perfect for a trial run. Before even eating or having my morning coffee or cigarette, I released the brake and held my breath as the blades slowly began to turn. Watching as the sucker rod went up and down, though unattached to anything, it all functioned so damn well I couldn't help but smile, it felt so good when things came together. One more major step, then I could really celebrate, or at least pretend to.

I was anxious to install the pump but hunger forced me to get something to eat. After my morning rituals I cautiously and methodically started the process of lowering the pump cylinder along with its component parts into the well. It was not only physically hard but also demanded concentration, constantly reminding myself not to drop it into the well as I lowered the assembly in ten foot increments. Invariably it got too heavy, with half still remaining I set a beam two thirds way up the tower and used a block and tackle to finish. This helped considerably but two people working would have been so much better, how often I wished for another pair of hands. Two days later it was finished, everything installed, ready to hook the sucker rod from the pump to the one coming down from the windmill. This had to be exact but I needed some wind to determine the exact top and bottom of the stroke before I could make the final connection, soon enough, but I was impatient.

I filled the time setting the five-thousand-gallon tank that would store the water. Easy enough, but time consuming, I built a mound from dirt and rocks with the tractor. Five feet high, wide enough for the rests. Simple to build but harder to get the tank onto, with several hours spent building a ramp with timbers.

The following day I rolled the tank up the ramps and onto the rests with the tractor. That went well but took several more hours of frustrating work spinning it to get the outlet on the bottom and manhole on top. I finished hooking all the pipes up with a spigot tapped into the line between windmill and tank, another spigot at the bottom of the tank facing the house, ready for a hose. I wanted wind.

Several more windless days, filled with sunshine. I devised a system to measure the stroke of the windmill to the stroke of the pump cylinder so I was able to make the final connection. That evening a slight breeze tickled the blades, forcing them to make half a turn. I was sitting on a chair outside, watching some dark clouds blocking the last of the evening sun. Enjoying a cigarette along with my evening coffee, lost in dreams of girls I almost had and girls I damn well had. These thoughts came often and were always welcome. I felt another breath on my cheek, this one stronger, lasting long enough to spin the blades for several revolutions before disappearing. I kicked the girls from my thoughts and focused entirely on the blades, motionless once again. I willed them to turn, as if willing would somehow be magical. I waited, holding my breath, unaware I was doing so. A few moments went by, nothing stirring, the smoke from my cigarette going straight up, a tiny wisp made circles as it rose.

Unannounced, a strong breeze hit the blades, the tail forcing a ninety-degree change in alignment. It held, the wind held strong and steady. Having no idea what was too much I feathered the tail, slowing the blades to what appeared a reasonable speed. I could almost sense the tension mounting in the metal, lifting the water removed the freewheeling effect of the blades, listening to the hum, it was rhythmic, the sucker rod going up and down. A spray of water came out from the packing gland, I had a wrench just for that, tightening just enough to stop to spray but still loose enough to prevent friction. I could hear the water going into the tank, such a rewarding, beautiful sound, I ran up the outside ladder and down into the manhole of the tank on another short ladder, set for this very purpose. I had a long handle brush that I now used to wash the bottom and sides of the interior, removing as much rust as possible with the stream of water that was now falling, spraying me with cold water, it was delightful. I pushed the rust and other particles with the brush to one end where awaited a two-inch hole. I had removed the plug earlier that day in preparation for this event. Satisfied it was clean as possible, I went outside, removed the ladder and brush from the interior, replaced the drain plug and listened to the sound of the water going into the tank.

I was so excited, such a long process by myself, no knowledge of what I was doing but plenty of help from others, for that I would be forever thankful. The windmill made a tiny clank with every revolution, almost melodic, as if to let me know it was working. I chased that sound off and on for years, never finding its source, most times I welcomed and enjoyed it, sometimes awakening me at night. That tiny clank would become my most constant and longest standing companion for many years.

I wanted to celebrate so I opened the spigot and filled a cup full of water, looking into the water, it appeared crystal clear but it was almost dark so I wasn't sure. I drank it, sweet and cold so I drank another. I wanted to celebrate harder, this being such a huge accomplishment. I found a half bottle of whiskey and started my party. It was a lonely party and it got lonelier as the bottle got emptier. What started with euphoria ended with depression and self-pity. I was alone, I would be alone forever it felt like, nobody really gave a shit about me or my water. I threw my bedroll onto the ground that night, next to my windmill. The constant clanking taunting me all night long, reminding me I was alone, probably drunk, and couldn't even keep a dog. But fuck if I didn't have water.

The wind must have blown all night. It still held steady the next morning, the weather gray and gloomy. My head hurt, but not too bad, luckily I quit drinking when I did. Checked the water tank, one quarter full, rhythmic spurts of water keeping time with the clanking, adding to the volume. I opened the tail, confident the wind wouldn't build, the clanking increased slightly, faint but constant, somehow reassuring.

My horse was making his way towards me, curious or lonely, I didn't know. Happy for his company I gave him a nice helping of oats and brushed him as he contentedly chewed. This small act cheered me considerably, his presence comforting. I sat on the ground, leaned against his front legs and had a smoke. Long after he was done with the grain, he continued to stand still, I sat there immobile, content with his presence, grateful for it. My ass getting sore, my stomach rumbling, I got up and filled a bucket with water from the tank spigot and gave Pinto a drink.

With some food in my belly and feeling better I found a lead rope, putting it around his neck I swung onto his back. I had no destination, merely sat and let him choose the route because it really didn't matter.

We worked our way towards the mountains, his head would reach down, move back and forth, then with a mouth full of grass we would continue on. There is a certain serenity that comes with sitting on a horse bareback, the warmth of his body spreading through your own. It felt welcome on cold days, on hot summer days it could be very uncomfortable.

About two miles from the house I slid off Pinto's back, removed the rope from his neck and walked back home, He followed me about half way then got preoccupied with a tuft of grass. The windmill was still pumping, clanking happily, welcoming me home.

It must have been Friday, I watched as the red Ford pickup came driving up to the house. My mother came and gave me a hug, smiling she squeezed me tightly, maybe grateful to have made the trip alive. My father didn't say anything, looked at me, nodded, then walked towards the windmill. My mom and I joined him as he watched the blades making their endless circles. "Is it pumping water or going around for no reason?" He studied the sucker rod intently, not really sure how it all worked.

"It's working. The tank should be half full by now."

"I'll be damned." He shook his head in amazement, smiling. This would be as close to a compliment as I would ever get, I took it as he meant it. "I'll be God-Damned" he added again, as if he was unable to fully comprehend my success.

We unloaded some groceries and their bags with clothes.

"We're staying for a week; this will be so nice to have water close by. I can't believe you did that all by yourself." She was smiling, it was so nice to see her smile, so rare. Shorter than me, average build with what would be considered an attractive face, lines were becoming etched more permanently. I suspected they were not laugh lines. I studied her, really studied her for what may have been the first time in my life. I watched as she bustled in the makeshift kitchen of her future home. This was her domain, even unfinished as it was, she was happy.

We had a simple dinner, there were no appliances yet. After, we sat in chairs outside on what would be our future yard and watched as the last traces of orange sky gave way to full darkness. My mother drank wine while my father and I drank whiskey, both of us feeling expansive. It was pleasant, I felt appreciated and useful. My mother had brought me several packs of Lucky Strike cigarettes, a great treat. We drank and smoked and talked until it was time for bed.

The next day my parents started painting the interior walls of the house, all the sheet rock was done. The house was plumbed and ready for water, I just needed to run a pipe from the tank to the house. It had minimal wiring but we had no electricity except for a generator which we used rarely. I started digging the ditch with pick and shovel, only one hundred feet but very hard-packed dirt with lots of rock. By the time I was finished and had the pipe installed, the painting was also done. We set some metal cabinets they brought with them, one had a double sink, water from the faucet adding to her excitement. It all went well and fast. By the end of the week my mother had a full kitchen with table. We moved their bed from the van into one of the bedrooms. They both seemed happy, my mother especially so. My father actually slapped me on the back that evening, damn near knocking me over, his manner of showing affection I guessed. A whole new experience for me, but cautiously I welcomed it. A brief thought of returning the gesture, but better sense prevailed.

With an enthusiastic announcement my father proclaimed we were going to the settlement that evening, I suspected he was in his cups but quite jovial, his good mood contagious. "There's a square dance at the school house, with a caller." My mother must have known; she was already getting dressed. I didn't know anything about square dancing or what a caller was, in fact it didn't sound all that much fun, hanging around with a bunch of old people.

I surprised myself, it was fun. The school house was full of people and music. I learned the calls quickly, there were some cute girls about my age having come clear from town for this monthly event. In spite of myself I had a lot of fun, some of the settlement boys that I had met several weeks ago in town, were there also enjoying themselves. Occasionally going outside to one of the pickups, we would take a generous turn from a bottle of whiskey, sometimes the girls would join us, shaking their heads and making horrible faces as the whiskey burned its way down their throats. No one cared, we would dance like crazy, sneak a drink that all the adults knew we were sneaking, everyone was sneaking a drink, alcohol was not allowed in the building. We all obeyed the rules. I was so damn happy, seemed like we were all happy, kids, adults and grandparents. The caller stayed several hours longer than he meant to, caught up in the frivolity. It ended too soon, but end it must. A whole bunch of new friends, though they all lived far away and there was no means of communication it still felt good. I hadn't been this happy since I spent days in a whorehouse, damn, life was good again.

MORE HORSES AND WHORES

There was not much sleeping in the next morning, too much to do. During breakfast we talked about clearing and leveling some land in preparation for planting something next spring. We decided twenty acres would meet the requirements of BLM under the Homestead Act for this 120 acres. We had 640 in total, 160 in my sister's name since I was too young to have it in mine. 320 in my fathers' name and 160 in my mothers' name. They joined one another and made a legal section, one-mile square. The 160 that had the house was a quarter mile by one mile. Being the one under my sister's name and having the reservoir and other improvements it seemed prudent to develop it first. The twenty acres that we marked out was a quarter mile long by about seven hundred feet, close enough.

We couldn't develop a good plan for clearing and leveling, not having any suitable equipment. My father argued it was simple, just pull the disk with the tractor until the bushes were all cut up into little pieces and by then the ground should be level enough. As so often between us, the discussion turned into an argument. I tried to impress on him the tractor was not big enough to pull the disk unless it was almost completely closed, which would make it useless. Also, the coarse brittle brush would puncture the tires, as it had so often before. By now I had more experience than I would have liked repairing tractor tires, arduous and frustratingly slow by hand. I told him nothing would get accomplished by me going back and forth in the desert over all that brush with a closed disk, except burning fuel and puncturing tires. By now it was getting heated, my father accusing me of always wanting more, constantly complaining and wanting everything to be perfect and easy. I wanted to retaliate, hurl back insults, make my own accusations to him, but I was unable. I wasn't sure why I was incapable of firing back at him, it wasn't fear, he wasn't a physical person, at least so far. I stood there, arms at my side, fists clenched in frustration and anger, his words hurt, they hurt deeply. I was seventeen, another birthday having come and gone over a month ago without any notice. Why this thought came I had no idea, my mouth opened and the rest transformed into words, cold and quiet. "I've worked harder than any man should ever have too, under shithole conditions. Most of the money I've made has been spent on fuel or other stuff we've needed." I could feel myself working into a fire stoking tirade. I stopped, looked right at him and said simply "Don't call me a whiner."

My cold stare and clipped tone must have given him pause, he probably expected me to be more defensive. At that time my mother announced herself, her voice a calming influence that was so desperately needed. "Let's go, it's a long way back to Sacramento and I've got a lot to do when we get there. This isn't getting us anywhere." She looked at both of us and added. "We shouldn't always leave here mad."

She was right, rarely did my father leave Dixie without some kind of parting shot at me, or at least it seemed that way.

"I'll do what I can." My way of saying goodbye, subconsciously trying to placate him so my mother wouldn't have to spend the next six hours with him totally pissed. I had no idea how their trips back and forth together went, I never asked and my mother never said.

I watched as the plume of dust from their departure slowly

dissipated. How many had I watched in the last year and a half. By now my emotions were almost predictable, anger, frustration, loneliness, slowly giving way to a general malaise. I was determined to start clearing brush and leveling the ground. I simply had no idea how.

Intending to service the tractor it was apparent one of the front tires had a puncture. Easy enough to raise the front with the loader. A couple hours later, tire fixed, tractor serviced I drove to the field and started pushing brush into low spots, covering it with dirt from the large mounds, some of them as huge as a house. Several hours later with the sun settling behind the mountains I heard the recognizable sound of air escaping from the right front tire. My efforts now focused on getting the tractor home before the tire went flat, every revolution causing a spray of dust as the hole was directed at the earth. I looked back at the pitiful amount of work accomplished. Coincidentally, I was just reading a book on mythology, remembering a character named Sisyphus, I felt a kinship with him. How frustrating, to spend so much effort with so little result. Nothing to be done, I made it home, fixed the tire just as darkness settled, ate some dinner and spent the rest of the evening reading, in a bad mood.

The next several days didn't get much better. Push some brush, push some dirt, fix a flat. I swore a lot those four days, used a lot of patches and moved very little dirt.

That evening as I sat moping over my meager dinner a pickup pulled up to the house. I didn't recognize it or the three men getting out. They stood next to their truck so I walked out to them. We introduced ourselves, shaking hands. They acted surprised when I informed then I was the only one at the house.

"We heard you could do some mine improvements; you did some for a friend of ours a while back." His manners were very polite. I studied his face as he spoke. "We each have several claims and need to get the work done before time runs out. Is it something you can do?"

"Yeah, you caught me at a good time. I'm just starting another project here but it'll keep." What I had been doing would keep forever I thought, so glad for the reprieve.

They gave me directions, about eight miles from my ranch, snug against the mountain range. They had cabins and would spend the night in them, I would meet them in the morning and look at the job. When I arrived the next morning we walked around discussing what needed to be done, very straightforward with no surprises. After several hours I gave them a price for all the work, rather than by the hour. This surprised them, but pleasantly so. I think they expected me to consult with my father or some higher authority before I could commit.

"What happens if it takes longer than you think it might?" The spokesman asked, his question honest.

"It shouldn't, but if it does it won't matter, the price is firm." I answered him with the conviction of a seventeen-year-old who had the confidence instilled by many years of making decisions.

"Is there any way you can get it done in the next three months? That'll give us time to get it all approved before the deadline." I could tell he was hopeful.

"What day is today?"

"Friday." He answered.

"What month is it.?"

"Almost the end of September, about a week left I think?" His head slightly tilted, studying me, as if trying to decide whether or not I was bullshiting him about not knowing what month it was. I wasn't.

"How about this." I stated after a few minutes thinking, as they waited silently. "You write me a check for half the amount. I'll have enough time to get to the bank in Fallon today, if the check clears I'll get some fuel and start Monday. By the end of October, the work will be finished."

"How do we know you'll do the work if you cash the check?" One of the other men asked, as he looked directly at me, knitted brows showing a slight concern.

"I don't know how to answer that." Returning his gaze, I spoke honestly, "I can only say it'll be done. Unless my tractor blows up or I die."

"That works for me. I'll give him a check and settle with you guys when we get home. My gut says he's good for it." The spokesman said as he was getting his check book.

Formalities done, they left and I drove my truck back to the house, cleaned up, threw some clean clothes and four empty barrels into my pickup and anxiously headed to town. I was excited to have a somewhat legitimate reason for going to town but I was more excited to see Brea, the girl that I had met last time I was in town. A moment of panic until I found her number in the glove compartment on the slip of paper she had given me, damn near running off the dirt road out into the desert. I slowed down after that.

First stop was at the bank. I opened a checking account under my name with the check and several hundred in cash, tired of wondering where to keep it. I had the bank make sure the check was good. Next stop I called Brea who was home from school and very excited to hear from me, pouting, accusing me of forgetting about her already. I told her I would meet her in two hours, I still had fuel, filters and some other things to do before the bulk plant and other stores closed. She wouldn't buy it, insisting she could go with me if I would pick her up. Damn right I would.

She sat next to me in the truck, getting out and going into every store with me. She sat in the back of the pickup and watched as I filled three fifty barrel drums with diesel and one with gas. She was intrigued, coming with me into the office to pay and set up a monthly revolving account so I wouldn't have to pay each time I bought fuel. I set it up in my name but I had no address. Telling them I would be right back we walked to the post office and they gave me an address. Very simple one, my name and then Star Route, Dixie Valley, with state and zip. They instructed me to get a legal mailbox and set it next to all the mailboxes that served the settlement, still twenty-five miles from my house, but at least I had an address and could now get mail. We walked back to the bank, they were also waiting for an address so they could order my new checks.

Two new tubes for the front tires of the tractor, oil filters, some other odds and ends and we were done with business. As we walked around town she insisted I hold her hand, I obliged but it felt strange. Don't know why, it just did, not something I had ever done.

We drove to a hamburger place and I got us some burgers and fries. It must have been a local hangout for teens, as we sat eating our food more and more young people kept showing up. Brea kept getting closer to me as if I would run away, no way in hell would that happen. She was very cute, built slim and nice, and all around fun to be with. The group got around to about a dozen young people and soon someone suggested we have a party at the local river several miles out of town. We all pitched in some money, one of them, must have been the oldest, said he would get the beer and meet us at the river.

Still an hour of daylight left, enough time to go swimming in our underwear. The beer came shortly, Brea and I shared one, neither one of us real drinkers apparently, I know beer wasn't normally my first choice in alcohol, not sure about her. We used up the waning light and afternoon warmth drinking and swimming and having a great time in general. It was fun, it was a lot of fun. As darkness came we built a fire, sitting and drinking, hugging and kissing, all the things teenagers do when drinking and unsupervised. There were never any problems, just a bunch of young boys and girls from town and mostly from the local ranches, clinging to the last warm days of summer.

I must have fit right in the mix, only one other guy made a few feeble attempts at harassing me about my height and not being in school. It went nowhere, I ignored him and some of the other boys told him to shut up, he sounded stupid. He did and we got on fine. Besides I was too happy to let anything interfere, this being such a change from my everyday life at the ranch, all alone.

We sat for hours around the fire but after several beers I was done drinking and so was Brea. We still sat and enjoyed the antics of the others as they continued the party, content to have her tightly next to me, my arm over her shoulders.

About eleven thirty Brea said she had to be home by midnight and didn't want to be late. I was fine with that. She was very sweet and I had no desire to get her in trouble. By this time, it was well established that sex would not happen until well into the future so I let that be and just welcomed her companionship, I just didn't have the heart to pressure her.

An interesting thing was happening anyway, the last hour as we sat by the fire my mind had begun to think occasionally of my future job doing those mine improvements with the tractor. Somehow being drawn back to my responsibilities and obligations. The feeling wasn't quite tangible but it was there. Several times as I sat staring into the fire, subconsciously understanding there was very little I had in common with these kids, other than my own age. No blame on them, but their conversations would be about school, college, football, basketball and proms. I was familiar with none of these things. They talked excitedly about the coming school year and plans afterward. It was fun listening to them, their enthusiasm, a little bravado from the beer about future exploits I suppose. They talked jokingly about parents setting curfews on weekends, chore expectations, how they tested their parents, constantly pushing. I was familiar with none of these things. I didn't remember any adult ever setting a boundary. It struck me that evening, maybe from the beers, maybe from being around kids with a normal life, maybe from many things. I would never be like them; I could never be like them.

We sat in the pickup outside Breas' house. She wanted me to come in, saying her parents would probably let me sleep on the couch so we could be together tomorrow again.

She was holding both my hands in hers, imploring me. Stressing it was the weekend and we had two days together. But she knew, she knew deep down inside herself that I was already gone. I made a feeble attempt at explaining how I had obligations for the winter and couldn't even see her for the next five months. It didn't help. I walked her to the door of her house, I think she understood words were futile. We kissed, hugged, I held her at arm's length for a moment, my last memory of her face having several tears reflected off the porch light slowly making their way down her cheeks. I knew she hurt, I hurt also, I turned around, walked to my truck. As I drove away I noticed she was inside already.

I drove home, much as the moth always goes to the flame. A long, lonely drive full of recriminations and pain. I chastised myself over and over for causing someone pain. I became morose, that deep understanding finally sinking in, I was different than other people my age, not better, not worse. I could never be like them, carefree.

The next day was spent putting new tubes into the front tires of the tractor, the old ones having so many patches I no longer trusted them. Changed the oil, greased the fittings, and gave it a good service. My actions were mechanical, comforting in their familiarity. My mind constantly occupied with Brea and my actions the day before. I felt bad, several times stopping what I was doing with the intent of driving back to town. I wanted to see her, be around people. I would be depressed for a little while, then become caught up in some little project and feel better for a while. The day wore on in this fashion, not the first time my emotions would be all over the place, I was familiar with them. So many times I had watched people leave as I stood in the desert watching the dust slowly make its way back to earth, sometimes the pangs of loneliness were almost visceral. So familiar.

I decided to make a tow bar so I could pull my pick-up behind the tractor to the work site. That way it would be possible to leave the tractor there instead of driving it back and forth to the house.

The work all done for the day, things ready for the next morning I sat in a chair outside, watching the sun slide its way down behind the mountains. It was warm and comfortable as I sat there having a coffee and cigarette. One of the luxuries of going to town, I could buy some cigarettes and not have to roll my own, such a big pleasure from such a little thing. I missed my dog, Smoky, a little, wishing for something to talk to.

The next morning was filled with connecting the tractor to the pickup with the tow bar, loading some clothes and food. Taking enough for two weeks, planning on staying in the cabin on the job site. I left a note with a brief explanation what I was doing and where I would be.

Mid-morning, the temperature perfect, skies a deep blue that only the desert can be when the air is cool and still. I got things organized and started right to work.

It was a good job, mostly soft dirt, no surprises. The tractor had lights so I was able to work late into the evening, with nothing else to do it was a good time filler. The days came and went, the tractor running well, no rocks large enough to cause me problems. Pushing dirt, leveling small plots, building short roads to join the claims, all the things they had asked for. The weather held fine, cool nights and warm days. A couple of small rain systems added enough moisture to help with the dust but not so much as to create mud. It was pleasant, simple, enjoyable, plenty of time for daydreaming. I lost track of the days. The work was going much faster than hoped for so I took a day off, driving back home to see my parents and do laundry. We had an old wringer washing machine that ran off the generator, simple and worked well. Plus, I needed more food.

That evening I arrived at the house but my calculations must have been off. Not sure if both my parents or only my father had come, but they had come and gone. My note was no longer on the table, and I could tell more work had been done on the fireplace in the living room. This was my father's primary focus, to get it done before winter set in. I was sad and relieved at the same time, wanting some form of human contact but at the same time glad not to have my butt chewed about something. Nothing to be done about that but still had no idea what day it was, I guess it didn't matter anyway, I'd still be alone.

My day was spent doing laundry, gathering more food. The canned situation was a little sparse, very little variety, mostly hash, beef stew, canned veggies and some fruit. I guess my father must have forgotten he had a son that needed to eat. Didn't matter, there was enough.

Drove back the next morning before it was light, so I started working as the eastern sky lightened, then gave way to a brilliant cool sunrise. How I loved the fall. My mind more and more drifting to my upcoming job once more as a buckaroo. Visions of days in the whorehouse, lazing idly with a naked woman lying next to me. The visions were so heady I almost stopped working long enough to make a quick trip to town so these visions weren't so pervasive. But I didn't, my stupid sense of obligation taking over. Damn. Soon enough.

Several weeks later the job was finished. Since I was far ahead of schedule I worked a couple extra days doing things they hadn't asked for but I knew would make their lives a little easier. I cleaned up the cabin and hauled everything home.

No idea what day it was. Unloaded and did laundry once again. Evidenced by the progress on the fireplace that my father had come and gone once more. A little disappointed that no effort was made to come see me, it was only a one-hour drive at most. So be it.

Early the next morning I drove to town, called the gentleman who employed me to tell him the job was complete and I would like to settle the account. Surprised to hear from me so quickly, he sounded dubious about the quality of work but assured me they would be there within three days, check the job and then pay me if it was accepted. Hesitantly he thanked me for my promptness. I told him that would be fine and I would be at my place when they were done.

I went to the grocery store and loaded up on food to take back home, I must have been hungry. Purchased some horse shoes, fuel, which I paid for and other items. Done with the necessities I was very tempted to call Brea. I knew she was in school so it was a decision that I really didn't have to make. I thought about driving by the school and seeing if I could catch her at lunch. That would seem a little desperate, plus there was nothing to be gained except more disappointment, for both of us. A little sad I started driving home. A short time later I realized I was driving like an old farmer, very slow, reluctant to leave town, but leave I must, so I sped up.

Didn't do much that afternoon when I got home. Unloaded and put away the stuff, in general just did odds and ends. Looked for my horse but he wasn't close by so I let the horseshoeing go until tomorrow. I knew I was dragging my feet about going back to the field and trying some more land leveling but my heart wasn't in it, so damn frustrating to work so much, burn fuel, fix flats and have nothing to show for it.

The next morning, I made a search for Pinto, finding him contently standing on a little knoll next to the mountain range apparently asleep. I kept whistling for him as I got closer. Finally, he must have heard me, his head coming up and turning in my direction. It took him several moments to decide it might be worth coming to investigate me, I might have some grain. I did and gave him a good helping on the ground, smoking one of my cherished store bought cigarettes as he munched on the grain, some falling back out of his mouth when he raised his head. I let him take his time, as I looked around the valley. I always felt better when I took some time and let the beauty of the desert register. The mountain ranges across the salt flat called the Clan Alpine were high and beautiful to look at. Forests of Pinyon Pine and Juniper where evident even at twenty or thirty miles, their dark shadowing in contrast to the lighter sage. Pockets of willow or aspen hinting at possible water in some of the canyons higher up. The last thousand feet of the peaks were barren rock with only some scrub brush scattered randomly. A harsh land, full of things that wanted to poke or prick you, bite or eat you, freeze or fry you. I loved it and felt at home.

I didn't put a lead rope on Pinto or ride him the couple miles back to the house. Just laying my hand on the bump between his ears, he kept his head down and walked beside me. Soon I took my hand off and just walked along with him keeping pace next to me. It was such a tranquil and serene moment I wanted to preserve it forever, no pressure whatsoever, just a boy and his horse slowly walking along like two lifelong friends. Then, unexpectedly, the little bastard shook his head and blew his nose, horse snot landing all over the side of me. I guess he wasn't feeling the moment like I was. I took small consolation at least, rubbing my arms and my side on him to get most of it off.

The rest of the afternoon was spent putting shoes on Pinto. He was easy, he didn't lean on you or pull his foot away, especially his hind feet. There is a moment when the nail comes through the side of the hoof that is a little risky before you twist it off with your hammer. I spent the rest of the evening riding bareback at the base of the mountains, killing time, enjoying the last of the day as the shadows crept up the mountains to the east.

The next day I reluctantly started to work back in the field, trying to level one mound of dirt that was quite large without getting a flat. No flats by lunch so went to the house to get something to eat. A pickup pulled in just as I was finishing. It was the three men whom I had done the tractor work for. They stood by the truck waiting for me to come out. This was a custom that may have been unique to ranches or people that lived remotely. The thought being you could hear someone driving up and choose to acknowledge them or not, your choice. I did and walked out to greet them. It went well, they were pleased with the job. I had them make out a check in my father's name. With an assurance that I would do more work for them next year, they left in a good mood.

Must have put a thorn through one of the front tires on the tractor, it was flat, no real surprise. As I fixed it my mind wandered to how much easier and productive my life would be if I had a bulldozer. It didn't have to be a large one, just something impervious to the sharp bushes, a rubber tired tractor was an exercise in frustration. Time to have a discussion with my father if we were to have a real chance of getting the ground level, ready for crops. I anticipated a struggle, normally he regarded my wants or needs as troublesome and should be ignored. Nothing to be done but try.

The next evening must have been a Friday, both parents arriving in a good mood. My father's got better when I gave him the check for $450.00 dollars. He was fine with me keeping the other half since I paid for all the fuel, inner tubes and other related items. More and more I came to realize he didn't have much interest in what I did as long as it didn't cost him anything.

He never asked what was happening, content as long as I had no requirements or made him aware of some need. Better yet if I bought all my own personal stuff like clothes and food. My mother was much more inquisitive, asking a multitude of questions about what happens and how I fill my time. Her concern for me she kept hidden, especially in front of my father, but it would show sometimes in her questions. I repeatedly emphasized that I was quite content, in fact I stressed that I considered myself fortunate to have so much latitude. Mostly I was serious, considering how many restraints most other people my age had. Plus, I knew there was a winter of riding again, and another trip to the whorehouse gave me many happy thoughts. The thought of lying in bed with a naked woman, tittes and other things available at any time, yeah I thought, I really have got it made sometimes. I did not share these things with my mother.

That weekend was spent finishing the fireplace chimney. In a day or two it would be usable once the mortar dried. The last night my father was impatient and built a small fire, using scraps of lumber left over from the house construction. It was a beautiful fireplace, built with local rocks having been selected for their color and shape. We enjoyed the small fire and sat there having a drink and smoking, my mother and I doing most of the talking. My father drinking much more than us, became very quiet, then went to sleep as he sat there. All in all, a very serene evening. Scary and rare to have this much harmony.

The next morning, he showed me how to nail chicken wire on the outside walls of the house. The walls were covered with heavy tar paper to keep the weather out. The wire was nailed with furring nails, a special nail made for plaster. They had cardboard washers to keep the wire a quarter inch from the paper so the plaster could be applied and have something to adhere to.

I had discussed my plans for the winter with them. My father thought it would be a good idea but I needed to get the house wrapped with the wire first. A week's job by myself, then it would be around the end of October so the timing would work well for me to head north. I think he was relieved not to have to feed me all winter or provide anything else, he was quite happy. My mom was sad and quiet, many times telling me to be careful and take care of myself, before they left that morning. I wondered how many times mothers had told their sons to be careful, the sons always assuring them they would be.

It was a bittersweet parting that morning, my mom hugging me, eyes moist, knowing she wouldn't see or hear from me for four or five months. My dad didn't give a shit, rolling his window down, his parting words, "I expect the wire to be on when I get back." With a half-ass wave he drove off. At least he was smiling.

It was mentally simple, nothing complicated in nailing wire up. I managed to keep it nice and tight. I worked as long as the daylight allowed, anxious to finish and get north so I could start my job, buckarooing. Also the whorehouse was calling very loudly. I kept a close eye on my horse, graining him a little every evening so he would stick around.

It took a few days longer than thought, but that was fine. The last day I spent putting everything in order, checking the anti-freeze in the tractor and my truck and all the other things I could think of. I entertained taking my truck and hauling Pinto to the ranch up north but then thought better of it, I might be a long way from the main ranch when it was time to come home and I didn't want to go back and get it. Plus, I enjoyed the ride. The weather looked like it would hold for a while, the temperatures still very moderate at night, with daytime temps perfect.

I loaded my horse before daylight the next morning, put my foot in the stirrup and swung into the saddle. I was sad to leave but excited at the same time, so many emotions. So different than the trip last year. I felt the confidence of familiarity that the next four months implied, the maturity that the summer had given me.

The well and windmill filling me with pride as I looked back one more time, the tail feathered, the blades still, resting until the next wind coaxed them into pumping water. Someday, I hoped, green fields of alfalfa would be visible and demanding attention. I still had that dream, in fact it became stronger the longer it was put off. Maybe next spring I could focus on that.

The trip went without incident, spending the night close to the same place I had the year before. No coyotes singing that night. I had a peaceful night sleeping under the stars. So many things to be grateful for, a good dependable horse, plenty of jam and tobacco, good boots, almost new clothes, money and a job to make more. That led to the thought of titties in my future, I was becoming obsessed with titties. With that thought I went to sleep.

The next afternoon brought me to the ranch, very familiar this time. I grained my horse then put him away. Taking my things into the bunkhouse I noticed there was one more bed occupied than last year but still several empties. Chose the same one as last winter.

Sitting on the porch and having a smoke the other buckaroos came riding in that afternoon, same men as last year except one new guy that I didn't know. George and Benson, the two Indians, saw me sitting there and rode over and dismounted, so did Chase, the foreman.

"Shit, the baby's back again." One of the Indians started right in.

"He looks shorter than he did last year, I bet his mom weaned him and he got stunted" The other added.

"We'll have to get some little ponies so he can ride with us." The first one laughed, not to be outdone. The ribbing was good natured, all last winter they gave me shit about being young and short. We shook hands. "Which one are you?" I asked, "All you Indians look the same to me." I wanted to get at least one jab in and that was all I could think of. It was good to see them, they weren't mean, but they sure liked to tease me.

Chase came up, shook my hand, "Glad to see you, we can use your help." With formalities over they put their horses up and we got ready for dinner.

The days got shorter and colder. A cold and wet weather system went through, keeping us miserable for half a week. The cold wind, full of snow, finds every little opening onto your skin and into your clothes. Try as you might by the end of the day you are just plain cold.

With six inches of snow on the ground the weather finally warmed up to a little over freezing and the snow got sticky, perfect for snowballs, if you were inclined, which I wasn't. It was grief for the horses interestingly enough. It would ball up in their shoes, packing tightly on the bottom of their feet until it felt like they were walking on baseballs. Most times they would come loose and fly off but on rare occasions the rider would have to dismount and pry the hard-packed ball of snow loose with a pocketknife. A pain in the ass but you had to do it. You could tell as you were riding, the horse's leg would wobble when he stepped on it.

A week later the snow was mostly melted, the ground wet and a hard freeze came along. The next morning all five of us were working a small bunch of cattle on an alkali flat. The four of us holding them in a loose bunch while Chase would work out a steer that would be headed to market at some later time. This is much easier done in corrals, but we were buckaroos and this is what we got paid for. By mid-morning the sun came out and started to thaw the first inch of slippery mud. The herd was done being held by the four of us and wanted out. One would make a break for it, one of us would try to head it off, as the horse and cow both would try to turn or stop it would realize too late how slick the ground was. Like one inch of grease on top of ice, impossible. Many times we all went down, horses and riders sliding an incredible distance across the desert floor. To watch this became a comedy. Ourselves, our horses and saddles so covered in slick, slimy mud, that clung to everything. Finally, Chase called a halt. We lost more cattle than we could hold and the rest were going at their own whim.

Riding back to the ranch we spent part of the afternoon washing horses, saddles, clothes and ourselves. The rest we spent drinking coffee, bullshitting and smoking cigarettes. Rare to have this much idle time while the sun was still shining. The new cowboy rarely said a word unless asked a direct question. Very even-tempered, in fact never showing any emotion, be it joy or anger. Medium height, middle age, thin face, large hooked nose with a generous bushy mustache. Dark complexion, deeply lined face. Damn good horseman, he liked working with the younger horses. He was good with them, his quiet easy temperament well suited to helping the young horses become good dependable working stock. I learned a lot from him that winter, how important it was to be consistent. What was bad behavior today will still be bad tomorrow.

The days took on a pleasant monotony. The weather was cold but stayed mostly clear. There is no sky as clear and brilliant as the desert on a cool day. No haze, no smog, visibility that went on for incredible distances. These were heady days for me, I was treated as a grown man, in spite of the Indians calling me baby or little boy or shorty. It was fine, just their way of passing time.

One morning Chase sent the new cowboy and myself to a valley over a mountain range. There were a couple dozen head that had wandered onto a neighbor's permit. We loaded our horses onto an old stock truck, grabbed our lunches and left, planning on returning that evening. We drove around the end of the mountain range, using a good two hours driving thirty miles. We spotted them at the base of the mountains where a canyon held promise of water. We unloaded our horses, tightened our cinches and trotted in a long circle, hoping to start them moving along the base of the mountain range. Things went to hell rapidly, a mile away and they spotted us. Heads up and tails up they took off into a wash that lead from the main canyon. If they started down the wash it would be okay. We got to the edge and spotted them going up the canyon. We both broke into a hard run and tried to get ahead of them so we could turn them back down. The canyon narrowed quickly and became very rocky. These cattle were wild and fast; we were unable to get past them. Stopping our horses to let them blow and not run the cattle any more than necessary we resigned ourselves to following and just keeping them in sight.

I had a vague idea that this canyon would lead us over the mountain range and onto the proper permit area. There were remnants of an old cat road along the bottom and we followed that. This wasn't the way we would have chosen, a long torturous winding path with frozen puddles of water that the animals broke through on occasion. We let them drink, along with our horses, when they could. By late afternoon it got very cold, the sun so low we never saw it again. We had enough clothes so we wouldn't freeze but it would be a long miserable night, and it was. Just before dark we ate our meager sandwiches knowing full well we would be hungry and cold by morning. We were buckaroos and never thought about leaving them and simply going home, it was our job to get them onto our ranch's permitted area and that's all there was to it. There was enough moonlight so at least we had decent visibility and could keep track of the animals. We would get off and walk on several occasions to get the blood back into our legs and warm up. Our reins were frozen stiff as cables by now but it didn't matter, they remained on our horse's neck, they simply walked behind us.

Sometime after midnight we crested the summit and started down the other side. The cattle wanted to stop but we kept driving them onward, this was easy in the narrow confines. By now we were both shivering with cold on occasion. We never spoke, no need, no complaining, just two buckaroos doing their job. The shivering and frozen fingers made it impossible to roll a smoke. Only one remedy, dismounting we would remove our gloves and put our hands between the hind legs of our horses, a tricky maneuver if they didn't want you to do it. Not something you would with a horse that was prone to kicking. When it worked it worked well but would burn your fingers until they started warming. Luckily, both our horses were older and had been down this road many times and gave us no trouble.

You can sleep in a saddle if things remain calm, we both would have little naps as our horses walked along trailing the cattle. Finally, the cold arousing us we would dismount, walk a while, roll a smoke and ride again to repeat the cycle. It was one of the longest, coldest nights of my life.

We came out of the canyon on the proper side of the mountain range and left the small herd to itself. It was still dark as we headed north, back to the ranch about ten miles distant. Two hours later, just as the sun was sneaking over the horizon to the east we arrived, cold and hungry. Taking care of our horses we were just in time for breakfast, as we had hoped. Chase and the Indians quietly watched as we sat down to eat, knowing we would talk when it was time.

"They decided to come over the mountain instead of down the valley." The quiet man said. I had expected him to let me do the talking. "It was a perfect moonlit night so we just tagged along behind them." The longest speech ever from him. I had to grin at his understatement. They all looked at me, I nodded and started eating. No more needed saying.

The next month was spent doing regular ranch work, different horses, places and cattle but the work was familiar and satisfying. My mind constantly on the next trip to town for a few days off. I wondered if Judy would still be at the brothel but didn't have much hope of that.

Finally, the day arrived. We were driven to town, the trip taking way too long. Just like last time, the Indians gave me no end of bullshit. The main topic seemed to be whether larger softer titties were more preferable then smaller firm ones. This was discussed in great detail, with no real conclusion. I didn't care how big or small, hard or soft, they were all wonderful.

After the stop at the bank I was dropped off, one third of my paycheck in cash in my pocket. The others were going to their own destinations. Damn near running to the front door I paused, a wave of nervousness hitting me squarely in the stomach. Taking a few deep breaths, I tried to calm myself, not very successfully. With a nervous finger I pushed the bell and waited.

The same large clown-faced woman from last year opened the door, recognition dawned, with a smile she pulled me in by the arm, simple for her since she outweighed me at least by one hundred pounds. Inside she gave me hug, "I wondered if you were ever coming back." She held me at arm's length as she looked at me. "You don't look any older or bigger than last year."

"You look the same too." I replied, "maybe a little thinner." By now I knew the merits of telling a female they looked thinner.

"That's a damn lie and we both know it, but it's still nice to hear."

In the parlor she sat at the table with me, "I'll buy your first drink, after that you pay. I suppose you want the same arrangement as last year?" She poured as she asked.

I agreed and we made small talk for a little while. She informed me Judy had moved on, no further explanation. I tried in vain to focus on her but my eyes continuously shifted to the three women sitting on a large corner couch. One caught my eye, her gaze direct and penetrating. Before long she slowly walked over to our table, artfully dressed, knowing full well she had my attention. She was my height, long dark hair, small nose and full lips. Grey eyes, that bore right into me, she had a poise and confidence that I had not encountered before. I remembered my manners and stood up. She introduced herself as Elisabeth but said I could call her Beth, as she shook my hand, very formal. She must have been close to thirty years of age, it seemed a little odd for me to be with someone this old but her attractiveness calmed any apprehensions. A double stranded pearl necklace gave a certain elegance and suited her perfectly.

The madam got up and left with a grin on her face, her job completed. Beth and I sat down. Just her sitting was graceful, very erect, shoulders back, chin up and those damn eyes drilling right into me. I desperately wanted to check all of her, actually and brazenly stare at the important parts but I only dared go as far down as the pearl necklace. I was so out of my league, even I was aware of it.

"Would you care to buy me a drink," her voice clear and pure, asked as a legitimate question, no coyness.

"Can I see your titties?" This must have been one of the most ridiculous statements that ever crossed my lips. Stupid and unwarranted, crass and immature, it would haunt me for many years. My face turned red, embarrassed, wanting desperately to take them back. These words must have been forced from me, I would never have said them willingly.

"My.... impatient little fuck" She deadpanned, then tiny little crinkles appeared at the corner of her eyes, along with a slight grin. "Perhaps in time."

"I'm sorry, I have much better manners than that." I was serious, she knew it. That was one of very rare times she would use a swear word. But who the hell uses the word "Perhaps?"

Things got much better after that. Same arrangement as before, I was to remain in the room when other men were around, the madam did not want others to see me. This was no problem, Beth and I spent a lot of time in her room. She had a car so we would drive out into the desert and watch the day fade away as we drank and smoked. Sometimes we would do things that were illegal in most states, in and out of the bedroom.

She had a way of communicating that was pleasant and refreshing, mostly direct, not given to coyness or evasion. I learned so much from her. Once again I lay there, comfortable, a naked woman next to me, whiskey and smokes on the nightstand. Some people go to college and some go to whore-houses. With way too much smugness, I wondered who got the better deal. To this day I am still attracted to a pearl necklace. This must be what marriage is like, I pondered, naked bliss, sex available at any time.

The time was short, way too short. Knowing better, I still fell in love. Maybe not only with Beth, just the feeling that for a few days I didn't have to make any decisions, I was able to simply enjoy myself.

The ride back to the ranch was torture. The Indians knew I was depressed, and relentlessly gave me shit about being a baby and in love with a little triangle of fur. After a while, as all things do or because of them, I got back to being myself.

The next month went by without incident. One day Chase said he needed to drive the Indians to town for some business, I could come along or stay at the ranch for a day, maybe two and do whatever I wanted, they wouldn't dock my pay. I decided to stay.

The next morning, I told Chase I would ride the young bay and check the waterhole in Sage canyon, about twelve-fourteen miles away. He nodded in agreement and they left for town.

Putting the saddle on it was clear the horse didn't like me, okay by me, I didn't like him much either. Twice before I had been on his back all day, rough gaited and stubborn I didn't think he would make a very dependable mount, Chase already mentioned they may get rid of him, nobody wanted an animal that was hard headed.

We covered a lot of ground in a trot, a hard horse to sit well, my insides took a beating as the miles rolled under us. I kept thinking how big this country was, right in the middle of Nevada, there probably wasn't another human within fifty miles of the main ranch.

My mind filled with many thoughts, mainly naked women and how I should have gone with the others to town and spent at least one day at the whorehouse. The fruit had been sampled and it was addictive.

Almost to the canyon mouth an outcropping of rock caught my attention, some interesting colors held promise of something, maybe. With time to kill and me being curious we trotted over. Just before getting close a dozen or so chukars started running across the desert floor, dodging sagebrush. I pulled my custom shotgun, a loaner from one of the Indians, the barrel and stock both cut short, much better for a saddle gun and it fit into most scabbards. Gun always loaded, I kicked the horse into a fast lope, intent on catching them and having some fresh chukar breast, a fine treat cooked over an open fire.

It was going well, right into the middle of them I was tracking one just as he started coming around and heading in front of my horse, then things went very bad. My horse's front leg hit a badger hole, his head went down and to the side, just as my mind screamed "Don't pull the trigger" my finger squeezed, the noise was deafening, my horse went down, a total collapse, pretty close to his head I thought, as I went flying through a red mist. It may have been accidental, a tightening of my finger muscles as my horse tripped, whatever the reason the horse paid dearly. I landed hard, right into a dead sagebrush, dry and brittle, a thousand pokes, none serious. I rolled several times, knowing I was in front of the horse and hoping he wouldn't run over me. I needn't have worried.

I stood up and checked myself for any major damage, clothes a little torn up, a few cuts and soon to be bruises, mostly okay. I picked up the shotgun as I walked back to my horse, the gun was dirty but otherwise unharmed. Not the horse, one ear almost blown off along with the last inch or two off the top of his head, I think it may have been fatal, the pool of blood collecting under his neck which happened to be bent backwards at an impossible angle made it certain. I knew he was dead, the one eye on the high side was beginning to glaze over. For some stupid reason I checked his front leg to see if it was broken, it didn't appear to be.

I gazed down at him, telling myself over and over, "Damn, I shot my horse. Damn, I shot my horse." I tried replaying the sequence in my mind, short replay and always with the same ending. Battered and bruised, a little pissed because now I had to walk back to the ranch, I sat on his shoulder and rolled a smoke, intrigued by the head wound. I didn't have any feelings about the horse one way or the other, just something to ride. I got my canteen off the saddle, luckily on the high side, undid the cinch and worked at getting my saddle free, it was a struggle getting the stirrup and cinch out from under him. That done I left the gun with the saddle, took a last look at the dumb shit that caused all this and started walking.

Dark before I got to the ranch but enough light to walk by. The others were not back from town so I had the bunkhouse to myself. Washed up and went to bed, sore, tired and hungry, but still much better off than the horse. They returned later that night.

The next morning at breakfast Chase asked how my day went.

"Not so good. We were loping along and he hit a badger hole and went down. I think he broke his neck. He's laying out in the desert, dead, I'll have to go back and get my saddle. I was trying to act put out.

Chase seemed ambivalent about the whole thing. "He wasn't worth a shit anyway." That was the end of it, I didn't offer any other details. I took another horse out bareback and retrieved my things.

Another month went by, the only break being on Saturday evening when we would all sit around in the bunk house listening to "America's Polka King" Frankie Yankovic and his Polka band. I enjoyed it, I felt part of a fraternity of sorts, I was at home.

The end of March came and Chase sat next to me one evening and we had a smoke together. Unusual, he mostly stayed to himself. It was pleasant, we didn't talk, just sat and smoked for a while, by now I knew enough to follow his lead.

"I know it's time for you to head home in a few days. I've got your money, but I want you to take my truck, I don't need it anymore and I'd like you to have it. Let's go take a look." He got up and started walking without even waiting for a response.

A 1949 Chevy ¾ ton with stock racks. He explained it burned quite a bit of oil but thought I should make it home, or at least most of the way. The battery was dead or almost, it wouldn't start the motor. No problem he assured me, we could push it to start and it would be fine as long as I didn't turn it off.

The next three days we worked cattle around the ranch so the days were easy. One of the ranch dogs had a litter of pups a while ago and they were well weaned and on their way to being working dogs. The new cowboy started training one of them and had us put some small rocks in our pockets. As we would leave the ranch on our horses in the morning the pup was unsure which horse to follow. If he stayed with the wrong horse, the rider would throw some rocks at him and he would eventually follow the right horse. Simple and effective, unless you were the dog, but he learned quickly and we were careful not to throw hard.

The morning to leave came. Chase put some gas in the truck as I loaded my horse. I thanked him for the kind gesture. I was a little sad to be leaving the ranch. Chase didn't look real healthy of late and I hoped he would take care of himself but I didn't say anything. One of the Indians came up with one of the young dogs. He said I needed something to take my mind off titties. I told him that dreaming of titties was a fine thing and I didn't need or want a dog. He just grinned and put the dog and a small bag of dry food for him in the cab.

Good-byes said and everything loaded they gave me a push with another pickup and I was on my way in a cloud of blue smoke. The truck ran well enough, the dog lay on the floor board on the passenger side and my horse was doing well in the back. It was a calm day and I left a trail of dust and smoke for several miles behind me.

The road was rough and bumpy, I drove slow to make it easier on my horse, I named the dog Smokey number two, as we crept along.

By mid-afternoon I was getting concerned about the oil in my motor. Cresting a hill, I pulled over alongside the road on a steep downhill. Turning the engine off I let the dog out as I checked the oil. Nothing on the dipstick. I added the one quart that I had. Still nothing on the stick. Nothing to be done, must have burned more oil than anyone thought it would.

I unloaded my horse, loaded my stuff and we headed out, dog following, twenty miles from home. Not bad, I thought, be home before bedtime. It was a pleasant ride; the temperature was comfortable and I sang as we went along. The house was fine, spent a nice night in my own bed.

The next morning, I loaded up five quarts of oil and left on Pinto. The truck was where I had left it. It took three more quarts. I loaded Pinto and closed the loading ramp. The truck rolled downhill at a good clip, I popped the clutch, the engine took off in cloud of blue smoke once again and I drove home, ready for another summer at my ranch.

Damn, I Shot My Horse

FRUSTRATIONS

I had no idea what day of the week it was, just that it was around the first of April, didn't matter anyway. The next morning was spent checking the windmill and water supply, all was well, so I serviced the tractor and my pickup most of the day. The old International flatbed was gone, I had no idea where it was, but my father's pickup that he used to drive back and forth to Sacramento was sitting in the driveway. Smokey number two followed me around most times then lay down in some shade that afternoon.

I heard a truck coming, looking up I spotted the flatbed loaded with an old John Deere tractor coming into the driveway. I watched as it came to a stop in the yard. My father and another man I didn't know exited the cab.

"Thought you'd come back sometime," he mumbled gruffly. I wasn't sure if he was happy or disappointed, no way to tell. "Brought you a tractor."

So much for formalities. With that both of them took a swallow of whiskey and started to undo the chains that held the tractor.

"Better back up to the ramp before you loosen the chains." Sound advice, I thought, but it fell on deaf ears. They ignored me. I studied the tractor, or more correctly the antique. Front wheels made of iron, rear wheels also, but they had five-inch metal lugs spaced all the way around. Two-cylinder engine that lay horizontal. No hydraulics for implements, it could only pull something, with no control over what you were pulling. It was better suited for some antique dealer's garage somewhere. The best to be said, no flats.

"Back it up to the ramp, be damn careful not to dump it off." I could only smile as my father cautioned me. This done we stepped onto the bed of the truck. "I'll show you how to start it." As he stood there looking at it, trying to remember. It was complicated, no starter. You primed the cylinders with gas in little cups. Then you grabbed the large heavy flywheel on the side of the motor, brought it around to compression and gave it a hard tug. Many attempts later it coughed, sputtered then settled into a very loud popping rhythm, blowing an endless stream of white smoke rings out the exhaust.

"Back it off and let's hook it up to the drag," he pointed in a general direction. I had no idea what he was talking about. As I was figuring out the transmission pattern looking for reverse, they both took another swallow of whiskey from a bottle in a paper sack, and walked off with a purpose.

I carefully backed it off the truck, the clutch was on a long lever run by hand, this took some getting used to. I followed them, seeing the drag, it looked heavy. That fifty yards was an incredibly rough ride on those iron wheels. I stopped the tractor, leaving it idling and walked over to where they were studying the drag. Two large bridge beams with three heavy beams as cross-members. All the bottom surfaces covered in angle iron. Two cables with eyes in the end leading from the front, obviously for connecting it to the tractor. I backed up and they connected the cables to the draw-bar. With the tractor in low gear I crept ahead to take the slack out. That done I engaged the clutch fully and the drag moved ahead, the old tractor barely able to pull it. The first little hill stopped us cold, wheels spinning, quickly digging a hole. I backed out of the hole and tried pulling at a different angle with even less success. Clearly the tractor was no match for this drag that was designed to level mounds and fill voids by sheer pulling force. Leaving the tractor idling I got off and walked over to where my father and the other man were studying this failure.

"Any ideas?" I asked, in a muted tone, trying to avoid seeming confrontational. It didn't work.

"Don't be a smart ass. You'll have to adjust it and learn how to drive." He glared at me, as if I was responsible for every failure. With that statement they walked back to the house, leaving me standing there, no invitation to join them. I wasn't upset, just another hurdle in a life with many hurdles it seemed. More accusations and ridicule thrown at me by my alcoholic father, I must be developing very thick skin, or losing any sense of what was normal, I had no yardstick to go by so I just made my own.

With no desire to dwell on that train of thought, I studied the drag. There was nothing to adjust, but I knew that already, it was simply built too heavy for the tractor that we had. I unhooked, drove the tractor to the shop and turned it off, a welcome silence from the loud sharp popping of the exhaust.

I didn't want to be around my father so I found things to occupy myself, mostly thinking on the situation at hand and how to remedy it, as I petted my dog and enjoyed a smoke.

The setting sun and my growling stomach eventually forced me into the house. The other two had already eaten so I heated a can of something, ate from the pan and washed all the dishes. With no way around it I joined them in the living room, poured a small amount of whiskey into a cup and pretended I was one of them, trying to join in the conversation. They didn't include or exclude me, mostly ignored me. I gave up and simply went to bed for lack of anything else. I was reading a good book anyway.

My mind wouldn't turn off for a long time that evening. I felt as if I were the only one feeling the pressure from the looming deadline that we would be facing in three more years. BLM would not give us the patent to the land if the requirements were not met in time. Only one of the three had been met so far, the dwelling. The well and twenty acres under cultivation seemed impossible under the current situation. I desperately needed one piece of equipment that would be suitable for land leveling, a bulldozer would be the best. Impervious to flats, it would make short work of the mounds of dirt that plagued and frustrated me so.

The next morning, I approached my father with the idea of getting a Cat so I would be able to make some headway on land leveling. Trying to keep it in a conversational tone so I wouldn't seem demanding proved in vain. It not only met a gruff resistance, it was deemed totally out of the question. Money being the number one reason, plus there was enough equipment to do the job.

"How many damn tractors do you need?" It was an accusation not a question. The anger becoming visible by the redness in his face. I pushed no further, having learned over the years to be quiet and get away from him when he became like this.

I went outside and finally got the John Deere started, hoping he might join me and demonstrate how best to make this work. I rolled a smoke, petted my dog and waited for them to come outside. They didn't join me for whatever reason so I drove over to the disk and hooked onto that. I was able to pull it as long as it remained mostly closed. This did nothing but cut the sagebrush into smaller pieces, much like doing dishes without water in the sink, I didn't care, I simply wanted to being doing something.

Within an hour, I spotted the long plume of dust announcing their departure. Not so much as a "Goodbye" or even a "Kiss my ass." What used to evoke a pang of loneliness was more and more turning into a sense of relief.

I wasn't bothered by their leaving. It was an ideal day, sun shining, moderate temperature, brilliant blue sky and enough moisture in the soil to keep the dust low. Every time the old tractor hit a rock with its rear wheel it would almost catapult me from the hard iron seat, annoying, but not enough to dampen my spirits.

I drove round and round, burning fuel and turning large sagebrush into smaller pieces of sagebrush. I was thinking about the future, the looming deadline from BLM. For some reason I was optimistic, the well would simply be a matter of money, and the twenty acres in production a simple matter of time and perseverance. I didn't think I was being naive; I simply knew I would get it done. It felt good having that much confidence.

After lunch I used the other tractor to drive and pick the larger rocks displaced from the disk. Throwing them into the bucket of the loader, it was simple work. Fill the bucket, drive over to the edge and dump them. By evening a good size pile had built up. I quit for the day, hungry, dirty, tired but happy. Not sure what tomorrow would bring.

The next morning. I noticed my dog was gone. I wasn't very concerned since he sometimes went exploring by himself.

This day was a repeat of the day before. That evening the ranch neighbor ten miles to the north came driving in, we learn to recognize vehicles as readily as faces.

"Your dog showed up at our ranch this morning, thought you might be worried and want him back." With that he handed me the piece of twine that was attached to my dogs' neck.

I invited him to stay for a cup of coffee, he declined. I thanked him and apologized for the inconvenience. I was a little embarrassed for not having better control of my dog.

I tied him up in the shop and set about building a dog house. I took my time and spent the better part of two days building one that looked proper. I tied him to it with a long chain. As he lay there dejected with a chain around his neck, damned if the same neighbors' two dogs didn't show up. I looked around for the owners but soon realized it was just the dogs. They came to me easy enough so I tied them in the back of my truck and hauled them to the neighbor's ranch. Returning the favor helped ease my conscious about dog control. One was a terrier and the other a heeler. The heeler was a bitch and in heat, the terrier was cut. My dog was an uncut male, how he knew there was a female in heat ten miles away was a mystery that would remain unsolved forever.

The rancher was like me, not too happy about his dogs causing other people problems. With that done I returned to my ranch.

The next morning, I untied my dog, thinking he would follow me around for the day. I didn't like keeping a dog tied up. He followed me around until mid-morning sometime when I noticed he was gone. I wasn't too worried, figuring I would drive to the neighbor's ranch the next day if he didn't show up.

I was just getting ready to drive north when my neighbor and his wife drove up. They asked if I had seen their dogs. I told them no and asked if they had seen mine. They also answered no. This was odd, the dogs could easily cover the distance in two hours so they should be at one place or the other. We agreed to keep our eyes open and let the other person know if they showed up somewhere. With that they left. She loved her dogs and seemed very concerned. I was the opposite, I was tired of this crap and didn't really care if my dog ever showed up.

I got my wish. None of them ever showed up anywhere. I was fine with that but the neighbors' wife came by several times the next week to check. She was very upset. I think she may have wondered if I had shot all three of them but she never voiced this, so it is only speculation. I felt bad for her.

One evening a man stopped by the ranch. His name was Bart, short blonde hair hidden under a baseball cap. He was a very large man, not only in height but also in girth, jovial and middle aged. He asked if I had a month's time and if I did would I be interested in helping him drive a tunnel at the mine several miles from our place. I told him I did and I would, adding I did have some experience with mining.

I started the next morning, glad for the break from going in circles, accomplishing very little in the field. It was hard dirty work. I was a "chuck tender." More commonly called a driller's helper.

We would drill a series of twenty-six holes eight feet deep, then load them with dynamite. The first stick would have the blasting cap, I would slide it all the way into the back of the hole, then compact it tightly and carefully with a wooden tamping rod. Then slide several more, compacting them carefully also. The fuses were burn type and had to be cut and ignited in a certain order to ensure the proper sequence of explosion. We would spend the next several days mucking out the rubble. This process was repeated over and over, the tunnel lengthening with each successive shot.

The worst part was starting the hole with the Jack-leg. I would hold the end of the drill steel against the rock face to keep it from wandering. Bart would open the air and water, the drill would hammer and rotate, spraying me with bits of rock and drenching me. Once the bit was in several inches I could let go and stand back until it was time to collar the next hole. He would let me run the drill many times so I was able to gain experience. I enjoyed it considerably. Bart was easy to be around, nothing seemed to upset him. Very vocal, constantly giving advice on things to watch for, smiling, thumping me on the shoulder with the back of his hand if he was empathizing something. It was good natured but he was a large man and if I wasn't prepared it would knock me off balance, which he did many times.

He lived at the mine in his small trailer while I stayed at my house but we spent the evenings together. He would tell tales of his mining exploits, some of which were in foreign countries under harsh conditions. I had a suspicion many of his stories may have been embellished but they were enjoyable to listen to.

My father came on one of the weekends and seemed quite content to have me gainfully employed. Indifferent to what I was doing he came and went with little fanfare.

Three weeks of driving tunnel went by. Bart informed me the next day we could expect company in the form of two men whom were financing this exploration. The next morning. they arrived well dressed and driving a brand new pickup. He introduced me as if I were of some importance. They were cordial but more interested in how their money was being spent. I left them to wander into the tunnel with Bart, him being very animated and full of promises, untold wealth just waiting for us to find it.

I found something to occupy myself, as they stayed in the mine for a good hour. Bart must have been very convincing, I even believed him. Shaking hands, assuring us there would be plenty of money to continue they left in very good spirits and a cloud of dust. I didn't see the backhanded thump coming in time. Delivered with lots of enthusiasm and a broad smile that showed several of his missing teeth, it knocked me several feet to the side. "We've got it dicked now." He laughed, unaware that I was rubbing my shoulder.

Another week of hard work. One evening Bart announced we would be going to Reno the next day to take a break and enjoy ourselves for a few days. I was ready for something different.

With a duffel bag of clean clothes, we drove to Reno, stopping at a bank where Bart got some money to pay me. It was a lot for one month's work but he seemed glad to give it to me. "It's not mine and you earned it. You won't need to spend your money. The next few days will be paid for by the company." I dodged most of the thump that I knew would follow this announcement, but his humor was infectious. I didn't really understand who the "Company" was or why they should pay for my expenses but I left well enough alone.

We checked into a large casino with rooms. We didn't share a room, Bart saying we might have need of some privacy, and money wasn't an issue, plus this would all be on a tab that would be paid for by the "Company." That word again.

After a late dinner we went to the lounge to relax and have a drink. In spite of our objections the bartender wouldn't serve me any alcohol but said I could sit in the lounge with a Coke or other non-alcoholic drink. That was fine with me, if needed I could go to my room and have a drink of whiskey, or sneak a pint in my coat pocket and pour it into my Coke.

The lounge was mostly empty with only a few men sitting at other tables, engaged in private conversations. I took notice of the lounge singer, accompanied by a piano. Late thirties, medium height, long clinging dress, mid-length dark hair. Attractive, not beautiful but good looking in a wholesome way, not making an effort to be a seductress, simply to entertain. Her music was soft, her voice mellow and pleasant.

Bart left me, bored and wanting more excitement, he said we would meet in the morning for breakfast. I sat for another hour, very content to listen to her sing.

Her break came and she walked to my table, asking if she could sit and join me. I was surprised, then realized I was the only person sitting alone. I stood and introduced myself, remembering my manners and shaking her hand. We were both friendly, if a little polite, just two people with no one else to sit with. She was more relaxed than myself, with her ready smile and easy going nature I soon felt at ease and we engaged in comfortable conversation. Nothing too personal, vague outlines of past and present. She was on her way to central California, stopping in Reno and earning some extra money. Married and divorced, no children. Simple, devoid of any coyness, engagingly direct.

She looked at her watch and stood up. "I've enjoyed you. I can come back on my next break if you're still here, if not take care of yourself." With those words she made her way back to the piano. I didn't know what to think, it sounded like someone telling their mechanic they would be back later to pick up their automobile. No hidden meanings or suggestions. Of course I sat there and waited, I was a male.

I sat there and enjoyed her singing, watching people come and go. She came and sat with me again. We talked for a while longer but the hour was getting late and I was having trouble staying awake. The hotel furnished her a room but she didn't invite me to share it with her. I sensed several times she was on the verge of inviting me up but then would change her mind. She did however invite me to go for a ride with her to see Lake Tahoe the next day. With that we went to our separate rooms.

She knocked on my door at ten the next morning, I was ready to go. She let me drive her Mustang. I am not very good at letting a woman drive while I sit in the passenger seat, I don't think that had ever happened.

It was one of those days that you don't want to end. When not on stage she was much more open about herself, relaxed, she enjoyed laughing. We swam in the lake in our underwear at a secluded little cove, the water was too damn cold to really enjoy it but she was easy to look at. I bought her lunch and filled her car with gas, I had plenty of money and she was well worth it.

She worked from six to midnight at the lounge so I walked downtown Reno for several hours that evening, not wanting to sit that long waiting for her. It was nice to be around people even though I only observed them, it was entertaining and time filling.

Bart came in and sat with me for a while as I waited for Alice to finish. "She keeps looking at you." He observed with a grin.

"You're going to drill that aren't you." A little crude but after several drinks it was tame for him and I wasn't offended.

"Easy to look at and a nice voice." I answered noncommittally.

"We'll head back in two days so good luck." He slurred just a little. I could see the arm getting ready to thump me on the shoulder as a good luck gesture, it looked like it might be a good one. Luckily I moved just enough and his aim was off.

"Let's go to my room." Finished for the night she didn't sit, no pretense, just assumed I would. Is it me or all men that easy, I wondered as I hastily stood and walked out with her.

It was damned nice. We spent the nights as two people would when naked and in bed. During the day we would drive around and see some sights. It didn't bother me that she was old enough to be my mother, inside I may have been a little proud. Maybe I was drawn to older women. Whatever the case I think we both understood this was temporary, a brief joy-filled interlude. No expectations, no fraudulent promises, no lies. Two people simply enjoying what was unexpectedly given them.

The morning of departure I didn't sneak out. It was a melancholy kiss as we said goodbye.

I met Bart and we left after breakfast. He had several Bloody Marys with his food. His eyes were bloodshot and he didn't look well. The ride back to the mine was quiet, I think his head hurt.

He dropped me off at my ranch saying he was taking his trailer and leaving for several weeks to another job that was pressing. He would return and we might do some more mining if I was around.

I never saw him again, or his investors. Somehow this felt a little like a scam. Work hard, get someone to believe in you and give you money in return for promised riches. Take some of the money and run. Another lesson in life.

The creek that fed the reservoir was not running anymore. The rains had been too few and it only ran half way to the property and receded as the weeks went by. The reservoir was only half full. Barely into June and the weather seemed hotter and drier than in previous years. Nothing to be done. Luckily there were no crops dependent on irrigation.

The water tank that serviced the house was showing signs of running out shortly. Maybe another week. The windmill seemed fine but with no wind it was useless.

The next morning, I drove to town and bought groceries. Stopping at a salvage yard produced a pump-jack in excellent condition. I purchased that, then drove to the farm supply store and bought a new five-horse gas motor, along with pulleys and belts. This took most of the money from my mining job but I felt good about spending it on these items. Lunch and a barrel of gas finished my money and the day. I still had plenty of money in my checking account so I wasn't concerned.

The next several days were spent pouring a small concrete slab and installing the pump-jack and gas motor. Fortunately, any problems that arose were solved easily enough.

When it was complete I unhooked the sucker rod from the windmill, hooked the pump-jack to the rod, started the motor and very soon I could hear water running into the tank. A welcome sound. I was a day or two from running out. I was no longer dependent on the mercy of the wind gods.

That evening one of the neighbors from the settlement came driving in with two other men. Introductions were made. The two men were from a Southern California university doing some geophysical exploration for an oil company. One had his doctorate and one was working on his. They came to do some seismic work and asked if I would be interested in setting out the seismic phones and doing the blasting. They asked if I was comfortable with explosives. Somehow they knew I had used them before. I assured them I was comfortable and I would be happy for the work.

It was in a remote valley to the south of us and we would work nonstop for about a month. They would furnish me with a tent and food but I would have to cook for myself as would they. I agreed easily and we settled on a price for thirty days' work. I was to meet them the following Monday morning and drive the equipment van to the job site.

The invitation for coffee was declined, they had too much work in preparation plus it was a business arrangement not a social visit. They seemed happy as they drove off but I think I got the better of the deal, I was always in favor of making money.

It was the middle of the week and I was very surprised to see my parents drive in. They seemed in exceptionally good spirits, particularly my father. After greetings they announced we were to have a house-warming party that weekend. The square dance caller and all the settlement, along with lots of people from town were to show up. Their excitement was infectious; I also became wrapped up in preparations. I pumped water until the tank was completely full. Both my parents watched the little motor as it ran the pump, my mother vocal about her pride in me, my father just cracked a slight smile and didn't say a word. It was enough.

That Saturday evening people began to arrive. Some of them I knew and some I didn't. The boys my age from the settlement, a couple with girlfriends and a couple without, also came. It had the promise of a very festive evening. A couple from town with their very cute daughter showed up. I didn't know them but they knew people from the settlement and I welcomed them. We introduced ourselves, I couldn't remember their names but it was easy to remember hers, Ivana. The music started much earlier than predicted, people must have been eager, I certainly was. There must have been sixty people, with more still arriving.

I watched Ivana covertly for several moments as she walked around with her parents, greeting people they knew. Very cute and fun to watch. Beautiful smile, short dark hair cut long on the sides and short in the back. A bare- shoulder top with straps and short skirt, perfect for a summer evening. My age, or maybe a year older. She exuded health and vitality along with a strong air of self-confidence.

Not wanting to waste any time I walked directly to her and asked if she would like to dance. We became inseparable.

The evening was just beginning and we danced straight for the next half hour. Mostly square dancing but sometimes the caller would put on a record with a slow song and we would hold each other tight.

Taking a break from the dancing we procured a pint of White Horse Scotch for ourselves off the table that held dozens of bottles of assorted alcohol. We sat outside on the porch swing, alone, talking and taking sips of Scotch. We stashed the bottle and resumed dancing. This pattern repeated for the next several hours, the dancing taking less time, we spent more of our precious moments on the porch swing embracing and sipping from our bottle.

Every two hours I had to put more gas into the generator tank as it ran. Ivana would hold the flashlight as I poured, she would start to giggle for some reason and I would have to stop pouring until I became steady again. We felt like conspirators but had no reason.

We danced some more and so did everyone else. No one paid us any particular attention, there was no need. It was a festive fun-filled evening, made so much the better because of Ivana. We had nothing in common except our youth and the future. We didn't care, we were young and making plans.

The night was going by way too fast. We were a little drunk but mostly giddy. We made many vows and promises to one another. Chastity, celibacy, honesty, faithfulness, we used words that weren't even clear to us, the list was endless. We promised our children would be the most loving and precious and best looking of all the children in the world as they frolicked through endless fields of grass on our ranch. It was heady stuff. The words of two young people hopelessly in love, fueled by time constraints. Mostly, I fear, it was fueled by the Scotch. Our words were sincere, so honestly and passionately given and received. She promised to write me a letter every day, to remind me of these words, to remind me of her. I explained I would be gone and out of touch for a month, a response would be impossible but I would devour and cherish every letter she wrote when I returned. I vowed to her I would never need reminding; she would be forever in my thoughts. We embraced and made more vows as we tilted the bottle to our lips.

The party lasted much longer than anticipated. It was still way too short. Her parents came to collect her as we knew they eventually would. They were very gracious and understanding. Inviting me to their house at any time it would be convenient for me, they sounded sincere. I accepted with gratitude. Ivana and I had both promised to remain stoic and resolute when the moment of separation came. We did not want to appear weak and childish as we parted. Her last words, "I'll write every day."

The next day my mom made breakfast for a dozen people who stayed over for the night, either in tents they had brought or just on cots outside. We all cleaned up the mess from the night before. My head felt tender but not overly so. Memories of the night spent dancing and just the company of Ivana was an excellent salve.

That afternoon everyone left. One of the few times my father left in a pleasant mood, with an actual good-bye to me. I felt lonely, the last twenty-four hours a whirlwind of activity then absolute silence. I got my stuff ready for the next morning. My head filled with thoughts of Ivana as I drifted off to sleep.

Dropping my pickup off at the settlement where Petre', the

head geophysicist and his associate Justin were staying. I drove the van with the equipment to the camp site. Petre' and Justin had already left the day before with a pickup load of water for us and another pickup loaded with all the food and camping gear for the month.

I arrived shortly before lunch. We had a sandwich then promptly drove to a predetermined location and started setting the seismic phones across the desert. Each one a little larger than a football, we would dig a hole and bury it completely until it was covered with about four inches of dirt. There were eight of them about fifty feet apart connected with a cable. We set three rows of them in a pattern then hooked the leads to some sort of graph machine in the van.

The next day they showed me how set the explosives. The powder came in one pound cans made by DuPont. The cap was threaded and screwed into the bottom of another can, each can had a threaded cap and receptacle in the bottom. It was possible to make an endless line, if one desired.

For our purposes I would normally put six of them in a row. The cans would then be attached to a metal fence post driven into the ground. Sometimes one post would have three rows of six each. Other times there would be as many as six posts with eighteen cans each, set in a very specific pattern. These would make a huge mushroom cloud when set off. The caps were electric, detonated with a plunger at a safe distance.

I was not involved in the pattern making decisions. Petre' or Justin would draw a diagram and I would follow it. After a shot they would spend the next several days analyzing the data, as I set up the next round and buried the phones in a different location.

I really enjoyed this work. Left alone to carry out my instructions, in touch via handheld radio to set off the explosives at their command. Many times we would delay the shot. A plane or truck driving on the highway many miles away would register on the seismic phones.

In the evenings I would sit and listen to them discuss the technical aspects of our shots and their conclusions. I understood very little of it. Just normal conversation, college, their lives in California were interesting and held my attention. Well educated, they used words that I sometimes recognized but had no idea of their meaning. I borrowed a dictionary from them and would look up the words when I could remember them. They would sometimes explain in more depth when I developed a glazed, lost look.

By early summer, the job ended. They paid me and we went our separate ways. I returned home to an empty house.

Early the next morning I was anxious to get the letters from Ivana that I knew waited for me in the mail box. My horse was handy and it was a beautiful day so I chose to ride instead of drive. Four hours and fifteen miles later I opened the mailbox door and there were seventeen letters waiting, I counted them, tempted to read them there. Putting my impatience aside I rode home. I wanted to enjoy them at leisure, with a cup of coffee and a smoke.

My horse put away and a fresh cup at my side, I rolled a smoke and started to read, starting with the first post mark.

Two pages of endearments and professed love made me want to forget the rest and just drive to town and see her. The next three were along the same lines, painting pictures of a blissful future.

After several more I detected a hint of doubt about my sincerity since there was no response from me. I had told her that communication of any form would be impossible for at least a month, it simply could not be. Maybe she would remember, I hopefully thought those words.

It was not to be. The letters continued to become more negative, spiraling into accusations of deceptions.

The last letter, was hard to read. My coffee now bitter and a knot in my stomach, I finished reading. She accused me of being an ass and a liar. Worse than any other boy she had ever met. In no uncertain terms she was finished with me and never wanted to see me again.

I sat there stunned, hurt, and a little angry. Wondering how I went from being almost married with children to a sad pathetic example of a loser.

I didn't know what to do. I did nothing but mope the rest of the day, mired in a wallow of self-pity.

The next morning was better. Another day that promised to be a perfect late spring day in the desert. Cool crisp night with warm sun filled days. The tractor with the loader had a leak on one of the hydraulic cylinders so I spent most of the day fixing that. I thought about driving to town in an attempt to patch things with Ivana. The last letter however, gave me little hope that things would improve if I met with her, I left it alone.

Later that afternoon the air became very still and muggy. It felt reminiscent but I couldn't put my finger on it. An hour before dark it all came back in the form of a huge black cloud rolling up the valley. I knew what was coming, a dark knot of fear took over. I was incapable of moving, transfixed as I watched it, remembering that night. That night that lasted forever with the howling demons shrieking in my ears. The night my tent flew apart, shredding me of the last vestige of protection and maybe my sanity. The night I cast God into the wind he created, hoping he would fly away into the very Hell he was tormenting me with. The night that lasted for days, becoming so covered in sand and gravel I thought I would surely be buried alive.

Sanity and the need for action shoved the fear to one side and I desperately began to prepare. First thing, completely turning off the windmill. Closing the shop doors, closing all the windows. Turning off the propane to the house. Laying heavy rocks on any loose pieces of plywood or metal. Opening the shop doors, I rolled three empty fifty gallon drums inside and closed the doors once more.

The front was only a mile to the south, the dark ominous cloud rising more than a mile into the sky. I stood outside and watched it come, hand on the open doorknob, ready to run inside, heart beating wildly as the roar preceded the wind by half a minute. I ran inside just as the house shook with the first gust.

In moments the house became dark, not total darkness, the sun had not yet completely set. It was a primordial darkness that your eyes see but your mind refuses to accept, it shouldn't be dark yet, not like this. You hold on to this thought deliberately, focusing on why it's getting dark, trying desperately to keep your mind on the hard science of cause and effect. I sat on the floor with my back against the rock fireplace, and rolled a smoke, difficult in the dark with shaking hands, but doable.

My thoughts were ripped from me as a howling, guttural roar came down the chimney. The ashes scattered on the floor and into the air. It sounded as if a freight train was rolling over the top of the house. I sat there on the floor, knees against my chest, hands over my ears.

I can take this I repeated to myself over and over, of course I could, there was no choice. Over the deep sonorous roar, I heard a new sound, barely discernible, the telltale metal staccato of loose roofing.

"Shit! shit! shit!" I muttered, then I screamed it loudly. Anger, fear, frustration, like three horses on a merry go round, each taking a turn, coming and going in an endless circle. With a shriek of protest, it let loose and flew off. Within minutes another rattle, faint, but a harbinger none the less. I could picture the scene, one corner of metal roofing that faced into the wind was slowly being ripped up from its nails, the loose portion growing larger as the wind gained an ever-increasing purchase. Even over the horrendous roar of the wind itself I could hear the shrieking of the remaining nails as the metal was ripped away, much like a woman might make as her baby was torn from her arms, a visceral, ear-piercing scream.

I sat there for hours, the horse of fear removed from the merry go round. Left now with only anger and frustration. There was no point in getting up, there was nothing to be done. I knew that as I listened to each piece of metal being ripped away. Four pieces per hour I figured, as I remained seated helplessly. If a heavy rain followed the wind we would sustain heavy damage to our new home, of course there was no insurance.

Sometime during the night the wind stopped almost completely. Only a gentle breeze evidenced by the rhythmic sound of a piece of metal still clinging to the rafters. I don't know if I was asleep but the silence was a welcome relief. It was still dark; no idea how much darkness was left. I lit a kerosene lamp and walked outside carefully. The light was too feeble to see anything so I went back inside, threw a sleeping bag on the floor and finished the night in restless fits, waiting for rain.

The rain never came; I was so grateful for that. With first light I went outside and checked for damage. A quarter of the roof was completely gone, several sheets of metal looked as if they could be nailed back into place. No other apparent damage. We still had plenty of metal to replace the missing portions. I had no hope whatsoever of finding any of the missing pieces. With that I went in, had some breakfast and spent the next four days replacing the metal and securing the remaining roof with more nails.

That evening as I finished the metal roof, my parents came driving in towing a horse trailer. We did our greetings. My mother had purchased a horse and was looking forward to doing some riding with me. A nice little sorrel gelding that she named

Sparky. Along with the horse, my two-year old niece Kerri. My mom and Kerri would spend the next four months at the ranch with me. I was glad for this development, I got along well with my mother and I wouldn't have to cook. I had never been around little children so this would be a new experience.

It was decided to build a corral, a two-stall barn and a small hay barn. We had plenty of material so it wouldn't cost anything and we could keep the horses close by.

My father left the next day so we started right into the project. We had some hay and used it to keep the horses around. Every few days my mother desired a ride. I would saddle her horse, Kerri and I would ride mine bareback with her sitting in front. I enjoyed these days. My mother loved to ride more than anything. Sometimes packing a lunch and riding for hours. Kerri loved it also, she was always happy and a joy to be around.

My eighteenth birthday came and for the first time that I can remember there was a cake. The three of us celebrated that evening, low key but fun none the less.

The weeks went by and we finished the corral and barns. Several weeks after my birthday the three of us drove to town and I registered with the Selective Service. The year was 1966, I knew the draft was calling up boys my age to go to some place called Vietnam and fight, I had no idea where it was or what the hell we were doing there. I had not seen a television in two and a half years and any news I received was fragmented and second hand. I did know that boys were dying there.

The days were getting shorter and the nights were cool enough to sleep comfortably. A geologist from a mining company was exploring our valley and some surrounding canyons. This was a common practice, they walked or drove their vehicles, searching for promising rock formations. He rented a room from us for a month. The room happened to be mine since it was the only other bedroom. I was fine with that and slept outside on a cot.

He was a considerate and soft-spoken man, so unlike my father. Medium height, a little portly, round face, thinning hair, around forty. He reminded me more of a bookkeeper. He would tell of his travels around the world, searching for the elusive gems and minerals. He smoked a pipe, with the most aromatic tobacco, we looked forward to the times he would light up. About half the time I would travel with him, knowing the country as well as I did must have been an asset to him. I learned a considerable amount that month. He went back to his family and stayed in touch via letters for a long time.

When I drove the tractor Kerri would sit on the hood in front of the steering wheel facing me. She would spend hours there, helping me steer. I enjoyed the company, even that of a two-year old girl.

I received a letter in the mail from the Selective Service informing me I was to report for my physical in Oakland, California on a particular date, all my travel arrangements were made and I was to be at the Greyhound station in Fallon at a certain hour to board the bus along with several other young men.

Another weekend came, along with my father. In the back of the pickup sat a one-cylinder diesel motor coupled to a generator by two fan belts. It came from a refrigerated boxcar off a train, having been replaced by a new one. It was a self-contained unit with its own twenty-gallon fuel tank. My father was so proud of this gen-set, he got it for almost nothing he bragged. We unloaded it with the tractor next to the old gas generator that had run intermittently for the last several years and was now completely worn out.

It was a hand crank start, the sequence self-explanatory. We checked the oil and fuel, both ok. My father announced with pride, "I'll show you how to do this." He took the crank and started spinning the motor with the compression lever in the release position. He released the lever and the motor almost started, then slowly stopped. He tried again, spinning for all he was worth, popped the lever and once again it almost started, coming to an agonizing stop, with a few anemic pops.

"You try; it probably hasn't run in a long time" He muttered between gasps. I gave it my best shot. With each attempt it would try to run for a little longer, just never quite able to make it over the hump and take off. I suggested we remove the belts to the generator. With that done I gave it one last Herculean effort and when I removed the crank it held its own, not increasing in speed but not stopping either. We collectively held our breaths, my mother included, we waited as it chugged along, then slowly, almost imperceptibly it began to increase rpm, until finally it reached its set speed. A huge cloud of gray smoke continued to belch from the exhaust, telling me it had very little compression.

We let it run for a while then stopped it and put the belts back on. I spun the motor again and laboriously it gained full RPM and we tested the generator with a drill. There were no gauges to indicate the proper voltage so it was a guess but we assumed it was set since there was no throttle, only an adjustment screw. We all went into the house and turned on some lights, they seemed fine. Next my mother turned on the record player, the music was fine, the singers sounding neither like chipmunks nor some deep- throated alien.

We let the generator run that evening, listening to an Italian singer, Catarina Valente sing in German as we ate dinner. My father was very proud of his acquisition, boasting we had plenty of power to spare, and it cost hardly anything. He ignored the starting problem and the propensity for the motor to sling oil everywhere. These were little things to be ignored he assured anyone who would listen. I was not so optimistic.

He left that Sunday after lunch. My mother and I started building a shed to house the generator. My father insisted we protect it from the elements. We tried starting it again, after two hours of cranking and cussing, removing the belts so it could warm up, we were greeted with success. I started hating that damn thing. It took longer and more energy to start than just doing what needed to be done by hand.

The shed was finished. One side had two swinging doors so we could lift it out with the tractor. An idea was taking root in my head and I started acting on it. Taking the motor off the windmill since it was used infrequently, I made a base that was hinged and connected the gas motor to the diesel via one of the belts, one remained to drive the generator. I simply started the gas motor, put tension on the belt to spin the diesel motor until it started running, then I let the tension off. No effort involved. The diesel ran nicely and the one remaining belt seemed sufficient to run the generator. We now had lights and music for a couple of hours in the evenings. Our record supply was very limited, the aforementioned album by Catarina, another by Eddy Arnold, Sons of the Pioneers and several albums of German polka music. My mother so loved her polka music, I eventually came to enjoy most of it also.

Soon enough it came time for my army physical. I boarded the bus in Fallon along with several other boys my age. We picked up many others as the bus made its way to Oakland. That evening, after settling in our rooms, I decided it was early so made mention of going to see a movie, there being a theater a block away. There was no interest so I went by myself and saw "Last Tango in Paris." This was the first movie I had ever been to in my life and I was sorely disappointed. The walk back to the hotel made me nervous, this was not the nicest part of town.

Next morning, we all got up early and boarded the bus to the Induction Center. The day was spent being poked and prodded in places that I was not comfortable with at all. This was also the first time I had been in the presence of a doctor, never having need of one before now. I rated the day worse than the movie of the evening before. There were hundreds of young men undergoing the same treatment and we succumbed quietly, some with apathy and some with enthusiasm. I was mainly annoyed at the indignity of being treated so inconsequentially. It all ended soon enough and I was listed as suitable for military duty. A letter would be sent telling me when to report for basic training. The draft was in full effect. There was a lot of talk about Nam. I had no idea what the hell we were doing there but it did not sound like a place I wanted to go, though I would if sent.

The trip home was without incident. My mother was glad to have me back at the ranch but very concerned about the war and my draft status. Having lived through World War Two, she knew firsthand how ugly and vicious it truly was. I was naive about the brutality of war.

We worked on the ranch, building fence and planting a long row of young poplar shoots along the fence for almost a quarter mile. The trees would be watered by the ditch or the windmill. The fence was a three board fence that we painted white, it lent a certain elegance to our new home.

At this time a notice was sent for me to appear in front of the local draft board in Fallon at such a date.

I did appear and was told to be seated facing a row of men that comprised the draft board. The spokesman had a letter from my parents explaining the time constraints of the homestead act and we had little time to spare. They asked many questions and I answered honestly. Several of them were ranchers and familiar with Dixie Valley and the remoteness and hardships that were involved in living out there. One sentence in particular from the letter praised me and so extolled my virtues that even I didn't believe some of the things that it said. I was given a "Hardship Deferment" and excused. I have no idea who wrote the letter, considering all the praise for me, I knew damn well my father didn't, probably one of his friends that had a better grasp of the English language than he did. I had mixed feelings about my deferment, as if somehow I was shirking my duties under false pretenses. I did understand that I was needed at the ranch, not that I was important, simply that I was free labor and on occasion would add money to the effort. So be it, I thought, on the way home.

The mine that was close to us and that I had worked in several times must have hired an exploration drilling company to seek more deposits of gold. The owner, named Jason, came to the house and asked if I wanted to work for several weeks. It was a large company that had several rotary hammer drills and one air-track. They brought a small dozer for road building so I ran that and also helped with the drilling. Jason, thin, rugged appearance, tanned face full of weather lines, gray eyes that never left your face, mid-fifties. A good role model, very serious about his work, you could believe anything he told you. I got along well with him, as with the others.

When their contract was finished Jason asked if I had any interest in working for the winter. The job would be in New Mexico and would last for about four to five months. I would drive one of the drilling rigs down there and they would furnish me with a small trailer at the mine to live in. The pay was very good. I didn't need to think about it very long so I answered in the affirmative. They would leave one of the rigs at the mine and I would start south in two weeks' time and meet Jason in the evening of a certain day in Fallon and we would travel together, each driving a separate rig. The one I was to drive was a large tractor truck with double axles in the back and extremely heavy. The drill tower would lay over the cab and extend a long way out the front. I told him I had never driven anything this large and was somewhat apprehensive. He must have been confident in me, simply saying by the time I got to Fallon it would all be second nature to me. With that we shook hands and parted.

I was alone at the ranch, my mother having gone back to Sacramento with my father. Once again I left a note on the kitchen table explaining what was taking place and that I would return in the spring. I felt guilty leaving the ranch but without any equipment there was not much to be done in the fields anyway. Better to make some money and help out with the bills.

I gathered my belongings, hauled them to the mine, loaded them into the drill truck and left the valley in my rear view mirror, sad and excited, as so many times before. By the time I arrived in Fallon I was at ease driving this beast of a truck. Met Jason and the next morning we left, heading south.

He was driving a brand new two-and-a-half-ton truck without a bed, only the frame and chassis. He followed behind me, I was so much slower being so heavily laden. Late that afternoon outside Tonopah, Nevada his truck broke down, the drive line had come loose, almost flipping the truck. He rode with me into town and made arrangements to have the truck fixed at a local garage. He would have to wait several days for parts so he gave me a credit card, and sent me on my way the next morning. Once again I was nervous, it seemed a huge undertaking by myself, still over a thousand miles, I had enough cash for personal needs and a card for motels and fuel. The trip went without any problems, I spent several days lumbering across several states, happy and content.

The crew was there already, arriving several days earlier to prepare some sites for the drill rig. The morning after arriving the foreman directed me to a site that looked impossible. The pavement ended and an incredibly steep road had been built straight up this mountain for a hundred yards. A heavy cable lay in the road with a shackle at my end, the other end was attached to a winch on a large D-8 Cat. The Cat was chained to a huge pine tree. This looked ominous. Without preamble the foreman hooked the shackle to the front of my truck and instructed me to watch the oil pressure on my gauge inside the cab. If it dropped to zero I was to shut the motor off immediately, the angle too steep for the engine oil pump to function. I would have to steer without assist. Looking up at this imposing wall scared the shit out of me. No problem, the foreman assured me, but if the cable snapped I was to bail out and save myself, I think he may have been grinning. Asshole, I thought to myself, why the fuck don't you ride it up this cliff. I didn't say anything, just nodded understanding, mad and scared.

He signaled the Cat operator to start his winch and I watched as the slack came out of the cable, I felt the truck lurch and move forward slowly, my engine idling with good oil pressure. The truck out of gear, the Cat was doing all the work, so much faith in a winch and cable I thought to myself as I stood on the running board with the door open so I could steer. The angle got steeper and steeper until I thought it would be impossible to continue but it wasn't. The oil gauge fell to zero, I shut the motor off immediately and held onto the steering wheel. There wasn't much to be done since it was a straight pull to the top. It went on forever, the truck frame groaning loudly in protest at the stresses, as if it was being ripped apart, nervous sweat dripped from my forehead into my eyes, I wiped it away with a trembling hand. By the time we reached the top, onto level ground my shirt was wet. The Cat operator came over as they unshackled the truck, "That was easy." he said, looking at me, grinning, spitting a huge wad of tobacco juice from a mouth full of rotten teeth. I didn't say a word, afraid I would only squeak something unintelligible. Getting back into the cab, I started the engine and backed where I was directed, with legs still shaking badly. After shutting everything down several of the men came over and slapped me hard on the back, saying I did okay. I felt as if a test had been passed. These were hard men, and I wanted to be like them, scared of nothing, never complaining.

We spent the remainder of the day setting the rig up and preparing for the next day's drilling. They drove me back to the mine and I became acquainted with my new home. A small trailer, one of many in a row. Stepping inside it was clear I could sit on the toilet and make my bed and cook without moving. Small but clean, still much better than a line shack in the mountains somewhere. There were community showers set off by themselves in a separate building along with a laundry. I caught a ride with another person to the grocery store, about an hour distant and stocked up on food. Very simple, ingredients for many baloney sandwiches and several cases of canned goods in a variety of foods, along with an ample supply of jam. With no appetite for cooking, I simply wanted something to put in my belly.

The next several weeks went by quickly, up early, at work by seven, ten-hour shift on the drill rig, back to my trailer for dinner and reading until I fell asleep. Jason, the boss, let me work on weekends doing maintenance on the rigs, grateful for the help. I wanted to make all the money possible and there was nothing else to do in camp. I was happy and content, the work was hard and dirty but honest. The money was very good. Jason also let me use a company pick-up to drive so I was spared the expense of owning one. A very generous benefit.

One Saturday evening several of the men were going to a bar for some dancing and evening entertainment, insisting I come along. They said I was boring and needed some excitement. Reluctantly I agreed but became more excited as I showered and put on clean clothes. As so many times before I was with older men and the recipient of a great deal of friendly ribbing on the trip to the bar. It was a large establishment out in the country. Restaurant, bar and dance hall in one building. We found a table that would seat all of us, and ordered drinks. The waitress refused to serve me alcohol because of my age but said it was fine to sit there if I only drank Coke or some other beverage. Not a problem the other men assured her, I would behave. I ordered a Coke, the others all ordered whiskey and Coke with one of them ordering two drinks. The waitress looked at him for a moment, shrugged her shoulders and left to fill the order. I paid him for the drink and the evening started with a toast to our good fortunes and a rousing Country and Western band.

The hall started to fill and though any girls my age were totally absent I still managed to find enough partners to keep me on the floor for most songs. A group of seven Mexicans came in, already well on their way, full of loud yells and good cheer. A boisterous group, their good mood was infectious. The oldest of the group, a female, about thirty-five who seemed unattached came over, grabbed my hand and led me out to the floor. She didn't say a word, just assumed I would dance with her and I did, happily. I eventually sat with her and her friends, introductions were made, her name was Carlita. My height, black hair to her shoulders, pretty and filled out her dress nicely. She was someone's Aunt, someone's sister, and maybe something else, nothing really sank in. I told them my name but I was simply Amigo after that. They were welcoming and friendly, all in their twenties it appeared, just out for an evening of fun and dancing. Carlita took possession of me and this suited me well, she was a real firecracker, never sitting, every dance calling to her, she loved the slow ones.

After several hours it was decided by the majority to leave and go to one of their homes, they insisted I come along. Once again Carlita grabbed my arm and pulled me along outside. We all piled into someone's Impala, it was tight, she sat on my lap, teasing me constantly. We drove through the country side for a half hour. A tiny little alarm went off in my head. I had no idea where I was, who I was with and where we were headed. This might end badly, the whiskey in my brain pushed the thought aside. Shortly we stopped and entered a nice house. We continued listening to music, most of it Mexican but upbeat as only Mexican music can be. Some of us still danced, we drank some more, I donated ten dollars to the pot for the alcohol. It was a great evening, full of laughter and amusement. They still called me Amigo, Carlita spoke English with only a slight accent so it was easy to understand her, the others spoke mostly Spanish but it didn't matter, they made me feel comfortable.

One minute we were dancing, the next Carlita prompted loudly, "We're going home", to anyone who would listen. I wasn't sure where home was, or whose home we were going to, I certainly didn't have a home worth taking her to, or even any way to get there. "We're going to my house." She answered without hesitation when I asked. As we exited there was a lot of hooting and cheering along with some comments in Mexican that I didn't understand, but they sounded ribald.

Fifteen minutes of her driving took us to her place. A very nice home, well-furnished and very clean. After a brief tour and without preamble she led me into her bedroom and instinct took over.

The next morning being Sunday, I awoke to the smell of breakfast cooking. I lay there like a lazy bum, already eight o-clock and I was still in bed. My mind drifted to my good fortunes, in a normal world I would be in my senior year of high school, wondering what direction my life would take. In truth, I had no idea what most kids my age thought about, maybe they were happier and luckier than I but I didn't see how that was possible as Carlita walked into the bedroom, dressed only in a shirt that happened to be unbuttoned.

She drove me back to the mine that evening. The next few weeks would repeat this pattern. Finally, I just stayed at her house with her invitation. I wasn't clear how she lived, it may have been a trust fund, perhaps a divorce settlement or maybe she was just wealthy, she was very vague about her finances. It didn't matter and I didn't inquire, we enjoyed each other.

The winter moved on. Work was going well. Carlita and I spent a quiet Christmas, she had no children and didn't care to be with her relatives, of which there were many in the area.

After several months staying with her it became clear I

couldn't handle staying awake until after midnight on so many occasions during the week. With her not having a job she was free to sleep as long as she desired. Many times imploring me to stay longer in the morning, impishly promising things. My resolve was strong as I left in the predawn cold, my job was very serious to me and I didn't want to jeopardize it. In time I began to spend some nights at my trailer, visiting and bullshiting with the crew in the evenings. The break from Carlita was a welcome relief for me and the camaraderie was refreshing. Eventually I moved back to the mine permanently. After two months of this torrid lifestyle we both decided it might be time to move on. She pouted as she kissed me good-bye after the last night. but we remained good friends and would get together on occasion.

One evening Jason told me most of the topside drilling was complete and I could run a small core drill deep in the bottom of a tunnel if I had an interest. I agreed easily enough, I was comfortable underground.

It was several thousand feet below ground at the end of a tunnel. It had been dug by hand decades before as that person followed a vein of gold. A small tunnel that led off from a main shaft, I had to crawl on my hands and knees for several hundred feet before reaching the end. I dragged the drill behind me on a rope, the size of a motorcycle engine, too heavy to carry while bent over. Back and forth for several days getting the drill steel, air hoses and all the things necessary to drill a hundred feet of hole with a core barrel. All this while there was three inches of water standing on the floor permanently, plus it was cold.

I mounted the drill on a metal post that was built for this purpose and slowly started the process. Dark, with only my headlamp for illumination, on my hands and knees in the water, unable to stand for the entire shift, it was deplorable conditions. Compressed air that ran the drill, incessantly adding to the discomfort, but I thrived. In some sick, perverted way, adversity challenged me.

I was by myself in that forlorn tunnel, my only visitor, a geologist that came to check on the progress and direction of my drilling. Content, he simply stated, "What a shit-hole place." as he crawled off. I grinned in acknowledgment to his receding ass.

I worked late this particular evening. I was at the required distance and wanted to pull all the steel and barrel out of the hole. This was common practice in case the rock shifted and seized the equipment. Glad to be finishing this site I didn't pay attention and hadn't realized the cover on the main gears towards the back of the drill had come off. The lever that turned the drill off and on was next to the gears. So much of this work was done by feel so I didn't even turn my head as I reached around to flip the lever. I felt a harsh pull on the index finger of my right hand and reflexively jerked it back. Now I turned my head so I could see what the hell happened. The end of the finger was mangled badly, ground into hamburger to the first knuckle with the nail gone. It was perfectly clear when I saw the nail still wedged between the two gears. The wound was full of grease and dirt, I studied it as blood began to trickle then run more freely. By now it was starting to hurt but I knew it wasn't life threatening by any means.

With resolve I ripped part of my shirt off and tied it around my hand to stop the bleeding. Then worked another two hours getting the steel and barrel out of the hole. I tried to drag the box full of cores with me as I crawled out but was unsuccessful so left them there for a later date. I found the shift foreman and explained what happened, somewhat embarrassed at my stupidity. He assured me these things were common and they had a company doctor in town. He called the emergency number before we left the mine and arranged to meet him at his office, even though it was two in the morning by now.

The doctor and his nurse were there and ushered me into a room. I think it was a room in the back of his house, none too clean and very spartan with one single bulb in the ceiling that barely illuminated the room. The doctor himself didn't instill confidence, short, portly, with a huge mustache, clearly Mexican and of a morose nature. His nurse, middle aged and nondescript had a kindly disposition.

The doctor didn't speak English so his nurse translated. He removed the bandage and held my hand under a sink as cold water ran over it. After studying it for several moments he said something in Spanish as he shook his head back and forth.

"He said it would be better to take the finger off at the main knuckle." She translated.

"I would like to keep my finger, or what's left of it." I replied. Holding it up.

"Maybe I can talk him into it, let me try." With that they got into a discussion that turned a little heated. He continued setting up a tray that looked ominously like some kind of finger removal tools.

They looked at each other for several moments. She must have convinced him, he walked over to me, grabbed my hand and held it under the sink again. He took a brush and scrubbed the remains with gusto. I think he was a little pissed at being challenged. It hurt like hell, I refused to give him the satisfaction of letting him know that, stoically gritting my teeth. He began speaking again, gruffly.

"He says there is nothing here for pain, you'll have to get that somewhere else." I looked at her and nodded my understanding, as I grimaced.

Content it was clean enough and happy with the amount of pain he had caused, he slipped a metal splint on my finger, more or less pushing all the meat parts in with the finger. I think he pushed it a lot harder than needed. He then taped my finger up roughly, all this time saying something.

"He instructs you to smell your finger for the next week, if it doesn't stink don't bother coming back." She didn't seem too happy about translating this. I simply nodded my head in understanding, thanked her and got the hell out of there, the doctor already having left the room.

"How you feeling?" The foreman asked as I got into his truck for the ride back to the mine.

"Fine." I answered. "Let's go home."

Jason wanted to put me on light duty for the next two weeks but I assured him I was fine and could continue drilling. With help I got my machine out and set up in another tunnel face and resumed drilling. Much better conditions on this site. As I finished, an opening came up for a driller to drive tunnel so I started in that capacity with my own helper. Day after day we would drill a round of twenty-six holes, load them with dynamite, back away from the face until we felt safe and count the shots as they went off. The next month went quickly and I finished the tunnel ahead of predicted time.

It was towards the end of March and I told Jason I would be leaving in about two weeks or when it worked best for him, I had no desire to leave in the middle of a project. I spent the next two weeks driving a short tunnel into another deposit of high grade ore.

Another driller who had come with us from Winnemucca asked if I could drive his vehicle as far as Fallon and he would pick it up there at a later date, since he had bought a new pickup and couldn't drive them both home. I readily agreed, happy to miss a bus ride.

I called my father in Sacramento, giving him a predicted time for my arrival in Fallon and asked if he would pick me up and give me a ride home. I said my goodbyes, a little saddened at leaving Jason and the other men. I spent one more night with Carlita, she seemed happy about this.

I stopped at a Sears store and spent hundreds of dollars on

craftsman tools. We sorely needed decent tools at the ranch, only having odds and ends to mechanic with was so frustrating. A roll away toolbox, grinders, drills, a three quarter socket set. Everything I might need and some things I might never need.

I allowed plenty of time for the drive to Fallon, or so I thought. A late winter storm came through and I drove hundreds of miles over snow packed roads, miserable conditions. I drove all that day, all that night without sleep, and all the next day until evening, finally arriving in Fallon two hours later than my predicted time. Tired and rummy.

"How come you're late." He asked gruffly as I sat on the bar stool next to my father. Five months since the last time I had seen him and this was his greeting. Drinking solitary didn't suit him, and he must have had several by now.

He seemed in no hurry to leave, telling me to relax and join him. Maybe he forgot how old I was, but there was no way I could join him in a drink even if I had wanted too, which I didn't.

I knew better than to pressure him into leaving, that would not end well. I was exhausted and just wanted to get home and into bed. Frustrated to the point of anger I asked for his pickup keys and told him I would move all my things from the other rig and wait for him to finish. That done, I crawled into the cab of his truck and promptly fell asleep. Sometime later I heard him open the door, sitting up and leaning on my side window, napping on occasion we rode home silently. Things never change, or people don't I corrected my thoughts. Tired, angry, and so frustrated, I hoped we wouldn't wreck and spill all my new tools across the desert floor.

THE SUMMER OF PIGS

It was a clear cool morning, with a brilliant blue sky that only the desert can present. My mother was at the ranch. She made us breakfast and we sat there at the table discussing what had transpired while I was gone. Nothing had been done in the fields, which didn't surprise me. I gave them a quick rendition of my winter at the mine, deleting my encounter with Carlita, they didn't need to know everything. My father was somewhat ambivalent, but my mother was quite interested and asked lots of questions. Mostly if I had eaten properly, if they treated me well, was I in any danger being so far underground? I guess these are concerns all mothers have. I assured her I was well taken care of and never in any danger, for the most part being truthful.

My father was in very good spirits and beckoned me outside, having something to show me. A road grader, old and in a very sad state. He was so proud of it, bragging how cheap he had purchased it from someone in the settlement. We walked around the relic as he admitted it might have a few problems. The major issue was a crack in the frame, just ahead of the controls, where the frame made a sharp upturn to clear the blade and swing table. It wasn't just a crack, one side of the frame was completely separated and the other side was split half way though. How he got it home without the frame completely giving way, was beyond me. We started the engine, a complicated process. An old International that started on gas and once warmed up a person engaged a compression lever, and switched it over to diesel. It had a starter but no battery, like so many things on the ranch. It did have a crank, and surprisingly, started well. He was aware a small amount of water came out the exhaust, but it was simple to add water throughout the day. This didn't look good, hopefully I thought it might only need a head gasket. He was very proud as we listened to the engine chug along, spewing white smoke and droplets of water.

I joined in his optimism, a week of work and I would have it in fine order. I looked forward to the challenge of repairing this sad old beast and getting to work, leveling some land. We unloaded all the tools I had purchased, anxious to start using them. My father's only comment being how much money they must have cost, but it was said in a positive manner so I took it as an affirmation. Nothing to be done anyway but working on the grader would be much easier now.

We had a relaxing evening, my mother drinking a glass of wine and I joining my father with some whiskey as we sat outside smoking and chatting, watching the sun set. It felt good to be home.

The next day after my father left I started repairing the grader. It took several days removing the cab and all the other things that were in the way. Several more days of grinding and welding to make the frame solid. Not content with the repair I decided to fish plate this area, it being a major stress point. My mother had stayed at the ranch with me so we drove to town in my pickup and I bought some heavy plate iron and two new tires for the front of the grader, the old ones being very sad and worn out. Two barrels of diesel, one battery, and some groceries later, we were ready to return home. Before leaving I treated my mother to a lunch in town.

It was almost another week before I had the grader fixed to my satisfaction and back together. New tires in the front and a new battery, I headed down to the field and started leveling. It went well, back and forth, the blade would move sizable amounts of dirt with each pass, moving high spots into the low spots. After several days I noticed some contamination of water mixed in with the engine oil. This is never good and resigned myself into pulling the head off the engine to determine the problem. A major job, but at least I had the tools.

When that was done it was apparent there was a crack in the head, very bad news. There was a retired machinist from the merchant marine living in the settlement, so I took it to him for advice. He heard me coming and met me outside his shop. I had met Mark several times but didn't know him well. Slight of build, normal height with thick glasses, hair cut short and flat on top, his clothes covered in grease and oil. Very friendly, he greeted me and invited me into his shop which was also his home, kind of. A square building about forty feet by forty feet there was barely enough room to walk amongst all the engine parts, tire rims, axles, springs, and all sorts of iron that must have been of some value. A counter top with a Coleman stove, sink next to it with a carburetor resting in it, a toilet standing by itself in a corner without privacy, and an unmade bed with parts laying on top. All kinds of machinist's tools in various states of usage. Clearly a bachelor.

He made instant coffee in two cups that may possibly never have been washed, except with gasoline. I accepted graciously, having a strong stomach, but it tasted more like solvent. I enjoyed him a great deal, direct, with a kind manner we made small talk, he seemed happy for the company. Eventually I explained my problem so we went out and he examined the crack very carefully in the sunlight.

Mark thought it worthy of an attempt at fixing, but would be several days before he could get to it. We moved it into his shop and I had some concern it might get lost in there, never to be found again. He instructed me to come back in five or six days and it should be ready. Mark offered another cup of coffee, I declined but sat and listened to him while he had a second helping. Deeply intrigued by his life aboard ships, covering the world. I left with a good feeling.

My mother and I caught our horses and spent the next several days riding in the mountains and generally enjoying ourselves, the weather perfect for this activity.

I drove to the settlement on the sixth day and true to his word the engine head was fixed and ready for me. Drilling small holes in the crack, then filling them with a bronze filler and peening them before milling the surface Mark felt confident it would hold. His charge was a pittance of what it could have been and I gladly paid him, along with drinking another coffee in the same cup that still had not been washed. It was fine, not having any ill effects from the previous one.

The engine went together without any problems and I was soon back to leveling land. The fix must have taken, there was no need to add water again, and the oil stayed clean.

The next weekend my father arrived late in the evening and the next morning as we sat eating breakfast he made a horrible announcement. "Next time I come I'm bringing some sows and a boar, we're going to raise pigs." He seemed genuinely pleased with this proclamation.

"I don't want to be a pig farmer." I exclaimed loudly and vehemently. Horror and disgust replacing my judgment. "I just as well be a damned sheepherder." I didn't know if being a sheepherder was worse than a pig farmer but it just came out.

"We can make some money and they'll be cheap to feed. What's wrong with pigs?" I think he took some pleasure at my distress.

"They stink and they're disgusting. I thought we were going to raise cattle." Even as I said this I knew it sounded petulant.

"You like pork don't you?" He smiled as he said this. I had no answer and knew there was no point in going any further. I wanted to shout at him that my death would be easier if he just slit my throat with a dull knife. I didn't though, I just sat back down, sullen and lost in my despair.

My mother wisely kept her own counsel. I looked at her for support but didn't receive any. Knowing there would be no placating me, she knew my attitude would be short lived, she would just let it play out.

"Let's go see where to put the barn and pens." I didn't want any part of this, but went with him nonetheless. My mother joining us after finishing the dishes.

He marked out a place for the birthing barn and six pens to keep them separate after farrowing. Another larger pen for general purpose, along with a stout pen for the boar when he wasn't needed. I hated this, just the word pig made me cringe. In spite of my reluctance to be involved I did help in the layout. I disliked myself all the more for not fighting harder to prevent this tragedy.

That afternoon was spent clearing the brush and leveling the site. The grader was the perfect machine for this. My father ran it for a short while, all the levers were mechanical and gear driven, brutal on a person's arms and shoulders. I took over, by now understanding how to avoid most of the bone shattering vibrations.

Two weeks later here they came, all was ready except my head. Six Yorkshire sows and one boar, let out of the trailer. The pickup full of expired loaves of bread from some bakery, half a dozen sacks of cracked corn. The corn we put into some barrels and we filled them with water to soften and ferment. That evening I could hear them grunting and squealing on occasion, adding to my sense of forlorn hope.

Feeding twice a day, making sure they had drinking water and a mud wallow. Letting the boar do what nature intended we kept track of breeding, soon all the sows were pregnant.

I continued leveling with the grader, happy to let my mother do most of the hog tending. We had a nice soaking rain so I graded the twenty miles of road to the settlement. In dire need of attention this helped ease the beating our vehicles took.

Every two weeks my father would bring a pickup load of expired bread. More cracked corn filled out their rations. On occasion a mouse or two would drown in the mash, the hogs loved these morsels. If left to sit very long the mash would turn slightly alcoholic and the pigs really developed a taste for this.

Spring was now here and the stream that fed our reservoir was down to a trickle, another poor snow year. There was plenty of water for our needs from the windmill but not near enough to water a crop if one was planted. It seemed pointless to plant anything on the twenty acres that was beginning to resemble a field. My father wanted to plant something in case it rained, it didn't take much to change his mind after considering the cost of seed and fertilizer. This was the desert and rain was pretty rare, if at all.

My mother went to Sacramento with my father so I was left alone. Ordinarily it would have served me well but now I was responsible for tending the pigs. That simple phrase, "Tending the pigs" would make me shudder with disdain. In spite of my feelings for them I was still a responsible person and took care of their needs, I just blocked that portion of the day from my mind. Over the years I was becoming very adept at disregarding the unpleasant, and just doing it.

The ground still had some moisture so I continued working on the twenty acres, making it as smooth as possible in preparation for seeding at some future date. Our two horses stayed close to the ranch and I would saddle my horse and go for a ride to seek solace and respite from the pigs. On a warm day I would find a knoll, parking Pinto with his ass to the sun I would sit on the ground and rest my back on his two front legs, rolling a cigarette and taking advantage of the shade he provided. He would go to sleep with his head drooping, content to stand.

One evening some people came by, they were taking a drive through Dixie Valley and wanted to stop and say hello. Cheerful, middle aged, no children, the four of them must have consumed several beers on the trip and I joined them for a couple more. We put some food together for an evening meal and they spent the night with me. They had three dogs and the next morning before leaving decided I needed a dog for company. I adamantly explained I had a poor history with dogs and didn't want one. They thought otherwise, and had the perfect dog for me, a one-year old Black Lab. A good looking dog and friendly he had taken a liking to me. Convincing me they had too many dogs anyway the decision was made, he was now my dog, I was not part of this decision process. They merrily went on their way that morning, as I stood there watching them leave, wondering how the hell this had happened. I named my new dog Smoky number three.

The weather was turning warm but still mostly mild. I hoped some rain would come but it never did. The stream was now dry, and there was little hope of planting anything in the fall. My parents came and went, surprised I had a dog but not saying much. I continued taking care of the damn pigs.

Smoky number three wouldn't go down to the pig pens with me, embarrassed by them I suppose, or he didn't like the smell. Whatever the reason he would follow me until it became apparent where I was headed then stop, turnaround and go back to the house.

There was still enough dry dog food in a sack left over from the previous dogs so I was okay for another several weeks. I let him sleep in the shop with the doors open so he could get out at night if need be.

This worked well until one morning when I was awakened just at daybreak by his whimpering. He was a pitiful sight, a long gash from his shoulder to his hip bone, his ribs visible, the large flap of skin hanging half way down his side. Must have tangled with a badger and lost, I thought to myself. I rolled a smoke and inhaled deeply, not sure what to do. He lay on his side looking at me with a soft whimper on occasion. My first instinct was to stop his pain with a bullet, simple and merciful. A trip to the vet was not a consideration, for several reasons, the main one being the expense.

I carried a curved needle in my saddle bag for suturing animals along with a can of KRS. A sticky black pine tar that we used to apply on castrations or other wounds that needed to be addressed. Horse tail hair made fine suture material, it was supposed to decompose in about a week. I wasn't sure if that was true or not but having used it many times successfully I thought to give it a try once more, fortunately my horse was home so I pulled some hairs from his tail, gathered my needle and can of KRS. I was not frantic, taking time to heat some water for coffee while I prepared, not so much cold as pragmatic, I had sympathy, just not much of it, for that I felt a little ashamed. There was nothing to be done, by now my personality was set.

He still lay on his good side, head resting on the ground, each exhalation raising a tiny cloud of dust. I squeezed some of the tar into the wound as I held the skin open. It must have burned. He struggled to get up and away from me but I was able to calm him and he settled down. I lay the flap of skin where it needed to be, took my needle that was threaded with horse tail and tried a stitch. Snapping at me with bared teeth I knew it hurt, he wouldn't let me get one suture in.

Time for some thinking and a smoke. At a total loss one idea did come to mind, ether. I had plenty of it for starting diesel engines. Not sure if it would work but out of options I sprayed a generous amount into a rag and held it to his nose, he struggled momentarily, then went to sleep or passed out. I didn't think it mattered. Four or five stitches later I had to repeat the process. A long time and forty stitches later I was finished. It wasn't pretty but looked effective. I poured some more tar on the closed wound and waited for him to come around. I tired of waiting, not sure what I was expecting. I came back several hours later and he was awake, with his head looking up, a good sign. Putting a bowl of water in front of him he sloppily drank his fill and lay back on his side.

The next day he gingerly stood on all four legs and walked around a small amount until he simply fell over onto his good side. Each day he went a little further and longer, eating a little and drinking water, promising a recovery of some kind.

My parents arrived one weekend and I explained what happened. My dad shrugged his shoulders, shit happens, that gesture said so eloquently. My mother showed some concern, I'm not clear what her concern was however. That her son was so cheap he wouldn't pay to save a dog, that I had to deal with it by myself, or that it was a shitty job of sewing. I never did find out. They left that Sunday morning and life continued.

The wound never got infected and showed signs of healing. I was beginning to worry a little about his traveling skills. If I was any distance from him he couldn't get to me. I would call him and he would walk towards me but could not hold his course, like a stick in a river trying to get to the other side, a straight line was impossible. Andy, my Indian friend from the settlement who was my age and came up on his horse to visit thought this was funnier than hell. Smoky three seemed happy, he would jump up and down like a puppy, but sadly could never get where he wanted to go.

I felt responsible for his brain damage, probably the ether, but the wound was healing well. I often wondered, left long enough would he travel in a complete circle, never realizing he wasn't going straight. It soon became apparent this was an impossible situation and I would have to deal with the harsh reality. One day I did, it wasn't easy, turning off all emotion, I took my gun and we went for a slow walk into the desert. I came back alone, a little sadder. There was still plenty of dog food.

A few days later, Mark the machinist and another boy about my age came driving up from the settlement in the evening.

"We're going to the whorehouse in Battle Mountain." Barry jumped out of the truck, very excited. A year or two older than me, he was a good looking kid. Tall, thin, ivy league looks. His parents had money and bought a ranch in the settlement. Nice enough guy with a hint of arrogance. I knew him but we had never done much together. "Get your ass in the truck so we can go." He added trying to hurry me along.

"Let him take a shower and put some town clothes on. The whores will still be there." Mark added as he exited the truck, never in a hurry.

Caught up in the excitement it didn't take me long. A long time apart from a naked woman certainly added to my haste. My chores already done, I took a good pull from their bottle of whiskey and we drove off in a cloud of dust. Mark drove faster than I thought was possible on this rough dirt road, much faster than he should have. Three men going to the whorehouse with money in their pockets, whiskey in their bellies, lewd thoughts on their minds. I sat in the middle, it didn't matter, we all bounced around like marbles in a can, heads hitting the ceiling as we bounced over a particularly deep wash. We didn't care, we were in a hurry.

About twenty-five miles from the house it went to shit. Through a deep wash, coming out the other side we got airborne and landed hard, bounced several times and kept going. Half mile down the road an explosion from the rear tire. A blowout, the tire with a hole the size of a grapefruit on the tread. Bad news. The spare was missing from the bed of the truck. Not strapped down it must have been thrown out at the last wash. By now it was dark so the three of us walked back with a flashlight that worked comparable to a weak candle. It didn't matter, we had all plummeted into a black mood. Our hopes and excitement gone as quickly and surely as the air in the flat tire.

We found the spare fifty feet off the dirt track after a considerable search, then took turns rolling it back to the pickup. Frivolity replaced with somberness, we changed tires and drove back, none of us wanting to chance driving through the desert for hours with no spare and only a half-bottle of whiskey for fluid. Barry giving me shit on the way back about raising pigs didn't help my mood. No more laughing, bragging or drinking, we silently went back, dropping me off at the ranch. Depressed and tired I went to bed.

Another week went by, the weather now getting hotter, upper nineties and lower hundreds. No promise of rain, an endless succession of blue sky. My mother came and stayed, just in time, the sows started having litters shortly thereafter. Within two weeks all the sows were done, each having between eight and twelve. A lot of little piglets running around squealing. I thought them a little cute in spite of my dislike. We lost three altogether from the sows rolling over on them; the rest grew rapidly, greedily sucking the teats. There was plenty of water from the house well, this kept the mud hole full and fresh.

The neighbor to the north of us stopped by one day. "I've got a heifer ready to slaughter, if you come up and shoot it for me and give me a hand skinning and butchering I'll give you a front quarter." We talked some more as we rested our arms on the bed of the truck.

"I'll be up in the morning."

"Don't forget your gun, left mine in town." He added.

"All I have is a .22"

"That'll work." With that he left.

Early the next morning I left on my horse with rifle in the scabbard. A nice day promised so I was content to ride instead of drive. Only a two-hour ride to the neighbor's ranch I was happy to leave my mother with the pig duty. She thought my disdain for pigs was a little humorous and teased that one day we would have hundreds of pigs. My mother never teased, this made me nervous.

Arriving at the neighbor's, I put my horse in a corral and we had a cup of coffee and a smoke while we discussed life and other nonsense stuff. Done with that I grabbed my rifle and we walked to the corral that held the doomed heifer. Normally ranchers don't kill their females for ranch meat but she clearly had a problem front leg, her ankle wouldn't support her so she hopped when walking. It didn't matter, a full-blooded Brahma, she had a slick coat and looked healthy. Standing in the corral, fifteen feet from me it would be an easy shot and a nice clean kill. The neighbor stood next to me, large knife in hand, he was ready to cut her throat when she went down.

Taking careful aim, I pulled the trigger and watched as a puff of dust showed were the bullet hit. I waited for her to topple over, I was certain it was the exact spot, having done this many times. She didn't topple, shaking her head as if to rid it of flies she continued looking at us. "Better shoot her again, looked like that shoulda done it though. I saw where it hit." Bart lamented.

Aiming one inch higher, another puff of dust showed the bullet hitting exactly where it was aimed. Once again we waited, another head shake with a tiny rivulet of blood exiting the wound. Frustrated, I shot again, another inch higher. Same result. "What the hell?" Bart muttered, clearly as perplexed as I was. The heifer continued standing still, slowly shaking her head. Waiting until she stopped moving I put another bullet into her, one inch lower than the first but all of them very close to her center line. Nothing, another bullet, still nothing, she just stood there, looking at us, a small line of blood running from the end of her nose. "What the hell?" Bart was becoming a little distressed. Now filled with anxiety, every time her head came to rest I put another bullet into it, the shots were well placed. Nine bullets in all, with empty chamber and no more bullets, I stood there stunned, looking at my rifle as if it were a Judas.

Bart and I stood there looking at her like two simpletons, transfixed, not saying a word because neither one of us could speak. For lack of anything else to do we rolled a smoke and watched her. As we finished and ground the butts under our heels the heifer's front legs began to buckle, slowly she dropped onto her knees then toppled onto her side. With a sense of relief Bart ran over to her, plunged the sharp knife into her throat and sliced through both juggler's and windpipe. He stood up and backed away watching the pool of blood spread into the dust.

Both of us breathing a sigh of relief we had the shit scared from us when she jumped up and started to trot around the corral. Blood shooting from her neck, she tried to bellow but could only make wet gurgling sounds. Several times she went around, still limping on her bad ankle, nine bullets in her forehead, both jugglers cut, spurting blood, wet slurping sounds as her neck gash opened and closed. A terrifying scene, it scared me, Bart was visibly upset also. This sickly, hellish thing finally came to an end as she toppled into the dirt.

"Maybe the Hindus are right, I bet they are sacred." It was all I could think. "I'll help you skin her, but all the same I don't want any of the meat." Shaking my head back and forth, I was deeply troubled. That said, I helped with the grisly task of gutting and skinning, all the time waiting for her to come back to life. I rode back home that afternoon, shaken.

I relayed the morbid event as my mother listened, she didn't say much except she had no appetite for the meat.

A few days later, Andy, my Indian friend from the settlement came riding up on his scroungy horse wanting to go for a ride and see if there were any Mustangs up a particular canyon. My mother said she would take care of the pigs so I gathered enough food for a couple of days and my bedroll.

We rode up the canyon, to some of the higher valleys where the temperature was cooler and welcome. We saw a small herd of wild horses working their way up a side hill the next morning but decided not to give chase, content to just ride and enjoy the mountains. The third day as we made our way home Andy let out a war-hoop, trotted his horse towards a large sagebrush and jumped off. Brush flew everywhere and soon he stomped down with his heel. He bent over and stood back up with a three-foot rattlesnake clamped in his bare hand, behind the heart shaped head. His gap-toothed grin didn't make his face any better looking, but he was really happy with himself.

"What the hell you gonna do with that?" I exclaimed, appalled at his boldness.

"Keep it for a while," he said, as if that explained everything.

I sat my horse, watching warily as he walked towards me, snake held out to the side. I half expected him to throw it at me but he didn't, nonetheless I sat tight in the saddle ready to bolt. It's just the way we were.

"Give me a hand and we'll pull his fangs out." Still with that stupid grin.

I dismounted and pulled out my fencing pliers from its case on the saddle. As Andy squeezed the head I held the mouth open with a stick and brutally extracted the large fangs one at a time, I'm sure it hurt.

"You gonna ride all the way home holding onto it?"

"Naw, you've got saddlebags."

"Are you a fucking retard?" I didn't want to ride around with a snake on my horse. "What the hell we gonna do with it anyway?"

"Make a pet out of it." He looked at me as if I asked the stupidest questions.

I gave in and we managed to stuff it into one of the saddlebags, luckily they were tight enough so he couldn't escape. All the way home I continuously checked to make sure he wasn't slithering around on my horse somewhere, that he was devoid of fangs little consolation.

We got to my place and Andy decided to spend the night. We must have acted suspicious, my mother asking what we were up to. By now we had the snake in a small canvas bag, much easier to carry, but it caught her attention. I pulled it out, showing the snake to her as it tried to rattle. She backed far away, startled and angry. Andy, the dumb shit, thought it was funny and started to chuckle.

"It's our pet." I mumbled feebly, glaring at Andy to shut the hell up.

"You get that thing out of here and I don't want to see it again." There was no doubt she was mad.

"Okay. But it can't bite." I quickly explained about the fangs. It didn't help, arm out to her side pointing with her finger, clearly indicating she wanted us and our pet gone. Women, I thought, they just don't understand men and our need to be adventurous.

Walking over to a shed so we could hide out while she cooled off we came across a large tarantula slowly making its way toward some shade. I had leather gloves on, picking it up we continued onto a landing in front of a storage shed. We assumed they were mortal enemies and would fight to the death if they confronted each other, the snake being at a disadvantage without it's fangs. With great anticipation I removed the snake and set him on the ground facing the hand sized spider, not three inches away. Neither moved, we waited, still nothing. Taking a stick, we pushed the tarantula right up to the snake, nothing, poked the snake in the head a few times, nothing. What the hell, we rolled a smoke, thinking it may take some time. An hour went by, nothing, in fact they may have gone to sleep in that time. Severely disappointed we stuffed our snake into his bag, agreeing he was a worthless pet. The tarantula we just left to his own devices.

Dinner that night was quiet, my mother still not trusting us. Andy left the next morning, bag with snake tied to his saddle. My mother in a much better mood as he rode off.

The summer was getting hot, very hot. 115 degrees and no air conditioning, we accepted the heat with resignation. Most of the time was spent building fence and doing small things around the ranch.

We weaned the young pigs, drove them to the auction early one morning while it was still cool and sold them. Not a great deal of money, but enough to buy a few things like barbed wire and other essentials. I tried very hard not to be spotted at the pig auction.

My nineteenth birthday came and went with only my mother as a witness. She made a cake for me, so we celebrated with cake, wine and cigarettes.

The neighbors from thirty miles up the valley came and visited my mother and me for several hours. They had a large ranch with several thousand acres of alfalfa. They did all of their land leveling themselves, having several scrapers and a D-8 push cat. Lance asked if I wanted a job running the push cat for a couple weeks, they were building a reservoir. My mother was fine with it so I readily agreed and promised to be there in two days.

I left home about three that morning, arriving just about daybreak. The Cat was a beautiful machine, almost new, hydraulic blade with two large rippers in the rear. Air conditioned cab that was pressurized to keep the air inside dust free. Automatic transmission. It was a huge imposing monster. A half hour of instruction and I was in the driver seat, feeling invincible. It had a decelerator, backwards from a regular gas pedal, you pushed it down all the way to the floor to idle the engine, letting up to gain rpm. It took a while to get used to it. I was in love with this piece of equipment and wanted the job to last forever.

We worked straight through for sixteen days, with me staying in their bunkhouse and eating with the family. With very good feelings all around Lance gave me my paycheck and said to come back if ever I needed a job. It was a happy drive home. All was well at the ranch, my mother glad to have me back, this gave her someone to cook for. The pigs were ready to have their litters again.

Once again the selective service gave me a hardship deferment, it was a simple formality since nothing had changed from the year before.

Walking into one of the sheds one morning I noticed a large paper container sitting upright in the corner. I walked over to inspect, puzzled, somehow it looked vaguely familiar. A one-hundred-pound sack of ammonium nitrate greeted me. Small pink pellets of fertilizer soaked in diesel used in mining or wherever explosives are needed. On further inspection there was a case of dynamite almost full, and a box of blasting caps sitting on a shelf, along with a roll of black fuse cord. I stood perplexed, looking at these things with no idea from where they came. Very familiar with them and their function I had no fear. Going to the house and questioning my mother only deepened the mystery, she had no idea and was a little nervous about it. She had a curiosity and wanted to see, so I took her to the shed, it was funny to watch, she approached as if there were some monster inside waiting to attack. I explained there was nothing to fear and I would separate the three items, especially the caps. I think she believed me for the most part but retained some skepticism about the whole thing.

That weekend I showed my father and asked him if he had any knowledge about this strange appearance. He knew nothing about it and didn't seem too concerned, as if this was an everyday occurrence in most people's lives. Plus, anything that was free could be good.

The next week with nothing better to do I spent several days hauling the nitrate and most of the dynamite up a canyon on my horse. There was a large fracture in a bluff that would make an incredible spectacle if I could blow it apart. I kept a dozen sticks of dynamite for some future use and slowly lowered the rest into the fissure with one of the sticks having a cap imbedded in it. Using a generous length of fuse, I was careful not to scrape the protective coating off. I poured the whole sack of Prill onto the cluster of dynamite, almost filling the crack. I looked down from the bluff to the canyon floor a hundred feet below. This will be incredible I thought to myself, so lucky at my age to have this much power without any supervision. I could barely contain my excitement.

The next morning after pig chores I told my mother I had something planned. She had suspicions that something was afoot but had never asked what I was up to. I explained as we rode our horses up the canyon, she was nervous and kept asking if I knew what I was doing. I assured her it was second nature to me, that I was familiar and comfortable around explosives. It was truthful and sincere, but I knew she wasn't convinced entirely, as any mother would be, I suppose.

We stopped in a small wash that would give us a great view and offer protection at the same time. She held the horses as I walked the remaining five hundred yards on foot. Taking my knife, I split the end of the cord to expose the powder making it much easier to light. One last look around, I yelled, "Fire in the hole" needlessly and lit the fuse. The impulse to run was strong but I didn't, knowing there was about fifteen minutes of burn time.

I cautioned my mother to hold tight to the reins of her horse. Her eyes large, her face alight with a large smile, complicit in some act that was surely illegal somewhere.

It went off, damn did it go off. The shock wave almost blew my hat off, we watched as the bluff slowly started to tilt away from the cliff, hundreds of tons of rock glacially reaching a point of no return, past perpendicular, speed increasing until it became an avalanche of boulders, dust, dirt and debris of all kinds. Even this far removed the earth shook, the noise incredibly loud. A cloud of dust billowed up, screening the sun with an orange filter, casting an eerie spectrum to the scene. Echos bounced around canyon walls for long seconds. The horses danced around, pulling on the reins, the whites of their eyes stark. We didn't lose them and they settled down. My mom and I looked at one another, her eyes also wide. "Alfred, was it supposed to do that?" Any time my mother used my full name and really emphasized it, I knew there would be a considerable amount of explaining and squirming. "Half the mountain was blown off. What if somebody catches us.?"

"Nobody will even notice, mines shoot all the time. We hear sonic booms every day. Nah, we'll be fine." It didn't sound as confident as I wanted. As we watched the cloud hang in the air, unwilling to go away I spent as much energy trying to convince myself along with my mother that no one would notice, but it must have registered on a Richter scale somewhere. She did trust me with some reservation so our spirits weren't the least bit dampened on the way home as we trotted our horses. It was the topic of conversation long into the evening.

The hot days of summer slowly gave way to the cooler days of fall somewhat reluctantly. One day still mildly hot, then several days that were perfect. A nice two-day rain came through so I graded the road clear to the settlement again. It took about a week and the moisture was ideal for this purpose. The second time in a month for this section of road, a major improvement.

There was a hint of fall in the air, the nights becoming crisp and cool. That weekend the decision was made to sell all the pigs, sows, boar and piglets. After considerable coaxing from me and a little help from my mother it was decided they were a poor return for the time spent watching after them. There were many jobs available to me, and my mother would be happy to return to Sacramento and work also. Fortunately, money could be very persuasive to my father. I was so damn glad to be rid of the pigs even though they required little care, the idea was repugnant. A week later they were gone, sold at the auction.

EXCITEMENT AND TEDIUM

My mother left the next weekend and I was once more by myself. A little sad, but overall it was nice to be alone. I put shoes on Pinto and spent a couple of days riding in the mountains, I spotted a small herd of Mustangs and watched them as they grazed up a juniper covered slope. I was content to idle away a few days, dreaming of girls and all the other things that young men dream of. I was happy, the weather ideal, a good horse and no pigs.

Two weeks earlier I had ordered some parts for our diesel generator. Tired of the hard starting and oil thrown everywhere it was time to rebuild it. Having lunch in town, I met a man who was obviously a cattle rancher and we began talking about the sad state of young Buckaroos, there seemed to be little interest in boys my age wanting to work out in the desert, away from the glamor of rodeo life. Soon enough this led to a job offer for the winter, this may have been his intention all along. A little on the portly side, mid-fifties, well-groomed and well-spoken he didn't appear to spend most of his days in the saddle. Later I found out he was an attorney somewhere in California and only spent a portion of his time on the ranch, a gentleman rancher was a common reference for this type of owner. Nevertheless, the pay offer was generous and I agreed to be there in two weeks with my horse. His ranch was closer to Austin so I would haul my horse rather than ride.

Rebuilding the engine back at the ranch went smoothly. I had Mark machine the valves and hone the cylinder wall. A week later the engine was back together and running well, starting easily and no leaks. I spent several evenings listening to music, as limited as it was this gave me considerable enjoyment.

Securing the house, I left a short note on the table simply stating I had employment for the winter and would be back in the spring. Loading my horse was an easy task, he stood in the back of my pickup even without any racks. The rest of my personal items went into the cab and I was off. So different from the first time four years ago, leaving my note in a tobacco can and riding for two days on faith alone. Watching the dust in the mirror the question entered my mind if the parents of other boys were so cavalier. Did they worry and wonder, or did they just assume all was well? I had no answer to that, only to marvel at how much lassitude was given me.

I drove slower than normal not wanting to throw my horse off the back end. I could see his legs in the mirror so I was comfortable in the knowledge that if his legs were there surely the rest would be also. Five hours and no problems saw me arrive at the ranch buildings.

A typical layout, snug in a small valley with all the normal buildings and a well-kept main house for the owners. Two other cowboys were sitting on the porch of the bunkhouse having an after dinner smoke. One of them, tall, lanky, very dark, heavy handlebar mustache came over and introduced himself as Al. He personified what a buckaroo would look like on a poster. Soft spoken, he gave me a quick tour of the corrals and bunkhouse. The other hand sat on his chair, said nothing so I did likewise, we just nodded our heads in acknowledgment. Al took an interest in my horse as he watched me unload him, impressed with his calmness and deliberation. I would learn he was one of the best horseman that I would ever meet, his approval was appreciated.

It was standard buckaroo work but we spent the nights at the ranch instead of line shacks, the ranch being small enough to haul the horses or just ride to our destination. There was no real foreman, the owner present enough to keep us lined out for the most part. We all knew what was expected and how to carry it out without daily supervision. One evening he sat with us on the porch and said there was a long-eared mustang bull that he wanted caught and sold. A mustang bull meant a male animal that had escaped castration, it was important not to let him breed back as he would be related to many of the cows.

He had been spotted about thirty miles from the ranch and I was sent to round him up and put him into a small corral, to be retrieved the next day and hauled to auction. It sounded simple enough but I was warned he was mostly Brahma and could be a little rangy. No problem I thought.

Early next morning I loaded my horse into the truck, a one-year-old Chevy one ton with duals, well-built stock racks with a spring loaded drop ramp. What a luxury to have such new equipment, even a radio, no reception didn't dampen my enthusiasm.

West bound on Highway 50, I understood how it was named the loneliest highway in America, a direct route from Utah to Reno it bisected Nevada across the middle of the state. Very little to break the monotony, a couple of small towns and roadside bars in the middle of nowhere. This was the type of country I was the happiest in.

I pulled off the highway in a small valley, unloaded my horse and headed north. Last seen here I kept a sharp eye out and spotted what might be him after about five miles. I circled around in a ravine so I could approach him from the north. Sitting my horse on a rise about three hundred yards I watched as he slowly grazed. His head came up abruptly, I was spotted but continued sitting there quietly. His tail came up and off he went toward the south at a trot. I followed him at a distance, not wanting to crowd him, content he was heading in the right direction. He was wild, a long yearling, light gray with a prominent hump over his shoulders. He would stop, face me and spin around taking off at a trot once more, head and tail both high. This was not a good sign, I wanted him to settle down and get into a walk but he was having no part of it. Working my way to the west slowly at a trot I began to haze him towards the east, the direction I needed him to go.

Soon he came upon Highway 50 and turned east at a good trot right down the middle of the road. I continued following at a distance, content to stay far behind. I knew by now he would be getting hot and losing any sense of reasoning that he may have had. Occasionally stopping my horse did nothing to calm him. Several times he would turn, trot towards me for several yards then spin around and continue trotting either on the highway or adjacent to it. This went on for half an hour and we were approaching the pen that I wanted to get him into. A hundred yards north of the highway with only one opening it would be a difficult if not impossible task to get him into it. It had wings that would help steer him into the gate but I didn't have much confidence that they would work, he was just too rangy and by now it was apparent a fight was looming. He began charging to test my resolve, tired of having me harassing him, each time veering off to stop a short distance away. Twenty yards seems like a long way until a person is staring at a bull, snot flying from his nose as he tosses his head and paws the ground with a forefoot.

Simple enough to walk away and leave him be I thought, but my job entailed getting him into the pen and that became my focus, just not sure how to go about it. I tried pushing him ever so slowly, he would have none of it and continued charging with his head down, each time coming closer before turning away. The last feint brought him within ten yards and I was in the process of spinning my horse to get away before he stopped and stood his ground. He was getting meaner and more confident with each attempt. He looked to weigh about the same as my horse, maybe a hundred pounds more, but his one-foot long horns looked ominous and gave me a healthy respect for any damage he could inflict. Not needle sharp they could still pierce me or my horse with ease.

This could not go on forever. The thought of just leaving him there and returning to the ranch was appealing. The thought of telling the other men I wasn't up to the task when I got there would be too shameful. Four cars parked alongside the highway, tourists standing outside the vehicles taking pictures gave me the impetus to be stupid and finish this, one way or the other.

My hands shook a little as I undid my lariat from the leather thong. I understood the commitment, once my rope was on him there would be no turning back, it could very well turn into a big problem. Normally I would have two lariats, one fifty-five feet long for heading an animal at long distances and a shorter thirty-three foot for heeling and close work. Walking my horse, a safe distance away I dismounted, threw my stirrup over the saddle, tightened the cinch and remounted. Cussing because I only had the short one I shook out my loop and slowly approached him. Wishing and hoping he would run away from me so I could have a decent chance of roping his horns and flipping him, my heart sank as he charged. It was an honest effort this time, head down he came straight at me, my horse moved to the side at the right moment and he went by us, brushing my leg with his horn. I threw my rope and started spinning my horse to face him. I knew instantly with a sick feeling my world was going to shit as I watched my loop perfectly settle over his head and come tight around his chest, the worst possible scenario. I barely had time to take my dallies and my horse was still broadside when he hit the end, the loop deep on his shoulders. I felt my horse start to go down, feet scrambling for purchase. I let go the dallies, the rope singing as it spun off the horn. Staying in the saddle as he got his ass end under him and came upright, I was aware we had dodged a serious bullet. The bull went down to his front knees, skidded for few feet then came upright to trot off twenty yards or so, facing and taunting me.

This was bad, really bad. My rope was on him, around his chest, and I had no spare. I mentally searched for ways to retrieve it or at least get it around his throat so I could choke him down. He was breathing hard, head almost to the ground, tongue protruding from the side of his open mouth. At a loss I decided to roll a smoke, not sure how successful it would be with my trembling hands. I spilled a lot of tobacco before getting the job done, lighting it took several attempts. Leaning on my saddle horn I felt the smoke starting to calm me, or maybe it was just sitting there gathering my wits. Giving my horse a pat on the neck reminded me how fortunate I was to be so well mounted, he was so tough and unflappable, I took some comfort from him.

I noticed there were about ten cars parked on the highway, doors ajar, men women and children standing next to them, some with cameras. Only thirty yards separated us, their features clear, excitement evident.

One way or the other they would get a show. Before my ego got in the way and I would do something even more stupid, a little luck came my way. Unceremoniously he lay down, more of a topple than a controlled settling. Not sure whether he was dying, resting, or admitting defeat I watched for several moments, undecided how to take advantage of this. The loop around his neck was now loose and had worked its way slightly up his neck, giving me some hope and better leverage. I slowly turned my horse around so his ass faced the bull and backed him up several steps. I didn't have a real solid plan, only followed my instincts. I continued repeating this, several steps backward then a pause, watching over my shoulder in case he jumped up and charged.

This proved successful, taking my time and no sudden moves brought us over the free end of the lariat. Still not threatened, I took a deep breath, gathered my courage and slowly swung down from the saddle. I understood how vulnerable I was at this moment, totally committed I bent over and retrieved the end, clenching it tightly in my fist. Heart racing, I heard that son of a bitch grunt, taking my eyes off the stirrup and turning my head it was soon apparent he was getting on his feet and coming for me. "Shit, shit, shit!" I thought as my first attempt missed the stirrup. My horse sensed my panic, taking a couple of tentative steps but mostly standing solid gave me a chance to get my foot in on the second effort. I knew he was close, it felt like I could feel his hot breath on my back, I felt the pounding of his hooves beating the earth. "Fuck, fuck, fuck.!" I was thinking now, remembering not to get tangled up in the lariat, so full of fear and adrenalin I almost flung myself clear over my horse in an attempt to mount.

Finally seated, both feet in the stirrups, horse gaining speed, bull almost poking him in the ass I gained control. We were almost at the highway, maybe twenty feet from the pavement. I edged my horse to the left and let the animal by us at a full run on our right. Cutting it a little too close he hooked my stirrup with his horn as he went by, pulling it off my foot, turning his head slightly it came free without any damage. I hollered "Whoa," gave a slight tug on the reins and set my horse hard on his haunches, while I took my dallies. It was a sight, that piece of shit hit the end of the rope, corkscrewed and did a flip, head landing on the pavement, breaking two thirds off one horn. I could hear a collective gasp from the onlookers, so close to them some had taken to their vehicles in a mad scramble for safety.

Again, my horse was almost pulled off his feet, it was a brutal jar. I stayed on as he scrambled to get all four under him once more. As soon as he settled I backed him up and put tension on the rope, the dallies still on my horn. The bull lay on his side, chest heaving in and out, blood shooting out two feet from the broken horn in a fine stream the size of a pencil lead every time his heart beat. Clearly dazed and spent, he lay there making no effort to raise his head, let alone get up. I knew this was my chance and I was taking it. Undoing my dallies and draping the end of the lariat over my saddle, I jumped off, ran up, put my knee on his neck, pulled his head around by his good horn, pulled the loop off and put it on his head, securely around the base of his horns, pulling it tight. It went fast and well, he never moved. Walking back to my horse I patted his neck, mounted, took some dallies and dragged that bastard over to a post that was a remnant of some bygone fence. It was a hard pull, Pinto gave all he had, it was barely enough, digging with all four feet, muscles straining beyond what they were designed for. Standing in one stirrup to help counterbalance and get away from the rope stretched taut over my saddle I encouraged him with only a word or two, I always wore spurs but there was never an occasion to use them on him. I paused Pinto several times in that short twenty yards, he was blowing hard. Making it to the post I stopped him, let go the dallies, jumped off again and made short work of tying the bull securely to the stout pole. I knew this whole episode appeared ugly and brutal, it needed to be done and there was no other way to accomplish it by myself. So be it, my only sympathy went to Pinto, his withers may be sore for a few days from the horrible jarring when the bull hit the end of the rope.

I mounted, watched the bull for a moment, I knew he was hurting but I didn't care, the bleeding from the horn was almost stopped, one side of his face was covered in blood that was dark and mixed with dirt. He would live, that's all that mattered. Confident there was enough slack so he could get on his feet and that he would still be there in the morning I slowly made my way to the highway where half the cars still stood idle. There were six, a considerable amount of traffic for this hellish but beautiful wasteland. One couple with two children was beckoning politely for me to come over. I did.

I had a feeling of what would transpire, they looked so much like city people, dressed in shorts, printed shirts and the women in their sun dresses. A couple of very young children hiding behind parental legs. I studied the large coagulated puddle of blood on the highway, a garish testimony of the last half hour, brutally reinforced by the horn remnant lying in the middle of it like some discarded body part.

A thousand questions at once it seemed, as I dismounted and loosened the cinch, easing the pressure on Pintos chest. I answered a few when there was a pause. They were honest questions, politely inquisitive, these people had never witnessed anything like what just happened. Enthralled, not by me, but the very complexity, speed, detachment and utter disregard for safety that was displayed. I tried hard to explain my own ass was at all times a primary concern. Not thoroughly convinced the attention soon began to center around Pinto. At any given time, there were easily five hands petting and stroking him. He didn't care, just stood there, eyes half closed and soon one hind leg bent at the hock, relaxed and resting. Some of the smaller children, now a little braver stared wide eyed at my horse and sometimes at me, you could plainly see they wondered if I had killed any Indians. I put a couple of kids on my horse, letting them sit in the saddle holding the reins. Soon they all wanted a turn, the parents took pictures. I happily obliged, it was fun and I enjoyed it. Very nice people and I felt a little chagrined for having judged them so quickly.

They began returning to their vehicles and continuing onward into the horizon. One family held back and asked if they could help in some fashion. Responding, I acknowledged a ride back to my truck would be very appreciated. About eight miles it would save two hours of riding and make Pinto's life a lot easier. It was in the direction they were going anyway. I led Pinto off the highway a short distance, removed his bosal and hobbled him. I kicked the busted horn off the highway.

A large station wagon, plenty of room so I sat in the back with a teenage boy who appeared a year or two younger than me, his sister who looked to be in her early teens and a young boy about eight who stood on the front seat between his parents facing me. The dad, soft and carrying twenty extra pounds, white complexion, surely worked in an office somewhere. The mother, still attractive had also given way to the comforts of middle age. The questions started as the car gained momentum.

"Where do you live?" from the mother.

"About eighty miles from here."

"Is that where your parents are?"

"No, they live in Sacramento." I wasn't trying to be evasive, I just didn't want to go into long explanations.

She studied me for a moment. "Who takes care of you? I mean what if you need something, or get hurt." It was a mothers' frown that creased her forehead.

"Mostly I don't get hurt, when I do, a shot of whiskey works pretty good." I knew it was a bad answer as it came out but I didn't want another mother. Somewhat taken aback she continued. "How old are you?"

"Nineteen."

"You're only two years older than Ben. I could never let him do this." She may have given a shudder at the thought of her son in my place.

Yeah, I thought to myself, a good week in a whorehouse would surely change him for the better. It was hard not to say this out loud but manners prevailed.

"I like it out here, it's beautiful in its own way." I tried to soften my image as I gazed out the side window.

"I would die if I had to live here." This from the girl, a scowl on her face.

"No way. There's nothing here, it's kind of ugly." This from Ben, long hair down to his shoulders, soft chubby arms.

I kept my own counsel, fighting a sharp retort. Dad remained silent.

"It must be so hard living out here. What happens to the cow that you tied up?" I wanted to explain this was all I knew and it didn't seem hard at all. Easier to answer her question, I didn't correct her about the gender, feeling it was pointless.

"We'll haul her to auction in the morning." Nothing to be gained by telling her it would most likely go to a slaughter house. I was very grateful for the ride and didn't want to be an ass. The young boy stood mute on the front seat, eyes never leaving me. Torn between scowling or smiling at him, I did neither, luckily we pulled off the highway and parked next to the stock truck. This spared me from further questions that I had no answer to.

Mom, dad and I got out. As I shook dad's hand, mom brought me an ice-cold Coke in a bottle, "Sorry I didn't think about it earlier." She gave me a hard hug, I have no idea why, maybe some kind of maternal instinct. It felt uncomfortable and good at the same time.

"I'm sure your mother worries about you." Such a strange thing to say I thought as she walked off. I watched as they drove away, shaking my head at this strange brief encounter.

With still two hours of daylight I pulled off the road and gave Pinto some water from a couple of milk jugs that we carried in the back, pouring it into a heavy rubber container just for this purpose. After he finished I took the tub and another jug of water to the bull. He was laying with feet under him but made no effort to get up. Cautiously I put the container next to the post and filled it with water. He would drink it at some point or spill it, out of my hands now. I felt nothing for him, understanding I may be hard, there was no desire to be cruel.

I loaded Pinto and drove back to the ranch. I felt good about the day. At dinner that night the day was reduced to a couple of sentences. "How'd it go today?" from Al.

"Pretty good, he slipped on the pavement and broke a horn off. Couldn't get him into the pen so tied him to a post for the night." They accepted this without any question. I liked being around men that didn't ask a lot of questions.

The next morning Al, myself and the other cowboy loaded our horses. A bigger two and a half-ton, there was room for all of them. I chose a big ranch horse, knowing it would be heavy work dragging the bull up a ramp and into a truck, even with three of us. The owner came along in the truck I had used yesterday. He would drive it with the bull to market.

It wasn't long before we got there. The bull still tied up but laying with all four feet under him. The owner parked with rear wheels in a ditch to lessen the angle on the ramp. We unloaded, tightened our cinches and rode slowly towards him. He stood up and flung his head several times. We sat our horses and the other two shook out their loops. I would untie mine once they had control of him. Al threw his lariat, it settled cleanly over his horn and a half, he pulled the slack quickly and took two turns around his saddle horn. The other cowboy made several attempts before he was successful. Held securely between them I dismounted but held onto my reins, not trusting this horse. The knot around the post was pulled very tight but finally came undone. I mounted and held the end loosely around my horn.

Between the two horses, both of them pulling hard, the bull had no choice. They dragged him along on his feet, with me following behind. They almost had him at the bottom of the ramp, he was fighting hard and made a supreme lunge at the cowboy's horse, Al's rope parted, it sounded like a gunshot. All hell broke loose; before I could get my dallies he hit the cowboy's horse in the two hind legs, knocking him down. The man rolled away and kept rolling into a small wash, the bull almost on him, blowing snot and spittle all over him. By now my dallies were hard on the horn and I spun my horse around and pulled him off the wide-eyed cowboy, terror clear on his face. I kept pulling hard, Al got his horse to the end of the loose lariat, jumped off, picked up the end and jumped back in one smooth motion. Just in time, now the bull started after my horse. Al knew what he was doing and got his wraps on quickly, stopping the charge and flipping him on his side. We had him again and simply dragged his ass to the back of the ramp with our two powerful horses. He was spent and decided to give up, not making any effort to get up, we were happy with that.

The cowboy got another rope from the truck, nervously walked close to the bull and got the rope around his horns. It was obvious he was shaken and scared to get too close. Walking into the bed he threw the end of the rope over the rack and cab at the front. Then got on his horse, trotted around to the front where the owner handed him the end of the lariat so he could secure the bull, while we followed suit. This was always the tricky part, the cowboy holding slight tension on his rope, we eased off on ours. The bull remained still, making no effort to get up or challenge us. At the same time Al and I tossed our ropes through the opening in the back and over the cab. Trotting to the front, our ropes were handed to us and we dallied hard. The owner went to the back where the ramp was and motioned us to pull. We pulled together, three horses, he slid into the truck without a problem. Maybe bruised him a little but it didn't matter.

We closed the ramp, sealing him in. I volunteered to get in with him and get our lariats off. Nervous and cautious I climbed over the racks halfway down the inside until I was able to reach his head. He didn't move, just lay there on his side, still alive, probably wondering how his world went to shit so quickly. All the ropes off, we were done with him.

"Had my doubts for a minute there." The owner deadpanned.

"I thought he had me." The cowboy said excitedly.

"We were just letting him play with you. Everything was under control." Al was grinning.

Nothing I could add so I stayed silent.

The cowboy quit about a week later, reasons unknown. It was fine with Al and me, we didn't care for his attitude. Most times sullen, hard to get going in the morning and very messy in the bunkhouse. Now we had to fill in for him and this involved our driving around in separate vehicles after dinner to pump water for the cattle. Taking about three hours I would drive to a windmill and start the gas motor for the pump jack. The cattle required much more water than wind-driven units could provide. After about three hours the motor ran out of gas but we would be gone by then, to come back the next evening. Three pumps each to service it would be long after ten before we returned home. This continued for several weeks until we confronted the owner and told him some other arrangements must be made. Too many hours for us, we did our own cooking and cleaning plus all the riding and each of us had a colt to break and ride.

With a promise to remedy this we worked another week without any help. It became apparent the owner didn't care one way or the other too much. I said to Al one evening I hadn't signed on to work fourteen hours a day seven days a week forever, I would be giving a two-week notice in the morning. He said he would also, same reasons as myself. Could I give him a lift to town? I agreed.

The next morning, we informed the owner. He wasn't any too happy but realized it wasn't open for discussion. After one week two men were hired and we spent the next week getting them familiar with the operation. Middle-aged and pleasant enough they seemed a little green, especially about horses and cattle. We spent an extra week as a courtesy to the owner and it gave him time to find one more person.

The owner was grateful and expressed it that evening as we settled up and prepared to depart the next day.

I put my saddle on Pinto and loaded him on the back of my pickup with no racks. My bedroll and duffel bag, plus Al's two duffel bags, saddle and bedroll were arranged around his legs. We put nothing under his back end for obvious reasons. We got it all in but there was very little room for him to move around. Forty miles west on Highway 50 then north for fifty miles on the dirt road to home. If all went well there shouldn't be any problems.

I drove slow on the highway. Fifteen miles from the Dixie turnoff was a roadside stop with gas, restaurant and a bar, called Middlegate. We stopped there for a sandwich and drink of whiskey. I kept an eye on Pinto, occasionally looking around, but he didn't move much. One drink led to another then another. An hour later and a little tipsy, we decided to leave. We drove off with alcohol-induced caution. Barely weaving, I made it to the turnoff and headed north on the dirt road, the horse still with us. Twenty-five miles and halfway to the house the truck made a sharp turn to the left all on its own, the steering wheel had no effect. We bounced across the borrow pit, the front bumper hitting the dirt then bouncing back up in a cloud of earth and dust that came over the hood and covered the windshield in a film. A loud thump on the roof above us. I hope Pinto didn't knock any teeth out, ran through my mind. Several more yards out into the desert over some sagebrush, finally coming to an abrupt stop. We both jumped out, the horse was still with us, all four legs bent, hunkered down, waiting for more. I knew it wasn't my driving, we were both mostly sober now. On closer inspection we discovered the tie rod had separated from the end. With an abundance of baling wire, a long bolt found under the seat, and fencing pliers we cobbled up a repair and limped slowly home, stopping several times to repair the repair.

We arrived at the ranch before dark, unloaded everything then backed up to a bank and unloaded my horse. Turning him loose I gave him an extra helping of grain.

"That is one good horse." Al said softly as we had a smoke and watched him chew the grain. I nodded in the affirmative.

"Nothing I did. He turned out this way on his own." I was serious.

The next morning, I welded the tie rod soundly back together, checked the alignment as best as possible. Content with the repair we loaded Al's stuff and headed to Reno, his chosen destination.

Arrived in Reno late that afternoon, Al gave directions to a hotel, it looked very seedy but he was paying. We carried his stuff up to the room, he wanted to go have a drink, my wish was to go walk downtown and enjoy the lights, so we split for the evening.

By now it was early evening and dark but the streets were bustling with people and cars. Standing by a stoplight waiting for the green signal I decided to roll a smoke. Lighting it and enjoying the first long drag a policeman walked up to me and asked sternly, "What you smoking, boy?"

"A cigarette, I just rolled it." I gave him a puzzled look

"I can see that, what's in it?"

"Tobacco." I almost added, "you dumb shit."

"Is it weed?" His question sharp.

"I don't know, is tobacco a weed?" I had no idea what the hell was going on. I wasn't trying to be a smart ass.

"Let me see the bag." An angry edge to his voice it wasn't a polite request.

I removed the bag of Bull Durham and put it in his outstretched hand.

Loosening the drawstring he put his nose over the opening and took a sniff.

"Doesn't smell like pot." He handed it back to me after examining the bag some more. "Where did you get it?"

"Any store sells it."

He studied me for several more moments then turned around and walked off without a further word.

I watched him fade away, finishing my smoke, missing several green lights. I had no idea what that was all about. As far as I was aware, it wasn't illegal to smoke in town.

A couple more blocks, waiting for another green light a man approached me. Late twenties, well put together and polite he made some small talk for a few minutes. Introducing himself he asks if I wanted to join him. He was headed to a party in a little while and it must have been obvious I was looking for something to do. I agreed, he didn't seem to pose any threat.

"I need to stop at my place and change. It's only two blocks." We walked off together in the direction he indicated. A few questions and answers that didn't matter.

Two flights up we entered his apartment. Well decorated if you like that sort of thing and spotless.

"I'll be right out. There's some magazines that might interest you on the coffee table. Go ahead and look at them." He closed the bathroom door.

Picking up the top one I started browsing, it was obviously pornography. Two woman, naked, doing things that might be banned in some states. I was not a prude and found it curious and interesting.

Setting it down I picked up the next one. Two men, naked,

doings things that were disgusting. An alarm went off just as the stranger came out of the bathroom with only a towel around his waist, smiling.

"Did you find them interesting?" A tiny grin on his face.

"Are you a queer?" I blurted, anger building rapidly.

"That was harsh." The grin removed from his face.

"Stay the fuck away from me, you queer." I threw the filth on the floor and walked out quickly, feeling dirty and disgusted. God damn pervert, I repeated to myself over and over.

By now the city held no more interest for me. I went back to the hotel, gathered my bag, left a message at the front desk for Al, I was going back to the ranch.

Driving back in the dark I was still puzzled by the strange behavior of the cop. I had no idea what pot or weed was, plus, I had never met a queer that I was aware of and damn sure didn't want to meet another one. I drove through Fernley, knowing there was a whorehouse in town. Sure as hell, a sign on the outside announced it was closed for the time being, whatever that meant. Now I couldn't even seek comfort in the arms of a naked woman. I drove home to seek solace in the desert and solitude.

I slept in the next morning, if seven is considered sleeping in. Mid-December and the temperature was in the mid-forties during the day, upper twenties at night, cool and clear with no promise of rain or snow. I was hoping for a heavy snow year so the creek would run well into the summer and keep the reservoir full. There was only one year left to prove up on the homestead entry and I was getting apprehensive about the deadline. I thought about doing some correspondence school work but that thought was soon replaced by some enjoyable daydreaming for several hours.

After squandering the whole morning, I decided to fix a tire on the grader that would go flat about every two days. One of the large rear ones, the job took the rest of the afternoon but I didn't exactly kill myself to get it done. The next several days took on the same note, doing things that had been put off for times like this. Except for school work, there never seemed time enough for that, I think I may still have been a sophomore technically speaking. Soon enough, I would hit the books hard. I knew that was a lie.

About midday it started to rain, flakes of wet heavy snow mixed in. It looked like it may continue for a while. Midafternoon Pinto and my mother's horse showed up at the ranch for the daily flake of hay, they didn't go very far, the smell of alfalfa kept them close by. As I was watching them eat a large two-ton stock truck came to a stop in the yard, two horses with saddles were standing in the back, visible between the racks. The driver exiting the cab in a hurry.

"Are you Fred?" Short, wiry, late forties, dressed like so many other buckaroos. My first thought, he reminds me of a Bantam rooster. I knew who he was, a rancher from the next valley to the east. A Basque, having come over with his family at any early age he started from nothing and was now the owner of a large well run ranch. His brand painted on the door giving proof of his identity.

"I have to get some of my cattle off a neighbor's permit over in Antelope Valley. I have ten days or BLM will trespass me. The ranch you worked for out of Battle Mountain has some too. They said if you're around maybe you could gather theirs." He was very excited and animated, arms moving all around.

"Sure, it'll take about a half hour. What about food?"

"We'll be staying in a bunk house. Should be food." He was pacing back and forth, sometimes a circle.

Horse loaded, bedroll in the headache rack above the cab and a few personal things, we were off.

There was an Indian sitting on the seat, he moved over but didn't say a word, I said nothing to him as he fell back asleep, smelling deeply of whiskey. Marco, the Basque didn't pay any attention to him and offered no explanation. Snow was coming a little heavier but wasn't sticking to the ground, melting quickly.

We headed north then east, on a rough dirt track, working our way over a mountain range that was several thousand feet higher than the valley floor. The snow swirling and blowing sideways as the wind picked up and the temperature dropped outside. We stopped once and all of us took a leak, the Indian taking a long pull on his whiskey bottle, then throwing it in a long arc to be lost in the darkness and snow. "Empty." He grunted. That was obvious I thought.

We continued climbing, not steeply but enough to stay in a lower gear, the engine howling. The snow blowing sideways. It looked miserable outside but we were warm in the cab. Close to eight inches of snow, we were able to maintain traction for the most part. When the rear tires would begin to slip Marco would let off on the gas until he felt them bite once more, then slowly apply more power. A good driver in these conditions. Feeling the truck leveling off we drove along on a plateau for another mile then started another easy climb, the road cut into a bank. Narrow, with a steep drop on one side things were going well, almost to the summit.

A jarring lurch threw the sleeping Indian and myself onto Marco, coming to an abrupt stop we could feel the horses in the back scrambling to get on their feet again. The truck was leaning over at a sharp angle in the back. Finding a flashlight in the glove box we got out and faced the blizzard to see what happened.

Both rear wheels were off the axle, ten feet back, laying in the snow. The hub having plowed a furrow in the snow.

"I just had all four tires put on before I came out here. Them dirty bastards didn't tighten the lug nuts." Marco said a lot more, most of it pretty bad language that doesn't need to be repeated here.

"No point in trying to fix it in this weather." With that said Marco started for the drop gate to get the horses. I helped while the Indian sat down in a snow bank, immune to the weather raging around him, clothes turning white as the snow stuck to him.

We fumbled around in the dark getting our slickers on and the rest of our stuff loaded onto the horses, only one flashlight and it was half dead. We left the Indian's horse tied in the back of the truck.

"What about him?" I asked Marco, shining the feeble light on the still form.

"Did he give you a drink of whiskey?" Shouting to be heard.

"No." Both of us shouting to be heard over the wind.

"That son of a bitch never offered me one swallow. I don't give a damn what he does." I could tell Marco was pissed. We rode off in the howling dark, leaving him there slowly being covered in snow.

At least the wind and snow were coming from behind. We rode single file, Pinto staying close behind Marco's horse. With no idea where we were, and less of an idea of where we were going I trusted to Marco and his horse.

It was a miserable night. Temperature dropping, we rode along in silence, hands in our pockets, bandanas wrapped around our faces, hunched over in our saddles. Pitch black, a few times we doubled back and found the road again, more instinct than visual. We plodded on through the night, the darkness giving way to a grayness that wasn't light, only less dark.

The snow finally stopping we spotted a feeble light in the distance. Riding up to the ranch we found the corral, took care of our horses and put our wet saddles in the tack room then carried our bedrolls through the door of the large bunkhouse. Four other cowboys in various stages of the day's preparation were inside. Marco must have known them, brief greetings all around but no introductions. Two other Indians asked about the one that that was with us. Marco gave a brief unflattering rendition, "Bastard was too drunk to come with us so we left him with the truck. Might be froze by now, but we didn't give a damn." I kept my silence but vowed to myself to always share my whiskey.

"How far and which way." asked one of the Indians.

Marco gave them directions grudgingly. They left in a four-wheel drive pickup and we cooked some breakfast, both of us hungry and indifferent to their quest.

Stomachs full and bodies warmed up we slept for two hours then saddled our horses again and rode off in the snow, the horses reluctant, as we expected. We spent the next seven days gathering Marco's cattle and eight pairs that had drifted off their range. These other eight were from the north and belonged to the ranch I had worked for out of Battle Mountain.

We never heard from the Indians again, they never came back to the ranch but we didn't care, neither did anyone else. A very unforgiving group of men, they mostly minded their own business, did the work that was expected of them and left others alone. Very few words exchanged, only what was needed. They did their work and expected you to do the same without complaint. Kind to the horses they took good care of them and would shun anyone who didn't. Being around these men would toughen a person or force you onto other things. Over the past years I had adapted and become more like them, viewing them as good role models but they were the only ones I had.

The next morning Marco and I loaded our meager possessions behind the saddles and left with our cattle. It was a cool day but sunny with most of the snow gone except small patches in shady areas. Around noon we separated his cattle from the small bunch that I would head north with. They didn't like being split but soon settled down, lined out and behaved. I drove them slowly, grazing a little as we went. If pushed too hard they would split and any control over them would be lost.

By evening we started up a narrow canyon that would take us over a low mountain range to the next valley. Confident they would stay there overnight I unsaddled and hobbled Pinto to graze for the last hour of light. I built a fire, had a meager canned dinner, smoke and coffee then crawled into my bedroll.

Frost in the morning, nothing new but still unwelcome I built another fire for morning coffee and to warm up. Back in the saddle I picked up my eight pair and continued on my way over the crest and continued down into the next valley. Back on their home range I pushed them another ten miles north, left them and turned around to start my way home, about fifty miles.

Almost dark I stopped, built a fire and made some coffee. Giving my horse the last of his grain and letting him graze for an hour I decided to continue on through the night and save the last can of food for breakfast. A cool clear night, the temperature was dropping. Pinto, with me on his back, walked along under a brilliant night, the stars giving plenty of light to see. I was getting cold and decided to wrap my sleeping bag around my body to preserve what little heat there was. Dozing in my saddle I was abruptly awakened by a jolt, opening my eyes I was startled to see Pinto loping ahead without me on him. Realization came about the same time my ass hit the ground, hard, still in the sitting position. A corner or string from my sleeping bag must have been dragging on the ground, his hoof stepping on it must have jerked the remainder under Pinto in one bunch. Startled, he must have jumped high in the air and took off running, leaving me suspended until gravity took over.

Luckily he stopped in about fifteen yards when I hollered

"Whoa."

After that I decided to walk, hopefully getting the kinks and stiffness out. I stayed on the ground until the sun was high enough to share some of its warmth with me.

I was hungry so I stopped and built a fire to warm up my last can of food. It didn't fill me but helped appease some of the pangs. A nice little patch of dried grass helped Pinto with his hunger so I stayed an extra half hour, drinking coffee, letting him eat a little more.

We took a fifteen-mile detour to the large ranch that had all the heavy equipment, having worked for them I felt confident they would feed me and my horse and let us spend the night. They did, happily so.

That evening after dinner the owner, Lance, asked if I wanted to work for a couple of months welding on his Cat rollers. I would be in the shop, out of the weather, and they would furnish room and board. The pay was very attractive so I agreed readily and promised to return in several days, via pickup and more clothes.

I left early the next morning, confident I could be home before dark. The day went without any problems. Mid-January, warm clear day. Once the sun got higher, it was a pleasant ride. Trotting at times, the miles rolled under Pinto's hooves. We arrived home with an hour of light to spare, enough time to wash and dry my horse's back before he went to roll. My mom's horse was very glad to see him. I had a pang of loneliness, there never seemed to be anyone to greet me. So be it, as I shrugged that sentiment off.

There wasn't much to do around the ranch, everything seemed fine so I packed my things and left in two days, driving my pickup.

The ranch had a huge shop with a full line of machine tools, large enough for industrial applications.

A full set of Cat rollers awaited me. These were small iron wheels that the bulldozer tracks rolled on. Rather than buy new ones my job was to add welds to them with a special rod. Once enough material was added they would be turned on a lath back to factory specifications by someone else. New bearings, shafts and seals would ready them to be installed under the swing frame.

A large arc welder, a chair, a table set up so I could roll the shell as I needed without lifting the heavy metal. This was my future for the next six or eight weeks, depending only on my ambition. They paid by the hour so I was free to work as much as I desired. It became mind numbing, the tedium excruciating. Hour after hour, listening to the sizzle of burning rod, chipping slag, inhaling fumes. I became even more adept at withdrawing into my own world as the hours went by.

I worked seven days a week, the days broken only by meals, showers and sleeping. They fed me well, as the Cat rollers increased in size so did my girth. Lance worked hard at keeping me there, offering a steady job with good pay and some benefits. I graciously declined.

Seven weeks, many dollars, and fifteen pounds later I was finished and on my way home, belt buckle to the last hole.

Damn, I Shot My Horse

IT GETS BAD

A surprise sat there waiting my arrival. A very old D-7 Cat, it looked well used, loose tracks, grousers worn flat and more rust than paint. Another relic from some bygone era, better suited for a scrap yard. A double drum winch in the back, one cable running over the top and connecting to the front blade via an overhead frame, the cable frayed and well worn, the other spool empty. A two-cylinder pony motor with rope start used to start the main engine. I shook my head, hoping it belonged to someone else, but knowing my father, I felt sure this was some new and inexpensive purchase of his.

I ignored it, walking away, hoping it wouldn't be there next time I looked. There was no note in the house, food looked pretty scarce but enough if a person was really hungry. Evidence they had been there but not sure when they would return I felt no sense of urgency to start any projects.

Waking the next morning the day promised to be another unseasonably warm day, maybe some rattlesnakes coming out I thought. Catching my horse and loading some canned goods I made the decision to go for a ride and check out a canyon ten miles to the north. Warm, with not a cloud in the sky it promised to be nice weather and I enjoyed these days of carefree riding and exploring. I didn't leave a note for my parents, planning on returning before they came to the ranch I didn't feel it was needed. Not sure if they cared anyway, except my mother may have, a little.

Ten miles or so north I turned into a canyon and made my way up the bottom. Easy for the most part with a few sketchy spots the colors were vivid and dramatic, pink, green, purple, and some dark brown with veins of quartz. I had no idea what minerals these held but suspected they may have given promise of gold if one looked hard enough. An old mine to explore might be in my future. I had my .22 rifle in my scabbard, hoping for a chukar or cottontail for dinner.

By evening we were a good six miles up the canyon, nothing to shoot, but a nice level wide spot in the canyon with grass and a stream welcomed me for the night. This would do nicely. Pinto hobbled and grazing on nice young tender grass I opened my ten thousandth can of food it seemed, had dinner and coffee, a smoke by the fire to finish the day. Ten feet from the bubbling stream I crawled into my sleeping bag and watched as the Milky Way showed itself, clear and pronounced. I fell asleep quickly, content and happy with my world, lacking only a naked woman by my side to make it perfect.

Early morning a sharp stabbing pain low on my neck woke me as I rolled onto my other side. Reflex taking over I swatted hard, my hand striking something. I jumped up and heard what I thought was the unmistakable sound of rattles. A distinct sound unlike any other, when the sound was close it would stop me in my tracks, heart pounding. I wasn't completely sure and it didn't matter, I was bitten, of that I was sure, as my neck began to burn. I was in a complete panic, only fifteen seconds had gone by and it began to feel as if I was being branded on my neck and shoulder. Not quite enough light to see with I felt for my boots, intending to put them on, stupid, I was too far away from any help. I fought hard to control myself, understanding flight was pointless, I would be dead before I got five miles on my horse.

A tiny wedge of reasoning wormed its way into my brain,

lance it, or cut an X, grabbing my pocketknife from my Levi's I went to work before my arm went numb. Not being able to see, I cut what I thought was a X, grateful my knife was sharp. I expected more pain but almost felt nothing. I took my t-shirt off and squeezed hard on the cut, brutally hard several times, that hurt. I could feel some blood running down my back, hoping some venom was coming out. I could feel my heart beating wildly in my chest, I was fearful, totally afraid, almost certain I would be dead in an hour. We had discussed snakebites many times around campfires, but no real consensus on a good course of action. The word cold, began creeping into my thoughts, keep it iced or cold. Easy enough to say, hard to do out here. My eyes turned to the stream the same time as my body crawled the few feet to it without thinking. I dragged my sleeping bag along, a plan taking form. I submerged my shoulder, neck and half my head into a small pool, the water so cold it had a burning sensation on the parts that weren't already feverish from the bite. I almost felt a small easing of pain but that might have just been wishful thinking. I pulled my sleeping bag over me as far as possible without getting it wet. There was nothing left to do but wait, already cold, my resolve to stay in the water was dissipating as fast as my body temperature. An unnerving thought crept in, my horse was still hobbled, if I died Pinto most likely would also, unable to break years of training I didn't think he would make a run for freedom if the grass was gone or the water dried up. Would he or wouldn't he, would my rotting, stinking corpse drive him away. I dwelt on that for hours, or maybe minutes, I wasn't sure. I wanted a cigarette badly but was shivering too hard to even think about trying to roll one. I knew the next twenty-four hours would be telling. Some had said snakes don't always inject venom when they bite, or only a small amount, sometimes the bite is only a warning, not intended to kill. This gave me a small glimmer of hope, I had no idea if was true or not but I held the thought with all that I had. I didn't want to die.

Between bouts of sleeping or being unconscious I watched as the sun made its arc across the sky. There was enough warmth to keep me from severe hypothermia, thanks to the sleeping bag covering me. A part of me numb from the icy stream, upper arm, shoulder, neck, and back of my head still felt as if it were burning but the pain was less intense. Mostly I was miserable, that gave me some comfort, knowing that as long as there was feeling there was life. My upper arm and shoulder were swelled considerably and a bruised discoloration, I was unable to see the back of my neck for obvious reasons. My arm was mostly immobile, either from the bite or the cold, my fingers could still move at will and remained a healthy color.

Many thoughts went through my mind that first day. Mostly how stupid of me for not leaving a note. If I didn't make it, not a person in the world knew where I was, or how long I had been gone. Would anyone even look for me, how could they with no clue as to my whereabouts. Who would even miss me? My mother most certainly, not sure about my father, though he would most definitely miss the free labor and monetary contributions. I knew that was unfair, deep down I didn't really believe he was that callous and cold. After years of tyranny my thoughts of him were not warm and endearing, but I was a realist by now and understood the meaning of a symbiotic existence. He needed me to build the ranch and I needed him so I could own one.

This line of thinking saddened me. Nineteen years old and only one and a half person gave a shit about me. Not even a girlfriend, that bothered me most of all for some reason. I should have gone to the whorehouse, just think how much better off I would be right now. My mind would jump all over the place, like a fly trying to go through a window, strike and bounce away, only to strike somewhere else.

In and out, sometimes clear and lucid, sometimes unable to comprehend anything, the pain my only constant. As the day wore on I became despondent, I didn't cry, I couldn't cry, I had never cried and saw no reason to ever to do so.

About an hour before sunset I came around, ravenously hungry and thinking about food. The need of a cigarette might have been stronger than my hunger. This gave me hope that I might pull through. Which should I try first. The smoke took priority. For the first time that day I dragged myself from the creek and crawled to my shirt which held my tobacco pouch. My right arm, stiff, frozen and mostly useless, it was frustrating trying to hold the paper. Several failed attempts later, I managed to roll something that didn't even resemble a cigarette, just a hump of tobacco rolled in paper. Lighting it and inhaling I felt the tingle of the nicotine coursing through my body. It felt so damn good, except my shoulder began to throb so I rolled back into the creek, not quite as deep as before, holding onto my smoke for dear life, so I could finish the whole thing as I lay there on my side, getting so cold. Most of that night was spent in freezing pain. Fortunately, I wasn't conscious for most of it. By morning, as the sky began to lighten so did my mood. I would survive this, there was no doubt. How long it would take before I could ride out was a total unknown, but I would ride out on my own, and a hell of a lot tougher than when I rode in.

My shaking was mostly gone, only an uncontrolled spasm infrequently, maybe a person only had so many shakes and I had used them all up. Removing my upper parts from the stream I managed to crawl to where my saddle and food was, all the time keeping a sharp eye for the snake that bit me. I lay there for a while, catching my breath, exhausted. My shoulder still very painful but manageable, interesting term I thought, what choice was there but to live with it. I lay there about another hour, gathering strength and warming myself before I made the effort to open a can of food. It was frustrating, how the hell did a one-armed person manage a can opener, I didn't know any one-armed people, so it was a moot question. Hunger forced me to improvise, I finally got the lid open far enough to get a spoon into the can and greedily shoveled some of the contents into my mouth. Half way through my stomach started to rebel, I stopped, thinking it may come back up but it didn't. I waited a short while and slowly resumed, taking my time. This worked better, thankfully I was able to keep it all down.

I sat for a few more minutes then rolled a smoke, wishing I had some store bought cigarettes. I rolled my aching shoulder back into the cold water, dreading that first immersion. It soothed the dull ache and I was able to enjoy my ugly smoke. The day continued, the sun making its arc across the sky as it had so many billions of times before, with no regard for me. So much time for reflection, I began to realize how tenuous and fragile life was. This was the first time my own mortality slapped me in the face, so close had I come, it was an unwelcome feeling. I tried to think of other things.

That evening, feeling a little better I thought about opening a can of fruit but the effort seemed too much so I didn't and my hunger abated. I spent another night with my shoulder in the stream, freezing once more but with less pain.

The days continued, three cans of food were all that I had brought, two were already gone in four days. Luckily I had come with extra pounds and for that I was grateful, but they were coming off rapidly. I saved the last can for a desperate time.

Feeling was coming back into my arm and the swelling was mostly gone but my shoulder was still a dark color, fortunately it was fading. I would soak it in the stream on occasion throughout the day but not at night anymore. Probably a week or more had gone by and my thoughts turned to going home, hunger becoming constant. I opened my last can, much easier now, cold Ravioli, a meal fit for Kings. Tomorrow I thought, home and food, a bed I could sleep in without worrying about being bitten again.

Pinto was close, removing the hobbles I noticed the hair was rubbed off but the skin was still intact, for that I was grateful. Putting the saddle on and tightening the cinch was problematic but doable with considerable cussing and effort. Leading him next to a rock made mounting much easier, I still felt like an old fat woman as I pulled myself up. My arm was usable and mostly free of pain, just stiff and unreliable. With one last look around I started my way home, grateful for such a dependable mount.

The ranch was a welcome sight but no sign of my parents' pickup. I was relieved, a couple more days of healing and no explanation would be needed. I had no idea how my parents would react about the bite and there was no desire to find out, especially my mother, a story for the future.

The next few days were spent doing laundry and general maintenance on the windmill and other machinery. The end of March and still very dry. We needed rain badly, White Rock creek was running about half what it should, the reservoir only two-thirds full without much hope of filling to capacity. A welcome rain did come, twenty-four hours, a slow and refreshing break. It didn't help the stream but added some much-needed moisture to the ground.

Headlights announced the arrival of my parents late one evening, must have been Friday. It occurred to me five months had elapsed since we last were together. My mother was extremely happy to see me and showed it with a strong hug, very unusual. My father, true to form looked at me deadpan and asked, "Did you run the Cat?"

"No. I wasn't sure it was ours." Since my snakebite I was making a conscious effort not to be confrontational, so I answered with a smile.

That same puzzled look on his face that was so familiar to me, not sure why he deserved to have a retard for a son. I was used to it by now and no longer took offense. With the pleasantries concluded we unloaded groceries from the pickup and settled in for the evening.

The next day over breakfast I broached the subject of needing to comply with the Homestead requirements. One year from this spring was the deadline and I felt considerable pressure to get a crop in and a well completed. The idea of the well met with stiff resistance from my father, too much money for the time being he argued, quite passionately. I dropped it, so did my mother.

With fanfare and his morning shot of whiskey he announced there was several hundred pounds of seed in the back of the pickup, ready to be planted. My mother was watching for my response.

"We don't have a drill. What kind of seed?" I was caught off guard, always assuming we would discuss together what kind of crops to plant.

"Somebody had some left over, I think it's wheat, should work. I brought a broadcaster. You guys can plant it with that." He was proud of himself, all the bases were covered.

I knew what a broadcaster was. A tool that went around your neck with a strap, a small hopper that held the seed, a hand crank that spun a disk and spread the seed as a person walked along. Suitable for lawns and other small plots of land. I held my tongue, so be it. This was my newly adopted phrase.

We unloaded the seed and he gave us an unnecessary demonstration with his highly prized broadcaster. He became bored with that after half an hour and a tiny square of land seeded. It seemed Herculean to plant twenty acres.

After lunch and a few more swallows of whiskey he gave me a discourse on starting and operating the Cat. Somehow it escaped him I was very familiar with all this, having operated a vast array of heavy equipment and to my knowledge he had never run something of this size. I let him carry on, no point in ruffling his feathers.

As with all pony motors it was possessed by demons. Two hours, a lot of pulling on the starting rope, lot of sweating and cussing we finally got it running. A sharp distinctive popping as the motor spun rapidly. I engaged the starting pinon and clutch, the main engine spinning with the compression off. By now my father was in over his head and I subtly took over, waiting for oil pressure to come up and the cylinder heads to warm sufficiently. Half throttle and compression lever on, the main motor took over and kicked the pinon out.

"Go ahead and drive it." A big grin on his face, so proud.

Jumping onto the seat that was mostly bare springs I disengaged the hand clutch and put it into gear, pulled on the lever next to my right shoulder to raise the blade. The winch in back which operated the blade made some horrible grinding noise, the blade raised almost all the way to its stop and came crashing back to earth with a loud crash, accompanied by a cloud of dust. The control lever having very little control. I tried again, only in small increments and succeeded in raising it several feet, enough to test the drive train. The main clutch was weak but maybe I could adjust that. Clanking and squealing, we lumbered forward, a thousand pieces of metal voicing protest. Testing a turn, I pulled on the right clutch and stepped on the right brake, it wouldn't lock the track but it did make a large turn. I tried the same procedure with the left turn, it jumped the track with a sudden lurch. Instantly I popped the main clutch and stopped the machine. I knew what to do. Finding a large rock, I placed it behind the left track, got back on, slowly reversed the Cat until I felt it come back onto its bottom rollers, thus engaged, the blade decided to drop on its own again with a loud crash, scaring the hell out of me.

Picking up the blade carefully, I drove the machine in a straight line and parked it behind the shop a short distance, my father walking behind me. I shut the engine off and stepped onto the ground. My father walked up, beaming with pride. "Works pretty good doesn't it?"

"It'll make things a lot easier." Nothing to be gained by pointing out the obvious flaws, of which there were many, some serious.

We had a nice evening, rare, but I was drinking a little also, maybe that made the difference. The next morning, he left for Sacramento. My mother stayed at the ranch with me and we started the tedious process of spreading the seed. I had my shirt off, she asked me why my shoulder was bruised. I answered nonchalantly, a horse fell with me and I landed on my shoulder. No big deal, hoping she would accept my answer. She did. We resumed seeding, one of us walking along, cranking the broadcaster, the other carrying a three-gallon pail with more seed. Back and forth, crank, refill, crank some more. Nine very long days later the job was done. I went over the whole field with a spike tooth harrow, covering the seed. Then we waited for rain.

Two days later, my father arrived with the rain. Another drinking friend keeping him company, both a little into their cups. My father, in a festive mood took total credit for the rain.

The next morning my father and his friend drove around the ranch, I'm sure he took most of the credit for all the work, I didn't mind. My mother stayed at the house, and with nothing better to do, I started to monkey wrench on the Cat. So many things needed adjustment and lubricating, some new parts that I didn't have but was able to make with a torch and welder. One week later, all that was possible was done.

The rain that came and went with my father was enough to sprout the seed in some low-lying areas. Many spots were vacant, for whatever reason but mostly because some of the ground contained a lot of gravel and couldn't hold moisture long enough. The ditch from the reservoir to the field washed out quickly because of the same gravel and steepness of the terrain. I managed to get some water onto the wheat but there was no way to control it. Soon it formed small creeks all over the field, doing nothing but wasting water. I had talked to my father about piping the water to the field and using corrugations to control the water, but he adamantly opposed that idea. Soon enough the water in the reservoir was depleted, the few shoots that clung tenaciously to life turned brown and died, no taller than eight inches. One month, from planting to failure, the outcome was predictable, with no real provisions for irrigating, depending on rain in the desert was ridiculous.

My mother and I both were predictably disappointed but without support and the proper equipment there could be no other result. My father didn't seem too bothered by it all, blaming us but mostly me for all the failures. It stung, though there were years of false accusations it still hurt every time.

I salved my conscience by plotting out forty acres on my dad's entry of three hundred sixty acres. Better soil and not as steep I could have it ready for fall planting with any luck. I used the Cat mostly, when it would start. Sometimes it would and sometimes it wouldn't. No predicting, one pull on the rope and the pony motor would come right to life, the next time it might take several days, frequently trying throughout the day before I was greeted with success. As long as I went back and forth mostly in a straight line it would stay on its tracks. The blade continuously would drop on its own accord, always startling me but doing no harm.

Meanwhile my father and a man from the settlement used the old drilling rig that completed my hand dug well four years prior, to drill a sixteen-inch irrigation well on his entry. After several weeks of drilling and drinking they declared the well a success. They found an old irrigation pump laying around somewhere.

With much ceremony and drinking they started lowering the pump into the well. Calamity, the well hole was too crooked, the pump only going a third of the way down, barely touching the water.

Much to my credit I mostly stayed away from this project, drinking and drilling was not a good mix. They pulled the pump back out, pulled the drilling rig away with a pickup back to the settlement. My father left my mother and me shaking our heads as he drove back to his job in Sacramento.

By now mid-June was upon us, the days getting very warm. I continued leveling the forty acres with the Cat. When it wouldn't start I would work with the grader and do some finish leveling. I took my money and my mother and I drove to town. There was a twenty-five-foot land plane with a hydraulic control, one of our neighbors informed us, that it was for sale. It would be perfect for the finish work. An eight-foot-wide bucket was a little large for our tractor but it would work well. I bought it and pulled it home behind my pickup, after locking the crazy wheels in back. I had no reservations about spending my own money on ranch supplies and equipment. It felt like I was contributing and there was some control over what was purchased.

We were coming up against our deadline for BLM requirements. I had filed for a two-year extension on all three applications. The inspector came, saw our intentions were serious, the two-year postponement was granted. I have nothing but good to say about them.

Another month went by, now into July and getting hot. I worked on the original twenty acres with the land plane, getting it much more level.

It was time for some serious decisions and commitment. I could level forever but without reliable water and a proper way to irrigate it would be a waste of time and fuel. My mother and I forced my father to sit and work it out. It wasn't pretty. A proper well, a pump capable of pumping twelve hundred gallons a minute, the minimum required by BLM. A diesel motor to run the pump and enough eight-inch pipe to get the water to the field properly. A lot of expensive equipment. A major loan would be needed. This set my father off. After considerable arguing, mostly between him and me, my mother would add support when needed but wisely stayed quiet. I didn't back down, remaining as calm as possible in spite of all the accusations hurled at me. After long hours of this, and the simple choice of we either go forward and spend the money or quit now and fold it up. I was tired and that was it in a nutshell. We went to bed and spent the night with our own private thoughts.

The next morning before leaving I calmly explained to my father it was time to decide. No more discussion, everything had been said. Yes, or no. I was smart enough to implore and not threaten.

He agreed, with anger. It would be up to us to get a driller, he wanted no part of that and didn't know why the hell we were in such a rush. All the other things mentioned would be up to us also. His face red with resentment, finger pointing at me to empathize his point, he drove off.

This kind of parting was difficult on me but more so on my mother. We knew it hadn't gone well, that was apparent. Most of the push was from myself, my mother understanding the necessity but reluctant to force the issue. It was done.

The local driller in Fallon was too busy but his son in Wells, also a driller with his own rig might be able to drill the well. We called him while we were in town and he agreed to come and inspect the site and give us a cost per foot.

One week later he arrived. Middle aged, tall, good looking, obviously an outdoor person, a great personality. He looked at the site, no problem, a price was agreed on, one dollar per inch diameter, per foot drilled. He took a keen interest in what we were doing and seemed impressed, being a rancher also.

He spent the night and we discussed me going to his ranch, close to Wells, to do some leveling on his fields. Several large humps in his alfalfa made it impossible to irrigate and he was plagued with large areas that never received water. We could trade some labor, therefore reducing the cost of the well. I would pull my equipment to his place and start in about a week. We spent the morning talking a few things over, mainly the well, he was of the opinion a sixteen-inch well would work the best. I loaded the tractor on the old truck that still had the piece of sagebrush plugging the hole in the radiator. Built a dolly for the land plane, hooked it to the truck and headed north to Winnemucca then east on I 80 to Wells. It would be an all-day trip. My mother stayed at the ranch to help out with things. Burl, the driller would stay at the ranch in a small trailer that he would bring along for that purpose.

My trip went well, midsummer and incredibly hot. Of course no air conditioning, but if a person never had it, I guess it wouldn't seem that important. That evening I pulled into their ranch. A beautiful old farmhouse with porch and shade trees everywhere. It was a nice place, clean and well maintained. One day my place could look like this, a pleasant thought.

Burl, working on a piece of equipment, was outside already so directed me to a place I could park and unload. His two teenage sons came over and introduced themselves, about my age, tall good-looking boys, just like their father, ready smiles.

Burl wanted to show me his fields and the problem areas before dinner. That was fine and just as we were driving off in his pickup a young girl came running out and exclaimed she wanted to go with us.

Opening the door and getting out, Burl let her in, she slid between us, grinning. Damn, she was cute, short blond hair, slim figure, a couple inches taller than me. She shook my hand firmly and introduced herself as Valerie, direct blue eyes and a smile that made you think she possessed some secret. The hour-long tour went by too quickly and I must admit my attention was not always on the upcoming job. I think Burl suspected as much but didn't seem bothered by it.

Dinner that evening was as all dinners should be with families, lively and spontaneous humor, especially from the two brothers, given to endless ribbing. They were both considerably taller than me, in fact the whole family was tall. It didn't take long before they poked at me about being short. Something like, I would always be the last to know it was raining but the first to drown in a flood. I was fine with it but their mother chastised them, without much effect. She was very attractive herself, poised and very self-assured. The whole damn bunch could have been on a poster for the "Perfect All-American Family". Somehow, whether by design or accident Valerie sat next to me and asked a thousand questions. Several years younger than me, she was very confident and poised like her mother. It was perhaps one of the most enjoyable meals I had experienced in many years. I wished desperately my own family could have been more as this one.

A spare shed in the yard served well as my bedroom, there were no spares in the house, better for me anyway. Breakfast, run the tractor till noon, Valerie would bring me lunch and sit with me, our backs against the big tractor wheel. Each day we would sit closer and lunch would take a little longer. After a week we became inseparable, except when I was working in the field, a testament to our will power that I got anything done. In spite of my efforts we did nothing that we shouldn't have, Valerie gets credit. It was a wonderful four weeks and seemed like only one. Burl was gone for most of it, coming home after two weeks of drilling at my ranch. He stayed for a couple of days to see how the leveling was going and other duties.

It was going well, straightforward, no problems except I didn't want to finish, but I did. He said the well would be done about the same time as I would be with the leveling. The drilling was going better than expected and he was confident it would produce plenty of water. He also informed me my mother was doing well and trying to fatten him up. After meeting my father, he was quiet about his opinion but evidently not very impressed by his brusqueness.

It was a sad day when I left, unable to think of any more pretenses both Valerie and I were resigned that this day would come. Her mom and brothers graciously left us alone. With her eyes wet and me with a sad heart I left her standing in the yard. We had made many promises and I intended to keep mine, I would write and call whenever possible. There were plans for the future and they were far ranging and sincere. I was in love, so was she.

No problems going home except a profound sense of loneliness, it did help keep my mind off the miserable heat.

Burl was just finishing preparing the rig for travel, another job waiting in Ruby Valley. The well was a complete success. He was very helpful that evening, instructing us on the proper size pump, how many feet of column to insure we were deep enough. What size diesel engine would work best for our needs. I wrote these things all down. He encouraged me to visit very frequently, and stay several days when possible. I assured him that was my plan, I had a strong drive to return, for an obvious reason, of which he was aware. We shook and he left the next morning, a cloud of dust to mark his departure, as with so many that I had watched.

The following day my mother and I drove to Reno, ordered a whole new pump, pump head, gear head and all the other things that would let us pump water. We also ordered several hundred feet of 8- inch aluminum pipe and another several hundred feet the same size with sliding gates that would allow a measured amount of water out with every foot of pipe.

Next we stopped in Fallon and arranged financing for all of that plus Burl's bill for the well, minus what was deducted for the leveling. The papers would need my father's signature, so we made arrangements for the following Monday morning to stop and have him sign.

After buying a couple barrels of diesel, we had a quick dinner. I called Valerie, so good to hear her voice, so sad to say goodbye. All in all, a very good day. We were in debt for a little more than fourteen thousand dollars. I knew we had to do it and I would help with the payments. We did fear my father's response, his temper just another hurdle.

It proved to be a big hurdle. He knew it had to be done but he sure made it miserable that weekend. Unreasonable attacks, never physical, just sharp accusations for which there was no defense except denial. I missed Valerie and her family, but I knew this would pass, it did after two long days. My mother had to drive with him to Fallon on that Monday morning for the loan signing. I would follow in my pickup and return with my mother, my father would continue onto Sacramento. I knew she would get the brunt of his remaining anger but by now most of it was spent and she was strong.

Two days later we drove the two-ton truck that I expected to fall apart at any moment, to Reno, picked up all the things we had ordered, paid for all of it and left with a heavily loaded truck.

The next several days were spent building a heavy tripod over the well, suitable for installing the weighty pump. It had to be foolproof, if we dropped the pump columns there was no way to retrieve them without hiring a boom truck with fishing tools. No way in hell did I want that scenario to develop.

 Clamps made, cable run through snatch blocks to the waiting grader that would be our power source for lowering the pump as it was bolted together. So much easier with a boom truck or the drilling rig itself, that's how it was always done, except here. My mother and I worked several days installing the pump. Adjusting the shaft that went to the impellers at the bottom, setting the oil drip system to lubricate the shaft. Hooking the large Cummings diesel motor would require some machine work but Mark, the machinist in the settlement made easy work of it, and the shaft was connected without any problems. The next day I took a barrel of diesel down to the pump motor, which was another of my father's acquisitions from some friend of his that promised it should run. It was so old it only turned at nine hundred rpm which required a special gear-head on the pump. I primed it with a small inline primer pump, bled the injectors, hooked up the two new batteries, it was twenty-four volts. It turned over for several moments then started, after a fashion. It belched gray smoke and ran very rough for a long time. I waited until it was hitting on all six cylinders then engaged the pump with the hand clutch. Brown water, full of sand. This was expected, soon it cleared up, I revved the engine until the whole eight-inch discharge pipe was shooting a powerful full stream. With a thin twine and weight on the end I measured the water level as we pumped a full stream. It held steady at sixty feet, only fifteen feet of draw down, static level was forty-five feet. We were ecstatic, we sat and watched it for a full hour, letting the water run free out through the desert. That night my mother and I sat on the front porch and had a few drinks in celebration.

The next day we drove to town, for more diesel and new fuel and oil filters for the pump motor. Plus, I wanted to call Valerie, let her and her dad know how great the well had come in, mostly I just wanted to hear her voice.

Best of news, she was taking the bus to Fallon the next day to visit her grandparents for a week. She had permission to come to the ranch and stay for a few days as long as my mother was there. Very excited, I promised to pick her up in three days, also to return her several days later.

It was good to see her again. A little constrained in front of her grandparents for decorum's sake, it was hard to keep our emotions in check, but we did. She met my mother and soon enough they were caught up talking about whatever women talk about. They got along very well, and I was a little envious, this should be my time with her. During the days we went riding, myself on Pinto and she on my mother's horse. Exploring canyons, picnic lunches next to streams high in the mountains, every hour falling more in love. Once again the days went too fast, soon I had to return her. It hurts to say goodbye to a woman with tears on her cheeks.

I was both depressed and excited for the next few days. Sad to see her go, I was compensated by the promise of the future, Valerie would be a part of it. The well also made the future look much better. I started building another reservoir next to the well. So much easier with the Cat, I was able to do in five days what had taken two months with the tractor. A couple of weeks more pushing dirt I would have another reservoir, this one much closer to the field where it was needed. I would connect the original one with a ditch and still be able to use the stream water when available, my world looked very good. The only glitch, the water pump in my pickup was out so we were on foot until I could get a replacement.

My father came home that evening and the next morning we demonstrated the well and I explained my plans for the new reservoir. He didn't seem very excited, probably the loan still nagged at him. The plans for the new reservoir irritated him, telling me it wasn't necessary and he didn't like me making decisions on my own. It was stated harshly and whittled at my self-confidence. My little mountain of happiness was immediately turned into a wallow of anger and frustration. As so many times before I said nothing.

I asked that he bring me a new water pump for my pickup as we had no way to get to town. His intention was to return in one week's time so there was no need to make other arrangements. For some reason I felt a strain between him and my mother, but didn't think any more of it.

My mother and I rode our horses for the next couple of days, she loved to ride. Normally it made her happy, this time she seemed distracted but said nothing. I didn't understand females so I just shrugged it off.

The next Friday evening a brand new Dodge pickup pulled into the driveway, I didn't recognize it. My father exited the driver's side, he was alone, angry and had been drinking.

"You and your mother aren't the only ones who can throw money away." He slammed the door shut, glaring at me.

"Did you bring my water pump?" I retorted. I didn't give a damn if he bought a new pickup.

Not looking at me he went into the house where my mother was. Loud voices immediately, mostly his, words indistinguishable.

I searched the pickup for my new water pump, nothing, no groceries either, the bed and cab completely empty except for a fifth of whiskey in a paper bag on the front seat. I didn't look to see how much was gone.

I stood there completely lost, my brain not comprehending, the voices in the house getting louder. I moved further away from the house, I didn't want to hear, it wasn't my business. I did want to be close enough in the event my father got violent, but I didn't think he would.

Both horses were standing a little way off so I walked over to Pinto, leaned against him with my back on his shoulder and rolled a smoke. My hands trembled a little, my stomach in a knot. Something was going on, I had no idea what, but it was serious.

I stood there as the evening gray turned to dark. A half-moon giving enough light to make out shapes. I rolled another smoke and leaned over Pinto's back, gazing at the mountain silhouette, his head came around to smell me or to see if there were any treats for him. I finished my smoke, the voices in the house louder still, only a feeble kerosene light visible through the window.

I got a pan of grain, giving the horses each a turn, listening to them chew gave me a small measure of comfort. I didn't know what to do, a small knot of fear twisting my insides. It was getting very late, the loud voices a torment in the dark. I sat down in the dirt, back against a corral post. Pinto came over to see what the hell I was doing, decided I was boring, relaxed one hind foot and went to sleep, head hanging over me.

I fell asleep sitting, leaning on the post, waking often to shrill voices. Sometime during the night, it got quiet. I listened for a while, it remained still. I fervently hoped it was over and slept a little more. Predawn light awakened me. I continued sitting there and finally rolled a smoke, watching the first glimpse of sun coming over the eastern mountains, I was hungry and craved a cup of coffee. The morning quiet broken by my father's angry voice. How could one person harbor so much anger I thought to myself as I got up and started walking to the house slowly, hesitating in my confusion.

My father came storming out of the house, striding up to me, eyes a sleepless red, dark circles under them. My mother followed slowly, eyes also red, mostly from crying I thought, she stopped next to me but a few feet distant.

"I'm done. You can take care of her now. You've both been against me the last couple of years." A quiet shout, so full of venom and acrimony it scared me. My brain tried to digest these accusations without success, there was no connection to reality. I stood there because I couldn't think of anything else to do.

"You're on your own. Both of you. I'm tired of getting fucked. You can have it all, that's what you've wanted all along." His anger visceral, so deep from within, so real. One last parting shot as he slammed the pickup door.

"I don't care what happens, you can both go to hell."

Wheels spinning as he left, I watched the dust cloud as my own anger built. I continued watching as it went for miles, testament to his leaving, a small tendril building into a cloud the longer it hung in the still air. I could hear my mother in the background, faintly repeating she was sorry. I longed for him to turn back, so I could scream how much I hated him at this moment. So much pain without explanation, we had very little food, less money, one broken vehicle, and standing in the middle of nowhere. As so many times before I was grateful he was leaving, I didn't know if he would ever come back.

MINING AND MARRIAGE

We sat on the front porch swing, lost in our own thoughts, not saying a word. I looked at her, hands trembling as they sat clasped in her lap.

"Do you think he'll come back?" I broke the silence.

"I don't know. I don't ever want to see him again. I've had enough." She deadpanned.

I waited for more. I knew she was hurting and didn't want to add to the pain. The questions could wait; I wasn't even sure what to ask so I asked nothing.

"You must be hungry." Still the mother.

"A little, I can wait." I was very hungry.

"Don't lie." A hint of a smile.

We sat for another fifteen minutes in silence.

"I'll make something to eat." She got up and went into the house.

I walked around, looking at everything and seeing nothing. My mind a blur, unable to focus on any thought. She called me in, food ready.

"We better have a discussion." Somewhat composed, her deep-rooted stoicism taking over. "He accused me of many things, all of them lies. Mostly he thought we were against him."

I didn't respond, thinking as I put food in my mouth. I tried hard to find any particular event that would support that. I couldn't.

"Do you think it was about the well and pump? That can't be it, we had no choice." I sincerely believed it.

"I think that had a lot to do with it." She paused for a long time, clearly organizing her next words. "I think he felt threatened by you. He kept saying you were making all the decisions." Another pause. "He never understood that you had to make them. He wasn't here."

"That's so unfair........." I stopped myself from continuing, knowing it might turn into a tirade.

"I know, it's all so unfair. I'm so sorry, I should have seen it coming." She was filled with remorse, truly heartbroken. Even a bad marriage is hard to throw away, add to that the profound affect it had on both our lives, given our circumstances.

"I guess we better make some kind of plan. Is there enough food for you for a week or two? I can get a job, get enough money to fix the pickup and buy some food." I was thinking out loud.

"There's enough food. What will you do for work?"

"There's a mine forty miles from here. I can probably get a job there. I'll just ride Pinto over."

"What about going to the settlement and asking for a ride to town." It was evident she didn't like that idea even as she said it.

"No. I don't want anyone to know what's happening." I wasn't too keen on sharing our private lives.

She was relieved, feeling the same.

That afternoon we took inventory. She had about twenty-five in cash, my dad had their checkbook. I had about two hundred left in the bank, the last several weeks, most of my money had gone to new batteries for the pump motor, fuel, oil and all the other things needed to keep the ranch going.

I caught Pinto and corralled him that evening. With any luck I would be back in a week, maybe two, with some money and parts.

The next morning, I left before daylight. It was so sad to see her standing in the yard all alone. No long goodbyes. I quietly rode away on Pinto, fearing she might not be there when I returned.

I was lucky and got a job immediately, knowing several of the guys helped. It was underground work, driving tunnel. Hard and dirty but it paid well. Just what I needed. I talked to the foreman about working as many hours as possible. A new, small Mercury mine that was just starting, there was so much work I could have worked twenty-four hours a day if possible. We each had a small trailer to live in so there wasn't much housekeeping. I worked between twelve and fourteen hours a day, this gave me enough time to water my horse morning and evening and move his picket stake.

They were good to work for, every other day some person went to town for building supplies and other necessities. The company paid for my truck's water pump since they didn't pay time and a half but were so grateful for all the hours I worked. They even brought back a bale of rich alfalfa hay for my horse.

Twelve days later, the end of the pay period came, along with a nice healthy check. I talked to the foreman and explained I had some urgent personal business and would need about five days off. After that I could dedicate myself to the job. No problem he assured me, take what time I needed but don't forget to come back. They would keep the trailer open for me.

The next morning, I left the mine long before daylight. The camp still asleep. Pinto knew we were headed home and traveling light we stayed in a trot for long stretches, eating up the miles. The water pump behind my saddle the only extra weight. I loved this kind of riding. A warm fall day, comfortable in a tee shirt, clear and brilliant sky. The only possible dark cloud was my mother, I wasn't overly concerned, she was mentally very strong and so resilient.

She heard me or was already outside when I arrived home. I think she was damned glad to see me. After greetings there was enough daylight left so I installed the new water pump in my pickup, an easy job. Serviced it and got it ready for a trip to town the next morning.

We left early, most of my mother's things already loaded, there wasn't much. A can of peas each for breakfast, almost the end of the food. A couple suitcases of clothes, some dishes, a few personnel items, such a small, dismal display of a lifetime's collection. I was depressed, driving her to Fallon.

We, but mostly her, thought it best if she moved to town and got a job. There was very little she could do by herself on the ranch, it was pointless to stay there and accomplish nothing. I agreed, reluctantly.

We talked a lot on the drive. Our world was in a shambles, the complications of the BLM entries and the large loans were paramount. The house and well were on Sonja's entry. My mother said she would call and ask her to give me a quit claim deed if that were legally possible. It should be, I was now over eighteen. I would have to pay the loan back, with her help my mother insisted. I know she felt partly responsible but it was not her burden to bear. The drive ended about the same time as our plans.

We immediately found her a small furnished apartment at a reasonable price. I paid the first two months' rent as I was the only one with any funds. This bothered her immensely and I knew she would try to pay me back at the first opportunity. She had such a sense of self-reliance, it could be annoying at times.

Next we drove to several casinos and restaurants. She was hired on the spot at one of the large casinos as a waitress. Her spirits were even more lifted when she realized she could walk to work and wouldn't need a car immediately. Some groceries to last until she got paid and things were looking a little better for us. She did insist on buying us a hamburger before I headed home. I agreed, knowing she wanted to contribute something. She smiled a little during dinner, almost as if a weight was lifted, for the first time in decades she was in charge of her own destiny. A lot of thinking was done while I was gone at the mine for those two weeks she told me. She felt good, she was ready, she was happy, or at least as happy as a person could be under these circumstances. I called Valerie's house, she wasn't there, I left word I would be up to see her in two weeks. I really missed her.

I drove back to the ranch that evening. The sad realization that no one would ever be there again worked its way into my mind, fueling my profound sense of emptiness. I was on my own.

It was a troubled night, apprehension robbing me of sleep. Getting out of bed as daylight approached I took stock of my food. Very little at the ranch, a few canned goods, that was it. The food that I purchased in town would go to the mine with me. I made a mental note to stock the house with more cans at the next opportunity.

I drove to the mine, arriving that evening, putting my food away and preparing to work the next day.

Two weeks went by slowly, working long days did little to fill the void, I stayed mostly to myself, the other men respected my need to be alone. I gave considerable thought to my father's abrupt leaving, and if I was culpable and if so, how much. I could never arrive at any answers. As the weeks went on these thoughts slowly faded and were replaced by thoughts of the future and Valerie.

Friday came at last, my pickup ready I jumped in and drove to

Wells, getting there mid-evening. My troubles left me at the sight of her. I couldn't be down around her. It helped immensely, the whole family so kind and gracious. I didn't say anything about the problems at home, maybe I held on to some forlorn hope of reconciliation. Knowing my mother, forgiveness was not in her vocabulary.

The weekend went too fast; we knew it would. Valerie and I talked about making it more permanent, the word marriage was used, not in haste but maybe as time progressed. We were both a little giddy with the prospect. I left feeling much better, a renewed sense of purpose, a reason to work hard. She was a woman any man would be so proud to be with. I felt so lucky, as a bonus her parents understood my dedication towards my own ranch.

Two weeks of work went by rapidly; in a much better mood I was also more receptive to my coworkers. In fact, one of them insisted I take a dog. What the hell was it with people and their dogs? My record with dogs was abysmal. One of his children could no longer keep it so now it was his and he wanted to make it mine. About seven or eight months old, it wasn't real friendly or affectionate.

"I don't want him. I'll take him out and shoot him if you don't take him." It wasn't a threat; the same tone of voice he would use to say he was going to make a sandwich.

I didn't care about the dog one way or the other. These were hard men and they did what needed to be done without apology.

"What the hell's he good for?" I asked, softening a little.

"Tie him to a dog house and feed him raw meat, it'll make him a good watch dog for you."

Not sure about that wisdom, I agreed to try him for a few weeks. Maybe some company would be nice.

"When you take him there's no bringing him back. You can

deal with it." Damn, his problem was now my problem. At least he was a dark gray so he became Smokey number four. At least he came with a half bag of dog food, I had to laugh, four dogs and I had yet to buy any dog food. We drove home that evening, the dog in the back of the pickup, just as well learn how to ride ranch dog style.

The next morning, he was tied to the dog house, so in keeping with my newfound training knowledge I took my 22. rifle and went for a walk. Soon I spotted a huge jackrabbit a short way off. One shot and he fell over where he sat, it didn't look like a kill shot, no blood but a bullet track across the top of his head. I picked him up by his ears and carried him to the dog who was lying in the sun dozing at the end of his chain, he seemed very interested in what I was doing. I threw the rabbit ten feet from him but within reach, the rabbit lay there kicking his feet, this might be really good I thought.

Smoky number four slowly got to his feet, eyes never leaving the rabbit, he slunk over to within two feet of him, tail between his legs, sniffing with neck outstretched. The rabbit sat up, saw the dog looking at him and let out a loud horrible screech. I waited for the dog to pounce and kill, no, that chicken shit ran into the doghouse and hid. A horrible, disgusting example of cowardice. This is where I normally tell people I shot the dog and chained the rabbit up, best damned rabbit I ever had. But in reality I didn't. Quick enough the rabbit ran off and the dog came back out, looking around for his adversary. Thoroughly disgusted I drove to Fallon to visit my mother, leaving him at the ranch.

All was well with her. She seemed happy but it was hard to tell with my mother. I asked if there was any contact from my father. She said no and didn't want any, there was no doubt she meant it. I left that one alone. We had an early dinner, I bought a few groceries and headed home, not enough time left to drive to Wells and see Valerie.

Sunday mid-morning my father showed up. Totally surprised I waited for him to start the conversation, having no idea how this would go. He was sober and contrite. An apology from him was a new experience, something I had never witnessed. He seemed sincere.

"Is your mother here?" He looked around.

"No, she's in town, working." My voice neutral.

"Tell me where she lives. I made a big mistake." He appeared beaten and very sad, eyes pleading.

"I can't do that." Extremely hard for me to say.

"Tell her to come back, we can work it out."

"I don't think she will." I wanted to add more but there was no point.

"She will if you tell her that's what you want." He was right, maybe. I didn't want that burden; it was too much.

"I can't, this is between you and her. I will tell her what you said. That's all I can do." I knew this was hurting him. It hurt to be this blunt. In spite of how he left us that day I had no desire to add to his misery. I stayed firm, denying him the one thing he so desperately wanted, a chance to see her.

The conversation over, I made no effort to invite him to stay. I had no stomach for this. There was no doubt I was being hard to the point of being cruel. I didn't like it; my guts were in a knot. I guess in every son's life there comes a time when he must stand up to his father, this was it for me. I hated the effect it had on him, there was no pride in me. I stood there, waiting for his anger, it didn't come, I wish it would have. He stood there looking at me, he studied me for a long time, maybe the first time he saw me without looking through a whiskey cloud. Nothing more was said. He turned around and slowly walked to his pickup, a defeated man. I was torn up, so much I wanted to say, to ease his burden.

"Would you please tell her I was here and need to talk to her." This was the first time the word please was used when talking to me, it seemed so out of character for him. I understood at that moment how deep his wounds were, they might never heal. He drove slowly, I kept him in sight for a long time, so many emotions, one of the most difficult days in my short life. So much emotional pain, I didn't know how to handle it so I walked over to my cowardly dog, sat on a rock and rolled a smoke, the nicotine was the one constant in my life that was predictable and soothing.

The next morning, after a very troubled night, I mostly secured the house and equipment for the coming winter even though the days were still warm and pleasant. After lunch with dog in the back I drove to Fallon, feeling compelled for some reason to honor my promise to my father and let my mom know what had happened at the ranch. I didn't plead his case, maybe I should have, I only repeated what was said. It fell on deaf ears. It struck home how cold and unrelenting she could be when wronged. A good lesson for me at my father's expense. I drove to the mine after calling Valerie, so good to talk with her, sad but always in a better mood. The coward, still in the back of the pickup.

Another long week at work by my own choosing. I was making good money and keeping my mind occupied.

Another weekend with Valerie at her house. We discussed marriage with more sincerity, being practical she wanted something simple. Her parents seemed happy with us getting married, it surprised me a little, I wasn't exactly the most stable son-in-law they could have had. Maybe they saw something in me I had yet to discover. I envied her for the family she had, and so happy to become a part of it in the future. I left sad but excited for things to come.

Back to the mine, another week of solid work, more money. The huge debt weighed heavy on my mind, that coupled with all the work I still needed to do on the ranch felt overwhelming, sometimes it all felt too much. I was tired, not just physically but mentally as well. I still felt sad at times when I realized things would never be the same, it would never be a family ranch, at least not with my parents.

When I went to visit Valerie I left my coward dog at the mine with enough food and water to last several days. The subject of the dog never came up with Valerie, she wasn't aware that I had one and for some reason I never told her. A premonition he wouldn't be around that long must have been lurking.

The weather was still pleasant during the day but the nights were frosting a little, pleasant early winter conditions. Arriving at my ranch with still an hour of daylight I was surprised to see children's toys in the front yard. I stood outside my pickup, uncertain, this was strange. I heard voices in the house so I knocked on the door, this felt bizarre, it was my house. A young woman answered, late twenties, blond frazzled hair, mid length. Two toddlers, maybe preschool, I wasn't a good judge, hanging on her legs, hiding from me. With some attention and a little less weight she could have been pretty.

She started with a barrage of apologies, starting and stopping, nervous and scared. A young family, down on their luck, with no place to live. She assured me her husband did have a respectable job and as quick as they could afford to, they would move on. She was frightened, on the verge of tears, eyes downcast, with some effort she looked at me. Though it was most unusual and unexpected, this was my house, but it wasn't in me to be an ass. She was already tormented, an arm on each child's shoulder, pulling them closer, a mother protecting. I couldn't imagine the fear that must being going through her mind.

I quickly told her there would be no problem from me. I backed up a couple steps to seem less threatening, it helped a little. I told her I would sleep in the hay barn but she would have to give me some blankets off my bed. Hesitatingly she offered for me to stay in the house, after all it was my bed, but she didn't sound convincing, I left no doubt I would be happy to sleep in the barn, for all our sakes.

"Can I at least give you a cup of coffee and some dinner. It won't be much; we haven't gone shopping yet." She handed me a couple of blankets as she said this. I could see in the front door the house was very neat and tidy, that eased my mind. I agreed to the coffee and said dinner wasn't important but it wasn't stressed and she saw through me.

"I'll be out in the barn, just call when it's ready."

It felt very strange to be in the house with another man's wife and children, it all felt surreal. The coffee was good, dinner consisted of hot oatmeal. She apologized again for not having more. It was good and I told her so. She was beginning to relax so we had a cup of coffee as the kids played in the living room. It felt too strange for me to linger, I think she felt at odds also, still concerned I might change my mind, or I might be hiding an ugly side of me that might surface at any moment.

I thanked her, and added I would see her in the morning. With that I left my house and slept in the barn. I was fine with it, I had no anger, mostly I had empathy. It saddened me a little to think some people struggled this hard to make ends meet. I harbored no opinions about her husband, it was simply one of those things a person must do in life.

I slept well that night, my coward dog sleeping in the barn also, I didn't let him sleep too close to me, a phobia of some sort I imagine.

The next morning, I told the lady I would go to town to do some errands and was there anything she needed. She said no but I didn't believe her. She asked if I would like some breakfast, it would be the same as dinner, the children really loved it, she added as an afterthought. I declined, that may be all she had, better to leave it for her and the kids.

The kids were playing with Smoky number four, at least he was a good kid dog. With plans to return that evening because I had no were else to go I left the coward to play with the kids.

I found my mother at her home so I invited her for breakfast. She didn't have to be to work until noon so we spent a pleasant morning catching up. Her divorce papers were in the works, her acreage in Dixie was quit-claimed to someone else already, that money was used to buy a new car. She was doing well. A few men were showing an interest in her she confessed. I was genuinely glad for her.

I told her about the strange experience from the night before. Her response was strange, normally detached, she chastised me.

"Are you going to take them some groceries?"

"I hadn't planned on it; I didn't think of it." I amended quickly in self-defense.

"Do you have enough money?"

"I've got plenty of money."

"Then I think you should. And buy the kids a cake or pie." She didn't need to be this stern, I already agreed.

"You know what it's like to wait for someone to bring you food, Alfred." I agreed heartily, when she used my full name I knew it was very serious.

"It reminds me after the war in Germany when we had nothing, so hungry all the time, it hurts so much to see your kids without any food. I never want to go through that again." She paused, "Nobody should have to go through that." I put my arm around her shoulder, very unlike me, and assured her I would gladly do the right thing, hoping to lift her spirits. Remembering Germany after the war never failed to dampen her mood.

"You were a gentleman?" Looking at me sternly. "You were

nice to them?"

"Yes mother, I always am thanks to you."

"Are you going to let them stay?"

"Of course, I don't need the house." I was being honest.

"I didn't mean to question you. I know you are a gentleman." She smiled faintly, "I guess it brought back too many memories of Germany. I have to get ready for work. Go buy some food, and not just junk."

We said our goodbyes, I drove to the bank and made several payments, I was about eight or nine ahead, that was a burden lifted. Still plenty of money. I splurged at the store, feeling generous. I felt very good about doing something for another person. Even something this small.

I didn't make a fuss when I got there. Stating that the house should have food, I needed to stock it anyhow. I didn't care what happened to it. Her small discomfort soon gave way to excitement. We unloaded, she put it away, made some coffee and we all had cake. It was a fun afternoon, the little girl reminded me of my niece Kerri, and the boy was lively and a real kick. I realized this was the first time I was ever around children. It felt good. I did notice my cowardly, traitorous dog was more interested in the children than his owner.

Under some pretense I said I had to return to work the next day and would be leaving shortly. By now I was a distraction for the children and they didn't want me to leave.

The young lady started to thank me profusely, I was uncomfortable and didn't want to start down a road of endless thank you's.

"You can thank me one time, that's it, the rest are wasted. Just take care of the house. Don't feel guilty and wish your husband well for me." I may even have known who he was but wasn't sure.

I stuck out my hand to shake goodbye. She hugged me, took me by surprise but it felt nice.

"Thank you." She whispered into my ear, letting me go. Two of the nicest words ever said to me. I felt very good. Thank you mom, for making me a good person. I drove off, she stood in the yard, kids at her side waving goodbye. I could see my Smoky number four in the back, thinking about jumping out to stay with them. I offered to give him to the kids but she rejected the idea, wisely. All in all, it was a good weekend and reinforced my desire to become a family man.

For some reason the week at the mine took forever, anxious to see Valerie I suppose. The next weekend was spent with her again. As were the next three, I didn't want to go to the ranch in case my house guests were still there. A month into the new year we were a couple months from the wedding. Still planning to keep it very small, I hoped it stayed that way.

I decided to try the ranch this coming weekend. Just about out of groceries and only enough dog food left for two days, that was stretching it. I would continue into town the following day and get some badly needed provisions. A two-day rain would make it tricky to get home, the road went through a low area for five or six miles that might be muddy as hell, and it was still raining lightly.

I left work a couple hours early, hoping to for better visibility across the muddy areas, if I got stuck there was no one to help me. Just before I entered the muddy flats I loaded a half ton of rock onto the back of my pickup. Slipping and sliding, changing gears continuously, one time sliding completely off the road, I gunned the motor, the tires biting with the extra weight we barely made it. I was drenched in sweat, a dismal place to get stuck, especially with no food.

Getting home with a little daylight revealed the front yard devoid of toys, that was a good sign. A brand new cattle guard grate was laying in the driveway next to a shed. A large heavy metal item, it would take a two-ton truck to haul it. One of those mysteries that would be solved at a later date. The inside of the house was cleaner then I would leave it, everything in its place, nothing missing with just a cursory glance. Fifty dollars sitting on the table above a handwritten note:

Thank you for the use of your house, we landed on the edge of the salt flat in our plane and got stuck in the mud. We stayed here for three days working to get it out with the help of your tractor and some planks. All turned out well, but we ate what little food there was. We left the house as we found it.

Bill, Steve, and Mary

Two strange events in a short time, one, a family living in my house and second a plane landing and getting stuck. All I could do was shake my head in wonder. Do these strange things happen to others or have I been singled out? It didn't bother me, they needn't have left any money, but it was a nice bonus. I was hungry and went in search of food, there was none, a half box of crackers, my only reward for five minutes of rifling through every cabinet. At least there was some coffee but the absence of any jam hurt the worst. That was my dinner, coffee and a package of saltines, not the first time I would go to bed hungry, I even shared a few with my useless dog. No doubt I would have to make a trip to town first thing in the morning. I took small comfort in thinking, I had plenty of food for thought, who left the cattle guard, how is the family that lived here doing, and how did the plane take off? A very heavy rain that night awakened me several times, concern over the road causing a fitful night.

The rain stopped just at daybreak, visibility only about four hundred yards, low clouds or fog, a dreary day. After a cup of coffee, I headed out in my pickup, it didn't look good. Two miles from the house a river of water was running across the road, several hundred yards wide. I knew the road well, the water would be at least four maybe five feet deep, and some of the road could be washed out, making it even deeper, I turned around, almost getting stuck and drove back home, pissed and hungry.

Walking across the yard I spotted what looked like a motorcycle that someone else had left, leaning against a shed. Getting closer it appeared very sad. Nothing left of the seat but the frame. The handlebars not aligned with the front tire, no kickstand, both tires bald but still holding air, so rusted I couldn't tell what make it was but I think it may have been a small Honda. I thought what the hell and checked the gas, there was some but no way to tell how much. The key in it and turn-able, I found the choke and gave it a few kicks. It sounded promising and after several more it ran roughly. Playing with the choke helped smooth it out and it actually sounded pretty good, even without a muffler. Why the hell didn't people leave me some food instead of all this stuff I wondered, hunger making me cranky. Going into the house, I grabbed my faithful old 22. and started the bike again, hoping to find a nice cottontail rabbit to eat. Not going more than one hundred yards a nice one ran from under some fence posts and sat watching me. An easy shot, so close I shot him in the head, saving all the meat I could. My worthless dog saw him too and got to him before I could get the bike started again. I tried calling him back nicely, that piece of shit took off running with my rabbit firmly in his mouth, paying absolutely no attention to my beckoning. He stopped a short distance off, dropped the rabbit in the dirt with the intention of ripping it apart so he could eat it. I called him again, he didn't even bother with a glance in my direction.

The bike running, I started slowly towards him, guessing my intentions he took off again, rabbit firmly in his mouth, it occurred to me he would not give this meal up. I stopped the bike, he stopped, enough of this crap. I took careful aim at his head and squeezed the trigger. The hammer fell on empty, out of bullets, this was too much. I grabbed the rifle by the barrel gunned the motorcycle and took off after my thieving, worthless, piece of shit dog. Both of us hauling ass out through the desert I got abreast of him and went to club him over the head with my rifle stock, I missed him as he dodged and struck a rock, shattering my wooden stock and breaking it. I threw the gun down and continued the chase, not sure what I could do. I got behind him as he continued in a straight line running full out, I simply ran over him, sending him rolling across the desert floor. I almost lost it on the bike but somehow managed to stay upright. I picked up my mangled, half chewed, saliva covered rabbit, daring my dog to just try and take it back. Not one of my proudest moments but I was hungry and he could damn well get his own meal, he was lucky there were no more bullets in the gun. He just stood there, a little goofy in the head from getting run over. He did follow me back to the house at a distance. I made two meager meals from the carcass, each time wiping the pan out with a paper towel and feeding that along with the bones to my dog, it appeared to agree with him.

Finding more bullets, I did manage to shoot a jackrabbit for Smokey number four, he couldn't seem to manage on his own. It was a long six days waiting for the road to dry out. One morning I went outside to find the dog had chewed on my saddle, he had been chewing on some other little things over the last several days. This did not set well with me, I had always placed a fifty-dollar limit on any animal, if they did more than that in damage or it cost more than that for a vet I would handle it myself. Never taking an animal to the vet and never seeing a reason why I would, that was a moot issue. So that left the damage amount. The time had come, over the last month he was becoming surlier and harder to control, I didn't want him to bite someone and he was displaying a tendency in that direction. We went for a walk in the desert, only I came back, not very sad.

Finally, I was able to get to town and the grocery store. The first thing I did was eat a burger and fries, so delicious. Visited my mother, she was doing fine and in good spirits. The divorce was final with no complications. A letter from my sister with attached quit claim to the property with the house and well. All my town things taken care of, I drove back to the ranch, dropped some groceries off and went back to work at the mine, making up for the days that I missed.

The next several months were spent working and visiting Valerie. The wedding day was upon us. A simple affair at their ranch house by a Justice of the Peace. A happy day for us, only her family present, but that was fine with me. I had said nothing to mine except my mother and she passed on her best wishes to us. With a lot of fanfare, we left and drove to the ranch for our honeymoon, if you could call it that.

The mine where I was working shut down until more financing could be arranged so I was free until I wanted another job. We spent several weeks at the ranch, she enjoyed riding horses, we spent days exploring canyons and thoroughly enjoying each other and the fine weather. Some friends our age came to visit, and wound up staying four days. I worked for a neighbor ranch again and was able to drive home every night like a regular person, even though the drive took an hour each way it was well worth it. I loved this life, and I was in love with Valerie. She asked for nothing and gave all she had to the marriage. There was no doubt in my mind I was a very lucky man.

I started back to work on my own ranch, I wanted to plant in the fall, intending to spend the summer paying off as much of the loan as possible. A job was made available to me through word of mouth, starting in several weeks. Valerie and I took this opportunity to drive to Sacramento and introduce her to my father. I had no reservations, she could win anyone over with her charm and personality and I wanted to show her off. My father was another story, I called to let him know and he seemed anxious to see us. I had not met with him since the previous summer after the failed attempt of reconciliation with my mother.

It went surprisingly well. Except one night Valerie informed me she was out of birth control pills. Not to be dissuaded I assured her the effects would last for several months and it would be fine until we returned to Fallon. She trusted me.

Returning to the ranch, preparations were made to go to work at the new mine. A mercury mine, ovens needed to be built and all the other things that would make the mine operational. Fifty miles from our ranch, Valerie and I elected to stay in a trailer furnished by the owner. Five other men were employed also, all staying at the mine, but no other females.

We all worked hard, pouring concrete, welding, building road and all the other back breaking tasks. Six weeks in and Valerie confided she may be pregnant, a total surprise, but a happy one. So much for my theory about the pill having lasting effects.

The summer grew hotter as Valerie's stomach got bigger. The trailer became an oven as the days got longer and more miserable, sleep at night became difficult at best. It tested her soul, sweating all day, nothing to break the monotony of a mining camp, no radio, no TV, no other females to confide in. The only break, the weekend trip to the ranch, way too short. The summer was relentless, I worked long hard days, unable to help her through the miserable tedium. I watched, helpless, each day eroding another grain of happiness.

Toward the end of summer, a job opening at another much larger mine presented itself. Well established, productive, it too was a Mercury mine. We moved there, also into another trailer, furnished. We had continuous power so we brought our record player from the ranch, though we had only one forty- five record, Holly Holy by Neil Diamond. Eventually it drove us nuts.

The summer turned into fall, Valerie now clearly pregnant. One night the stove in our trailer had a gas leak and caught fire with a small explosion. Needless to say we both catapulted from our bed and ran outside to escape the flames. With help and many fire extinguishers we managed to put it out, luckily Valerie had enough foresight to grab a robe, I was in my underwear.

The trailer was a loss and unusable so we moved our things into a vacant spare, most of our personal things were fine but smelled of burnt plastic smoke.

I could see Valerie was becoming despondent. Because of the trailer catching fire, being pregnant, or mainly because of the miserable situation I had put her into, maybe all of them combined, she longed for her family and the comfort it provided. The vivacious, happy young woman that I married was thrust into a life she was ill equipped for. We didn't fight, there was no acrimony, I felt responsible. It was such a hard life, I had placed her into this isolated, cramped, sometimes miserable existence without much thought to her wellbeing.

We ordered a new car, 1970 El Camino, needing reliable transportation the only reason. It arrived, only a vehicle, it did nothing to help us, we didn't think it would.

A couple weeks later, she asked to go home for a break. That next Friday afternoon we made the trip. She stayed and I went back to the mine.

A week later, heart pounding I called and asked if she wanted to come back. She cried and said no. It broke my heart. I didn't see her again, or the baby for eighteen years.

ENOUGH

I was morose, sullen and withdrawn, going through the motions, doing my work without feeling. Eating lunch one day, sitting with the other miners, one of them voiced an opinion.

"Enough of this shit. What the hell did you think would happen? You bring a pretty young girl out here, knock her up, then pretty much ignore her." Rare for any of these men to get involved or voice their feelings. A retort was forming, he continued before I could speak.

"You deserved it. All you do is work." Looking at me as he took a bite of his sandwich, "Think about it."

I did, fighting an angry response I stayed quiet. It wasn't said harshly, only one man telling another the brutal truth. I didn't think a forty-year-old man, never married, no girlfriend, no children that he claimed, was the best person to give advice on how to treat a woman. Deep down I knew there was some truth in what he said. I let it be, my anger turning onto myself.

The week wore on, then another, time and work removing some of the sting. I went to my ranch for the weekend, a sharp pang of loneliness hitting me as I walked into the house. It seemed so vacant I almost left, but I had nowhere else to go.

My Shangri-La vision of the future was gone, replaced by a more honest reality, years of work ahead.

My resolve faltered, I didn't want to do it alone, the work didn't bother me, I enjoyed most of it. I only wanted to share my future and dreams with someone. That weekend was extremely difficult for me.

I did some field work, making preparations for spring planting, hoping to fulfill the BLM requirements and finally get the long awaited deed. The creek running well, it held promise of filling both reservoirs, giving ample water for spring irrigating.

Each passing week at the mine, returning to the ranch on weekends, I was slowly returning to my former optimistic self. With the money I was making the loan would be paid off rapidly, a huge burden lifted.

One of the workers got extremely sick and was taken to the hospital. Two days later a group of state officials came to the mine and shut it down immediately. The man was in the hospital suffering from renal failure, caused by mercury poisoning. They discovered the condenser tubes were full of pinholes and leaking mercury vapors, the whole camp was severely contaminated.

It had been going on for several weeks and we were all ordered to get medical examinations. I had mercury poisoning, my numbers very high, along with the others. Mercury poisoning is called salivation for some reason, at least that was the term the doctor used. I had no symptoms and the doctor was uncertain if and how it would affect me, maybe my knees, my teeth, my kidneys, my hair, could even make me sterile. He had no idea, there was very little literature but he did know there was no treatment to remove the mercury. I was on my own until something developed.

The tubes were fixed and we were allowed to return to work, I stayed just long enough until it was time to plant my field at the ranch. I bought a good ten-foot drill for planting seed to pull behind the tractor, a huge improvement over the tiny broadcaster my father brought us so long ago.

I bought some cheap sorghum seed, a hearty plant, not worth much as a crop but suitable to plow back into the ground when mature, adding much needed organic matter to the clay soil.

It worked well enough to pass inspection, I had earned the deed, a huge burden lifted. It felt good, I now had time to do things properly. The irrigating worked well enough but soon the water made its own course through the field and only the low spots stayed green and grew tall.

I spent that summer buckarooing for local ranchers so I could stay close to home and continue working at my ranch, a welcome relief to be on my horse again. I was becoming a recluse by necessity and wasn't happy about it. The words, "All you do is work," never rang more true. A truth I was becoming more and more aware of.

Later that summer a rancher from the settlement asked if I could work for him leveling some land for about a month. A nice job that I enjoyed, running equipment was second only to riding a horse but paid much better.

The rancher had a brother named Pete visiting from Las Vegas, late forties, unmarried, tall and dark. A carpenter, he took a liking to me and inquired if I had any interest in going to Vegas and being a carpenter. His brother interjected, I couldn't leave until I was finished leveling. I agreed to both, with a promise of very good money and some kind of social life it was very appealing. I got his phone number, planning to call in another two weeks before heading to Vegas.

The leveling finished, I spent a day with my mother in town. Things were going good for her, a man having a very serious interest in her created a spark that had been absent for a long time, she deserved some happiness. No word from my father for months so I called him and we had an easy conversation about nothing. He too was seeing someone. I got a letter from Valerie with a picture of our baby girl. So kind and thoughtful, pictures and letters continued for many years. The divorce long settled I started making child support payments, untroubled by these, I understood the importance.

After pulling Pinto's shoes off and securing the house, which meant only putting things away that might get blown off in a wind storm, I loaded my El Camino with my personal things and left the ranch, unsure when I would return.

Four hundred miles went quickly, Nevada was an open speed limit state, any speed as long as it was safe for conditions, except through the towns. Pete was staying in a motel, a little strange considering how long he'd been there. It did save him doing any house chores and it was inexpensive so I joined him there, staying in my own room.

A housing boom, Vegas was bustling. Huge housing tracts with five to six hundred homes was the norm. Everything was done by piece work. One person might only snap the lines on the concrete for the walls then put the top and bottom plates on. The next person would cut all the headers and cripples for all openings, nailing them together and placing them where they belonged. That was my job at the beginning. A cripple nailer they called me. I got payed so much per house, I could do all the houses I wanted, if I caught up with the layout man I could do something else. It was big money, the checks huge every two weeks. The Unions hated this. Nevada was a right to work state but they fought piece work continuously. My first introduction to Unions and politics, it left a bitter taste in my mouth. It became an ongoing fight with me, I detested Unions and all they stood for.

Long hard days traded for big checks. After work I would stop at a Der Weinersnitzel, eat something for dinner, go to my room, get my lunch ready for the next day, shower and go to bed. Not very exciting but profitable. Weekends I would go to a large dance hall, meet girls, dance and drink until exhausted. Every other weekend back to Dixie Valley, drive there Friday evening, work Saturday and most of Sunday then back to Vegas. I was trying desperately to get another forty acres ready to plant. The winter and spring were spent in this tedious but rewarding monotony.

One Saturday evening a girl about my age caught my eye, shoulder length blonde hair, nice body, pretty smile and did she love to dance. Before long Katie and I sat at her table and we danced the night away. This became a ritual every other Saturday night, sometimes meeting during the week for an hour or two. She worked for a doctor's office and had very steady hours. Katie, like myself suffered from a dissolved marriage, an unfortunate bond. Catholic, she was hesitant about some things.

Soon she started going to Dixie Valley with me. She was nervous the first time, so far removed from civilization with a man she honestly knew very little about. It turned out fine, over time we began to fall in love. Both of us a little slow and cautious, hesitant to make another mistake.

Spring turned to summer, still driving to Dixie, but now every weekend with Katie, she worked every bit as hard as I did. Too much work to be done, planting more acreage would just have to wait another year.

As the summer progressed so did Katie and I, still staying at our individual places but spending as much time as possible together. My spirits high, I charged at life with all the exuberance I could muster. It was hot on those concrete slabs midday, one hundred fifteen very common in Vegas throughout the summer. Most of the guys would quit about one or two in the afternoon, I didn't, a whore for money, I worked as long as my body could stay upright, salt tablets all day long, drinking untold gallons of sugar water.

My last loan payment for the pump and well was sent, such a huge burden lifted, even paid my El Camino off. Debt free,

Katie and I celebrated, not lavishly but celebrated nonetheless. Another month, we drove to Fallon and I bought a large Case tractor. Diesel, huge rear wheels, plenty of power to pull anything I could think of. Used, but pretty new it was in pristine condition and reasonably priced. They hauled it to the ranch for us. Another payment but well worth it. My world became easier.

A larger tractor had been on my mind for a long time, but recent events hastened my decision. The grader and tractor with loader that I had used for the last six years were gone. Last conversation with my father warned of this eventuality. Feeling they were his, he sold the grader to the same person that bought his quit claim deed on his three hundred twenty acres. The tractor and most other things he felt were his, were also claimed and hauled off to Sacramento.

I wasn't upset, they were his to claim. Too bad he didn't haul the Cat off, might have if it would have started. Nothing was gone that I felt shouldn't be. A sense of relief, having severed that final tie, it did force my hand but the time was right.

By now my mother was remarried and her new husband was very helpful when time allowed. They would come out to the ranch when we were there and help as much as possible. Her new husband Randy was always eager to drive the tractor or the Cat when we were able to start it. We got along well, the evenings were pleasantly spent together.

Late that fall Katie and I married, a small ceremony at a chapel in Vegas with most of her family present, none of mine were there, I had not told any of them. Most of the winter was spent in Vegas, Katie continued working for the doctor's office and myself still as a carpenter. By early spring the Union rep. was on my ass full time. The last holdout, I had a choice, either join them and pay my dues or they would make my life hell. I quit, it went against my principal to pay someone so I could work. It was time to go back to the ranch and get some work done on the new fields. Katie stayed in Vegas and continued working. I would drive down and visit most weekends.

I worked as hard as possible, burning a considerable amount of fuel and with tractor payments and living expenses I worked for some local people, sometimes buckarooing, sometimes running equipment. Whatever was handy and close, the extra cash flow made a significant difference, mostly mental, it was hard on my conscience having my wife as sole means of support.

I was getting tired, every day long and hard, working as many hours as possible. Katie was pregnant, we were ready for a child and welcomed this news, she continued working. That fall I went to work for a land-leveling company in Fallon, a large one, with a dozen scrapers and huge D-8 Cats to pull them, several with rubber tires for longer hauls. The Soil Conservation Service would survey a field, small to hundreds of acres. Stakes would be marked and the work would begin in preparation for flood irrigating. My kind of work, something about running big equipment, it just felt manly. A big job would take months to complete.

The company furnished me with a house. Sitting vacant on one their hay fields, it was isolated, several miles from town. I only slept there, one bed and a kitchen table with four chairs my only furniture. I didn't need anything else. I didn't turn the heat on, keeping my water and what little food I had in the fridge with the light continuously on kept it from freezing. Mostly I just slept and made my lunches there. I showered at the main shop, I worked there most evenings anyway.

The owner of the company, Carl, and his son Dillon, were two of the most honest, hardworking people that ever came into my life. Carl, mid-fifties, incredibly tough individual, I looked up to him and he became a mentor and template. His son Dillon, maybe ten years older than me was just like his father, they treated me like part of their own family

Katie had our son in January, born in Vegas. I was glad to be there, it went well but I felt sorry for her, he was like a bowling ball. Heavy and healthy, we named him Erik. She took some time off from work and I stayed with her for a week. We were both beaming with pride.

Reluctant to leave my family, the decision was made for her to move and stay with me as soon as the weather turned warmer. Her whole family lived in Vegas so she had a lot of help, that took some of the guilt away from me leaving.

About a month later Carl and I were repairing some equipment at the home ranch about five miles from Fallon. I was bent over cranking a generator, the crank slid off and hit me under the chin. It was a very heavy crank, smoking pipe in my mouth I bit through the stem, the bowl went flying. My front teeth were loosened, and a large flap of skin hung down from my chin, blood running freely. I managed to stay upright, head spinning, eyes rolling around in their sockets, using my hand to help staunch some of the blood.

Carl walked over and looked at me, he appeared fuzzy and wouldn't stay in one place. He handed me his handkerchief, full of oil, grease and anything else that may have needed wiping up at some time. I tried taking it from him but my hand would not connect with it so he removed my hand from the injury, stuck the rag on and placed my hand back over it. "Just push hard, it'll stop."

Things were starting to hurt, I stood there a few more minutes scared if I took a step I'd fall down.

"You better go to the hospital, that's gonna need some stitches." Intent on what he was doing before getting interrupted, he went back to it, all his concern for me used up.

A step then a pause, another step, another pause, it took a long time to find my rig, I couldn't remember where it was. The sequence of starting the motor and putting it into gear and all the coordination that was entailed seemed impossible. It took several attempts before I got it right. Somehow I managed to get to the hospital without any further damage, thanks to isolated country roads.

All the blood down the front of my shirt gave me immediate attention and I was whisked right into a partitioned area. The old nurse removed my hand and took the blood-soaked rag off, clucking like a hen the entire time.

Many stitches and some Novocain later, I made my way back to my rig, after searching the lot for the longest time. Some of the pain was gone but I was really goofy. By now it was evening, I drove to Carl's ranch, telling him I would be back to work in the morning. He answered with "Okay." No questions.

Things healed up but my ears continued to hurt, to the point of becoming difficult to speak and chew. Two weeks later as I told Katie what had happened she got me right in see the doctor she worked for, who just happened to be an ear, nose and throat specialist. A few tests later he informed me the small bones by the ear canals were either broken or cracked. Not much to be done, he gave me something for the pain and said it should start feeling better on its own in another week or two. It worked for me, at least I had some idea of what was happening, and it was free. A great man.

Always so hard to leave Katie and Erik but soon enough, maybe two more months and we could be a whole family.

A month of running equipment and diminishing pain except when I yawned. The days getting longer and warm enough not to freeze anymore. Carl came by to check on the fields where my house was one evening. We sat in the kitchen having a cup of coffee.

"What the hell is that smell?" Carl said. As he looked around, sniffing in disgust.

"I don't smell anything"

"You don't? It smells like something's dead in here," more disgusting looks.

"Maybe you got some cow shit on your boots." We both checked our boots.

"It smells dead, rotten."

"You're imagining it." I was puzzled, there was nothing in the house to stink.

"I'm gonna find it, I know what dead smells like." He got up and started going through the kitchen cabinets. I helped but we found nothing after a thorough search. Same for the bathroom. The other bedroom and living room had the same results, they were bare so it was easy. That left the bedroom, I searched through my two duffel bags of clothes on the floor, glad I kept a clean house. The bed had only my sleeping bag which had a snap in liner that I tried to launder every week. Carl was bent over looking under the bed, "Shit, there it is." He exclaimed quite loudly. "It's bad under here." Taking a deep breath, he reached back under and pulled a crow carcass out. Holding it arm's length he walked to the door and carried it by one claw to a ditch, throwing it in.

"How could you live with a dead bird under your bed all winter?" Shaking his head in wonder, smiling, "and not smell it?"

"I don't know, maybe I'm not sensitive like you." I chided.

"Let's see how he got in, maybe a broken window." We went back in to solve the riddle.

After some searching it was clear. A stove pipe in the living room ceiling with no cover. It must have come down sometime during the winter, got under the bed and froze to death during the cold weather, recently thawing out and decaying, causing the stench I couldn't smell.

He gave me crap for the longest time.

I would call my father every couple of months. Remarried, now living in Oregon. Having started his own masonry business things were going well for him. Half dozen employees, his hands were full. I should come up and be part of his business, an invitation that I was not willing to entertain.

Katie and Erik moved to Fallon, into the house where I was living. What had been an empty cold shell was transformed into a warm comfortable home, amazing what a woman can do with a few simple things. I continued driving heavy equipment for Carl until spring. The three of us moved out to Dixie, more driving for me, still working for Carl ten hours a day. But it gave us a chance to make the ranch our real home.

We bought a milk cow, then would buy day-old dairy calves, feeding them the milk along with supplements. Katie would do the milking sometimes, lucky for us the cow was very patient. It didn't turn out to be very profitable and it was an incredible time constraint. By fall we gave it up and sold them all. Katie enjoyed having the cow, something comforting about resting your head against the flank of a tranquil animal as you milked it.

I wanted to have another forty acres ready to seed by fall but there wasn't enough time to get the ground ready, always so much work. By fall I was worn out again, Katie took as much of the load as she possibly could but there were limits, especially with Erik starting to become mobile. We managed to keep the bills paid easily enough, and there was always plenty of money for food. I couldn't save enough to run me for a year or two until I could get the fields producing. I kept trying.

That fall Carl and son bought a ranch in another valley about one hundred miles from Fallon. Already in hay production, some of the fields were very uneven, the profit potential greatly reduced. It was decided to move some of the scrapers to the ranch and level hundreds of acres.

That fall it was arranged to move the equipment to the new

ranch. A large home came along with the property, so Carl, his wife, Dillon, Katie, Erik and I all spent the winter living in it, there was plenty of room for all of us at the house. Carl's wife and Katie got along exceptionally well and would do the cooking. We left Fallon early one fall day, sixty miles east on Highway 50, then north on a dirt road for another thirty miles. Two behemoth rubber tired scrapers and one low boy with the D-8 push cat.

Katie would follow us in our pickup in the event of a problem. Carl had just given us a dog a week ago, saying every young boy needed a dog. Four months old, grey and very friendly. I didn't want another dog but of course I was overruled by the others. He became Smoky number five.

The drive was going well, I was the last scraper with Katie and Erik visible in the cab, the dog in the back of the pickup, first time for him. I happened to be looking back as we were driving down the highway when Smoky jumped onto the roof of the cab. Katie wasn't aware of it yet, then he jumped onto the hood, turned around, sat down and stared at Katie and Erik through the windshield, proud as could be. Going thirty miles an hour of course Katie hit the brakes, the dog slid off the hood onto the pavement, then rolled under the pickup, bouncing like a pinball between the road and the undercarriage. I watched all this unfold, horror on Katie's face, I saw the dog running out through the desert, stopping a short distance off. I stopped my scraper, Katie behind me, visibly upset, expecting the dog to be a bloody mess underneath. I figured the dog was okay and didn't wipe the grin off my face in time. It wasn't funny but it was, Katie didn't see the humor in it as she looked under the pickup. I pointed the dog out to her as it made its way back to us, hesitantly. I could see a few raw spots on its hide but otherwise it seemed to be okay. She was putting him into the bed of the truck as I started driving down the road in my scraper, she soon caught us. Smokey number five still laying in the bed of the truck as he should be.

We arrived that evening without further incident.

Days turning to weeks, then months, we leveled land, spent pleasant evenings and I put ten pounds of fat on. Two women cooking and idle evenings, even after working ten-twelve hours a day, all three of us men became victims of excess eating and short winter days.

We didn't go to Dixie often that winter. The house was cold, the water off, snow on the ground sometimes and not much to be done that time of year it, seemed pointless. We did go to Fallon on occasion and visit friends. It was as close to a normal life as I had come to in years and it felt good. I talked to my father still whenever possible. His business was going strong and he continuously encouraged me to join him in some form of partnership. I declined, things were going fine for me here and I remembered some of the ugly things that happened between us. I didn't hate him, I didn't even dislike him, I was wary of him. I knew some horrible things happened as a result of the war, I knew there were demons in him that tormented endlessly. I had no understanding of these things, I just knew they were real, I also knew it wasn't my responsibility, I was like a head shy horse.

Spring came and the job was finished, we moved back to town, bringing our extra fat along. Katie, Erik and I moved back to Dixie, so much work to do. We bought three lines of hand move sprinkler pipe, each a quarter mile long, enough to irrigate forty acres. I had to pump the water into the sprinklers to get enough pressure, an added cost.

I continued working for Carl in Fallon, the hours long and grueling. Three hours of driving a day, ten hours leveling for Carl, then pipe changing twice a day. I could manage but the extra fat came off quickly. Katie helped as much as possible but was limited, unable to change pipe by herself, not just the physical demands but with Erik now able to walk around a little he demanded more attention. Twice that summer Katie had come across rattlesnakes right by the house, this demanded so much time and caution for her, not to mention the anxiety.

We did catch Pinto and my mom's horse and go riding sometimes. It was fun, the three of us enjoying the rare day that Katie insisted I take off. She was nervous on a horse but handled them well. Erik would ride with me. I loved these short intervals, especially being on Pinto but the guilty feeling would never be far away, I was wasting a whole day.

Not long after the neighbor stopped by to tell us some bad news. My mother's horse had been shot, he came across the dead horse as he was riding and recognized the animal. No idea how or what happened, a bullet hole clearly visible, saying he was sorry for giving us the bad news he left us standing there, we were perplexed and angry, but could do nothing.

My father came to visit one weekend. Not a total surprise, we had communicated several weeks earlier. His business was making incredible money and he wanted to share the opportunity with me.

He seemed like a different man, maybe his new marriage was having a positive effect. He drank nothing but coffee while there, no trace of the volatility I remembered so well. I asked about his drinking, expecting a sharp response, it didn't come, only a statement referring to it as something in the past. He continuously stressed the future would be much easier with him than out here, struggling the rest of my life, putting my family through the same struggle. I assured him I had a good job and my life was just where I wanted it. It was a good visit, we enjoyed having him there for the day, he never apologized for some of the things that he did, I'm not sure I wanted or expected him to. They were things in the past, maybe I was a fool or just too tired to worry about things that had been.

That summer, the relentless heat took a toll on my fields. I couldn't keep enough water on it, slowly they turned brown, giving up the struggle to grow. It was sad to watch, there was nothing I could do. Katie and I began to talk more about our future. As with Valerie and my dying field I saw the toll this life was having on her. We had no idea how to handle Erik's schooling, too far from town for him to attend any public school we would have to teach him ourselves. A possibility but not a good one. We discussed many things sitting there on our porch that evening. I began to think of a normal life but I had no idea what a normal life was. We discussed selling, perhaps considering my father's offer. Not as a way out, just a real and better opportunity. I expressed concern, my history with him nothing like Carl and Dillon, who in spite of differences seemed to make it work so well. Maybe I wanted something similar with my own father, Katie thought we could make it work. She didn't push, so smart in her ways, she simply let me know her feelings, it was my decision to make. We watched Erik play in the yard, as parents ever vigilant for rattlesnakes, Smoky keeping him company.

I walked around behind the house, looking over our land, Katie leaving me alone with my struggles. I could no longer envision endless acres of alfalfa, cattle lying contentedly in the pasture, the visions of an optimistic young boy, full of wonder and hope. Instead I saw years of toil, frustration and fruitless labor ahead. Life being sucked from my family as certain as life was being sucked from the plants.

Maybe reality, maybe exhaustion, maybe a cynicism that comes with maturing, I saw things with a stark, bitter truth. There was not enough ground, even if all of it was producing, it would never be enough to support us, I would always have to work for someone else.

I saw all of these things, I didn't welcome them, I hated them, they came in a flood, they were true. I sat on a bucket, legs weak. I said out loud to myself, "I've had enough." I rolled a smoke in tribute to my acceptance. Done, I walked around the house, watched Erik and Katie playing with the dog in the yard. I told her about my decision, I think she was relieved but didn't show it. The next day we would go to Fallon and call my father, if the offer was still good that would be our course. I would also give two weeks' notice to Carl.

The offer stood, he asked me to come immediately, I told him there were things that needed doing but I would be there soon as possible.

We stopped at Carl's during lunch time, knowing he would be home. They invited us to lunch with them, ever so gracious. I explained what had taken place the last several days, and my decision. He didn't seem surprised, in fact he somehow expected this. Thinking back, I remembered how he would comment about my need to continue against such impossible odds. Said very subtly at the time it held some meaning now.

Carl said to forget the two-week-notice, they would be fine. It was difficult to say goodbye

Next we drove to Bishop, California where my mother and Randy, her husband were living. He worked for a power company maintaining the roads for high power transmission lines. I didn't know what kind of reception the news would get. My mother reluctantly appeared in favor, knowing August gave her caution, but having lived there herself she clearly understood the loneliness and hardship.

"You have other people to consider now. I think it's a good decision." She started to say she had reservations about working for my father. She didn't, stoic as always. We said goodbye.

We rented a trailer and returned to the ranch. Loaded the trailer, the pickup that would pull the trailer and our El Camino. It took several days, I didn't think about what I was doing, I couldn't. There wasn't all that much. Two bedrooms, and personal things. The living room furniture was too bulky to haul that far, plus it was time for some new things. The propane refrigerator, stove and washing machine stayed.

I would have to make one more trip for my tools and other things that we didn't have room for.

We rented a place as soon as we arrived, spending only one night with my father. Unloaded and put things away. A nice small house, well suited for our needs, reasonable price. This was the first time in my life I had to pay rent, what a strange feeling, utilities also. We bought a new fridge, washer and dryer. Katie was set, I started back to the ranch alone in the pickup, leaving the El Camino with her.

I stopped in Fallon, meeting with a realtor who specialized in ranches and spent several hours listing our place, it seemed such a final act, almost a betrayal, I shut my mind off. Then returned the trailer, no further need of it.

The long drive up Dixie Valley to the ranch was melancholy and filled with sadness. It was still beautiful even with all its inherent hardship. Thinking about the ditch that went on forever, that incredible frightening windstorm ripping my tent apart exposing all the fears a boy of fifteen harbored.

The house felt lonely, the rooms echoed my footsteps, reinforcing the emptiness. I went into the shop and focused on loading my tools, each handful taking a bite out of my resolve to leave. I stopped several times, wondering if it was all a mistake, remembering all the things that were fixed with these tools. I went slow, dragging it out, hoping for some kind of reprieve, it didn't come. I finished that miserable task. Everything loaded, one last job, pull the shoes off Pinto.

He was there, standing in the yard, looking alone and forlorn, his friend of years dead, a rotting corpse out in the desert. I grabbed my tools and pulled the four shoes off, thinking this will be the last time I ever do this, it was gut wrenching, I didn't tie him up, there was no need of it. I kept the shoes but couldn't say why. The decision to leave him in Dixie was made weeks ago, inconceivable to lock him in a pasture somewhere in town. I couldn't do it, he would spend his remaining days in the desert, free.

I couldn't leave, not yet. I leaned over his back as I had so many times before, his hind foot coming up to a relaxed position. I surveyed all the mountains we had traveled together, all the canyons that we explored together. Thinking about the time he slid down the rock into a wash and how many days we spent getting out. How many cold frozen nights were spent in the saddle. The hours behind a herd of cattle in the sweltering heat, breathing their dust. The bull we fought for hours on Highway 50, a show for all the tourists. Each remembrance, tearing at my heart. My first trip to the ranch up north, a real buckaroo job. He was a true friend, uncomplaining, my one constant in life, eleven years, a big part of it on his back. I rolled one last cigarette, leaned with my back against him, his head coming around to smell me. Finished, I wiped his eyes, they seemed misty. Of all the times I'd said goodbye, this was the hardest. I patted his neck and rubbed his ear for the last time.

I couldn't take any more. I drove off slowly, watching him and Dixie Valley fading in the mirror.

The End

Epilogue

I worked for my father a long four years learning to become a mason. The ranch sold the following year after I put it on the market, it sold again to the Navy a couple years later. They bought all the ranches in Dixie Valley except a couple at both ends and used it for the Top Gun school that was located in Fallon.

Each of these four years working for my father enabled him to once again become the victim of alcohol. We parted as bitter enemies, never to see each other again. I took my family and moved to Joseph, Oregon. He died about four years after our parting, from some kind of alcohol-related problems I assume.

Katie and myself divorced seven years after moving to Joseph. Several years later I met and married my current wife of thirty years, Marsha.

My mother and her husband moved to Joseph and spent the last few years close to me and my family. They died a year apart, peacefully.

I feel fortunate to have lived such a rewarding life, sailing and living on a boat as we explored the West Coast, Florida Keys, and the Bahamas with my family for seven years, six months at a time. Marsha and I are now living in the mountains of Eastern Oregon, running trails.

I harbor no resentment or anger towards my father, he made me what I am today. Sadly, his demons finally devoured him.

Sonja, Anita, mother Chris and Fred.

Fred, 11 years old, first cigarette in front of his parents.

Fred with sisters
Anita and Sonja in
Canada

Looking east across the salt flat towards the Clan Alpine
mountain range.

My mother walking through the yard gate towards the house.
The bulldozer that caused me so much misery.

One of the few pictures of Fred and Pinto, 1972.

Horse race at Gibson ranch, Fred in the lead momentarily. The other boys are the owners' sons.

Damn, I Shot My Horse

While his peers were in high school, Fred received his education in the wild open spaces of Central Nevada. He raised three children and lives with his wife Marsha in the mountains of Northeastern Oregon.

(He has no dogs.)

Damn, I Shot My Horse